INTERNATIONAL FRANCHISING
AN OVERVIEW

International Franchising – An Overview

Papers presented to the International Franchising Committee
at the SBL Conference, held in Toronto, October, 1983

organized by
SBL - Section on Business Law
of the International Bar Association

edited by

MARTIN MENDELSOHN
Adlers
London, U.K.

1984

NORTH-HOLLAND
AMSTERDAM · NEW YORK · OXFORD

ISBN: 0 444 87548 4

Publishers:
ELSEVIER SCIENCE PUBLISHERS B.V.
P.O. Box 1991
1000 BZ Amsterdam
The Netherlands

Sole distributors for the U.S.A. and Canada:
ELSEVIER SCIENCE PUBLISHING COMPANY, INC.
52 Vanderbilt Avenue
New York, N.Y. 10017
U.S.A.

Library of Congress Cataloging in Publication Data

SBL Conference (6th : 1983 : Toronto, Ont.)
   International franchising.

   1. Franchises (Retail trade)--Law and legislation--
Congresses. I. Mendelsohn, M. (Martin), 1935-   .
II. International Bar Association. Section on Business
Law. III. Title.
K3966.A55 1983   341.7'54   84-10139
ISBN 0-444-87548-4 (Elsevier)

Printed in The Netherlands

FOREWORD

"It is with great pleasure that, as Chairman of the Section on Business Law of the International Bar Association, I write this foreword to 'International Franchising - An Overview', a publication which owes its conception to Martin Mendelsohn of London, Chairman of the Section's Committee on International Franchising Law.

There is no doubt that this book will make a valuable addition to the libraries of all practising lawyers required to advise clients on franchising problems in a number of countries. It is based on the programme presented by the International Franchising Law Committee at the Section's sixth Conference held in Toronto in October 1983 and contains papers presented by lawyers covering more than 20 countries.

An enormous amount of work has been done by Martin Mendelsohn in organizing the Conference programme, in collating the papers and in masterminding the production of the publication. This book represents a landmark in the history of the IBA in that it is the first joint venture undertaken in conjunction with the North-Holland Publishing Company. Various Committees of the Section have already published proceedings of topics discussed at Conferences and Seminars and I hope this new business partnership with North-Holland will successfully continue.

I must express the gratitude of the Section both to Martin Mendelsohn and to the many other eminent lawyers without whose efforts this work would not exist."

RICHARD C. MEECH Q.C.

TABLE OF CONTENTS

Foreword   v

The International Bar Association and its Section
on Business Law   ix

Editor's Introduction   xiii

List of Contributors   xxi

Chapter 1

An Introduction to Franchising.

                              by **Lewis G. Rudnick**   1

Chapter 2

Franchising: Trade Mark Practitioners' Perspective.

                              by **Iain Baillie**   75

Chapter 3

Character Merchandising.

                              by **Nicholas Fyfe**   107

Chapter 4

Regulation of Franchising in the United States:
Implications for International Franchising.

                              by **Philip F. Zeidman**   129

Chapter 5

Legislation and Regulations Affecting Franchising
in Canada: An Overview.

                              by **Harvey A. Shapiro**   153

Chapter 6

Franchising in Latin America.

by **H. Stephen Brown**   211

Chapter 7

Focus on Franchising in the Asia/Pacific Region:
Joint Ventures, Regulation of Investment, Tax.

by **David R. Shannon**   249

Chapter 8

Franchising in Europe - United Kingdom.

by **Martin Mendelsohn**   271

Chapter 9

Franchising in Europe - EEC.

by **Stanley A. Crossick**   333

Chapter 10

Franchising in Europe - France.

by **Olivier Gast**   379

Chapter 11

Franchising in Europe - Germany.

by **Dr. Walther Skaupy**   389

THE INTERNATIONAL BAR ASSOCIATION AND ITS SECTION ON BUSINESS LAW

The IBA was founded in 1947 as a federation of Bar Associations and Law Societies. It now represents 80 national organisations and has some 7,200 individual members in 113 countries throughout the world.

Its principal objectives are:

to establish and maintain permanent relations between member organisations and individual members;

to discuss problems of professional organisation and status;

to provide members with means of improving their services to the public;

to promote uniformity and definition in appropriate fields of law;

to promote the administration of justice under law in accordance with the principles and aims of the United Nations.

Activities:

The IBA organises Conferences, Seminars and Regional Meetings throughout the world and publishes a Journal, a Directory of Members and studies by its members.

It has consultative status with the UN and the Council of Europe, and is strictly non-political.

IBA SECTION ON BUSINESS LAW

The Section was established in 1970 to promote an interchange of information and views amongst members of the IBA as to laws, practices and procedures affecting business, financial and commercial activities throughout the world.

It has twenty-five committees which deal with specialist subjects of interest to a commercially orientated lawyer.

Activities:

Conferences and Seminars

The Section holds Conferences and Seminars regularly worldwide and each committee meets at least annually.

International Business Lawyer

The Section's own Journal, the International Business Lawyer, is published eleven times annually and contains articles on business law contributed by members; articles commissioned from non-members; reports on committee meetings and Seminars; book reviews and up-dates on international law developments.

Directory

A Directory of Members of the Section, from over 100 countries, is published on a regular basis.

Handbooks

Twenty-two Seminar and Work Study Proceedings of committees

have already been published by the Section.

Liaison with other International Bodies

The Section works closely with the EEC, FIDIC-FIEC, ICEL, ILO, IUBSSA, OECD, the Council of Europe and the United Nations and its various associated bodies etc, to advise on draft legislation or codes.

Further details of the IBA, its Section on Business Law and the International Franchising Committee may be obtained from the International Bar Association, 2 Harewood Place, Hanover Square, London W1R 9HB, Tel: (01) 629 1206, Telex: 8812664 Inbar G.

INTRODUCTION

The International Franchising Committee of the Section on Business Law of the International Bar Association was established at the end of 1982 with the following aims and objectives.

"To provide a forum for the exchange of views, experiences and discussions of the problems which arise in the field of International Franchising - a method of distributing goods and providing services through dealers licensed to use the Trade mark and/or business format developed by the franchisor.

It is the intended to hold meetings and seminars:

to enable emerging issues to be discussed and studied

to provide the means for the dissemination of information about developing franchise trends

to identify those areas of law which affect franchising and its practice and discuss and evaluate their effect on International Franchising

to provide the means for lawyers to analyse and compare current terms usages and practices in International Franchising."

Although the Committee was established only at the end of 1982, it already numbers 81 members from seventeen countries. Not surprisingly, the largest contingent is from USA but, surprisingly they do not amount to as much as 50% of the membership.

The immediate interest which has been shown in the Committee underlines the growth of International Franchising. As franchising grows the need for laws to regulate unfair practices and abuse will inevitably also grow.

In the USA, Canada and Australia, as well as the Andean Pact Countries, there already is regulation and the trend is likely to continue.

The problem for the lawyer who has never been in touch with franchising before is that he is faced with bringing together into the one transaction a number of topics which in the ordinary course of practice would never be handled by one practitioner. In those countries where franchising is newest the alertness of the practitioner in identifying the problem areas and in coping with them is a source of great difficulty.

Apart from the need to cope with such a wide range of legal topics the franchise lawyer is also required to show a considerable understanding of commerce and the commercial considerations which affect his client in the structuring of his franchise system. It is all too easy for a lawyer to say what cannot be done; it takes greater effort to conceive the requirements and advise on how one's client can best achieve his objectives.

It will be among the prime objectives of the Committee to ensure that it provides:

- A vehicle for the dissemination of information about the problems of International Franchising as they become apparent

- A forum for the discussion of problems and techniques available to overcome them

- A system to enable it to monitor Internaional legal developments and alert members to their existence

- A vehicle for the making of representations to Governments about the effects on International Franchising of proposed franchise legislation.

In order to assist the Committee in achieving its objectives the members must be prepared to make a contribution:

- by remaining on the alert for developments of interest which can be drawn to the attention of other practitioners.

- making available expertise and experience for others by speaking at the seminars and programmes which will be presented by the Committee

- by finding the time to write articles and perhaps from time to time by serving on Working Parties to prepare and publish reports on topics of interest and where the Committee would like to make its influence count

- by educating the International legal community about franchising by all these means to ensure that there are colleagues around the world who are knowledgeable and have the expertise to give advice to the International franchising client. It is the duty of the International legal community to ensure that it is able to serve the need of its clients and by working together in the framework of this Committee we can get to know each other and develop relationships which will greatly assist the understanding of our subject and the improvement in the quality of the service which can be given to our clients.

The first opportunity which was available to the Committee to present a programme was the occasion of the 1983 Biennial Conference of the Section on Business Law in Toronto. Since this was to be the inaugural programme it was decided to pinpoint specific topics of interest in various zones in the world. With this approach the practitioner could have available could have access to valuable source material which was not otherwise available.

The Committee was indeed fortunate that from its membership it is able to draw upon the most experienced practitioners in the field of franchising from around the world.

The first session which was held was a joint session with Committee L of the Section of Business Law which is concerned with Patents, Trade Marks and Copyright. This session was by nature introductory and the three papers which were delivered covered "Franchising as a basic business concept" by Lewis Rudnick; a Trade Mark practitioner's view by Iain Baillie and a look at the world of Character Merchandising from Nick Fyfe.

The four zones into which the world was divided and the chosen topics were;

North America (USA and Canada) - Statutory Regulation

South America   - Transfer of Technology

Far East   - Regulation of Investment

Europe   - Methods of doing business

The first two zones were dealt with in one session when practitioners from jurisdictions as yet untouched by franchise legislation were introduced to the wide scope and nature of the USA experience by Committee Vice Chairman Philip Zeidman. The wealth of statutory regulation at both Federal and State level which has developed in such a short time span is so astonishing that one is left to speculate about its necessity and its effectiveness in achieving its objectives. This legislative approach has been followed in the Province of Alberta as explained by Harvey Shapiro when renewing the position in Canada and has been viewed favourably in Japan and Australia where franchise laws are being considered. In order that some perspective of franchise legislation might be obtained the Committee has established a Working Party with the following terms of reference.

"A working party to review the stated purposes of Franchise laws; to examine the evidence supporting the need for such laws; to evaluate their effectiveness in achieving these purposes; to identify areas in which the cost and burden of the laws as applied in practice may exceed their benefits; to offer comments and recommendations where appropriate."

The study by the Working Party will take some time to produce results but it is the first attempt to evaluate the legislators' approach to franchising.

The South American zone, with which Stephen Brown dealt, creates its own problems and the existence in the Andean Pact countries of franchise laws may well have come as a surprise to many.

The Far East embraces a wide area which has provided very fertile growth for many franchise companies and the paper, which was delivered by David Shannon, gives a very good indication of the legal problem with which they had to cope.

Europe covers so many jurisdictions in which there are no franchise laws that some selection of countries had to be made. The final choice was to cover England, France (Olivier Gast) and Germany (Walther Skaupy) in which three European countries franchising has expanded most extensively. In the absence of franchise laws the methods of doing business and the effect on franchising of other business laws are more important. The possible influence of the EEC Antitrust laws was considered by Stanley Crossick. Although franchising has so far escaped the attention of the Commission and of the European Court, many analogous transactions and practices which are features of franchise arrangements have been considered that some franchise transactions may well be affected.

This work is the first step by the Committee with the support of the Section on Business Law of the International Bar Association to publicise its work which of course is one of its objectives.

I would like to express my thanks to Richard Meech, Jan van de Ven and John Salter, the Section Officers, Madeline May, the Executive Director of the I.B.A.,and Joan Rawinsky, the Section Administrator, for the help and assistance they have so willingly given to assist the Committee in its efforts to become established.

I would also like to thank Wendy Reed for preparing the copy for the printing of this work.

Martin Mendelsohn
Chairman
International Franchising Committee
London   March 1984

LIST OF CONTRIBUTORS

IAIN C. BAILLIE

Iain C. Baillie was born and educated in Scotland, graduating from Glasgow University in 1953. He has practised in both industrial patent departments and in private practice in Great Britain and in the United States. He is qualified as a Chartered Patent Agent for practice before the U.K. Patent and Trade Mark Office. In 1954 he went to the United States and after graduating from Fordham University J.D. (Juris Doctor) in 1956 he was admitted to the New York Bar and the U.S. Federal Bars.

In 1976 he became the Senior Partner of the London office of Ladas, Parry, Von Gehr, Goldsmith & Deschamps and Managing Director of Langner Parry, Chartered Patent Agents, and is now Senior European partner of Ladas & Parry.

He has written and lectured extensively on International Patent and Trade Mark Law, Licensing, E.E.C. Competition Law and Copyright.

He is a Fellow of the Chartered Institute of Patent Agents (U.K.), a Member of the American Bar Association and serves on several committees; a Member of the Institute of Trade Mark Agents (U.K.) and of the International Franchising Committee of the Section on Business Law of the International Bar Association and other professional groups.

H. STEPHEN BROWN

H. Stephen Brown is a Partner in the law firm of Brown & Reese in Memphis, Tennessee, where he practises in Franchising and Corporate Finance. He has made a particular study of and acquired outstanding experience in franchising in Central and South America.

He is a member of the Board of Governors of the American Bar Association Forum Committee on Franchising and a past Editor of the A.B.A. Franchising Journal. He is a member of the International Franchising Committee of the Section on Business Law of the International Bar Association.

He has delivered and written numerous papers on Franchising in South America and is the author of various articles on International Franchising.

STANLEY A. CROSSICK

Stanley A. Crossick is a Solicitor, Lecturer and Legal Author. He graduated from London University in 1956 with a Bachelor of Laws Degree and was admitted as a Solicitor in 1959. He is now Senior Partner in the Brusells law firm Community Law Office Belmont, where he specialises in and practises European Community Law.

He is President of the European Secretariat of the Liberal Independent and Social Professions (SEPLIS) and Honorary Vice President of the International Union of Lawyers (UIA).

He is a former Deputy Secretary General of the Consultative Committee of the Bars and Law Societies of the European Community (CCBE) and former Secretary General of the International Union of Lawyers (UIA).

He is the Author of European Insurance Law and European Banking Law published by Financial Times Management Report and of numerous articles on Community Law and current affairs. He lectures widely on Community Law.

He is a member of the International Franchising Committee of the Section on Business Law of the International Bar Association.

OLIVIER GAST

Olivier Gast is Avocat a la Cour and a senior Partner in the Paris Law firm Gast-Douet-Bord and the President of the European Franchising University.

He graduated from the "Institut Superieur du Droit des Affaires", and has specialised in business law.

He wrote a thesis of "Doctorat du 3eme Cycle" on the following subject: "Les Groupements de concessionaires ou de franchises." (Unions of concessionaires or franchisees).

Oliver Gast is Co-Author, with Martin Mendelsohn, of the book: "Comment negocier une franchise" published by the "Editions du Moniteur, Usines Nouvelles" (Second Edition).

He has written and lectured frequently about franchising and antitrust laws.

He is a member of the International Franchising Committee of the Section on Business Law of the International Bar Association.

MARTIN MENDELSOHN

Martin Mendelsohn is a Solicitor and partner in Adlers, practising in the City of London.

He has been involved with Franchising as a lawyer and as a Director of franchise companies for 20 years.

He is author of "The Guide to Franchising" (now in its 4th edition); "How to Evaluate a Franchise" (now in its 2nd edition); "Obtaining a Franchise" (a guide published by the Department of Trade). He is co-author of "How to Franchise your Business" and in France (with Olivier Gast) of "Comment Negocier une Franchise". He also contributed the U.K. and E.E.C. Sections of the American Bar Association Publication "Survey of Foreign Laws and Regulations affecting International Franchising". He is the author of many articles on the business as well as legal aspects of franchising which have been published in the U.K., Europe and North America.

He frequently lectures on the business and legal aspects of Franchising in the U.K., Europe and North America and is a Course Director at the College of Marketing.

He is currently Chairman of the International Franchising Committee of the Section on Business Law of the International Bar Association.

LEWIS G. RUDNICK

Mr. Rudnick is a partner in the law firm of Rudnick & Wolfe, Chicago, Illinois and graduate of the University of Illinois, Columbia University Graduate School of Business and Northwestern University School of Law.

Mr. Rudnick specialises in franchising and business law.

He was General Counsel to the International Franchise Association from 1973 until 1981 and is now its Special Counsel and was Chairman of the American Bar Association

Forum Committee on Franchising from 1980 until 1982. He is a Member of the Governing Committee of the American Bar Association Forum Committee on Franchising, a Member of the Industry Advisory Committee to the Franchise Regulation Subcommittee of the North American Securities Administrators Association a Member of the Illinois Franchise Advisory Board, and a member of the International Franchising Committee of the Section on Business Law of the International Bar Association.

Lew Rudnick has written and spoken widely on various legal topics relating to franchising in many parts of the World.

DAVID R.SHANNON

David R. Shannon was born and raised in the wheat, sheep and cattle country of Eastern Australia. He took degrees in Arts, Law and Business Administration in Sydney, and commenced his professional legal career with the litigation section of the leading Australian law firm Allen Allen & Hemsley in 1969.

In 1972 he joined the Sydney office of Baker & McKenzie as an associate. He was elected to partnership in 1977. In 1982 he transferred to Hong Kong.

Throughout his legal career David Shannon has specialised in "marketing law" - the law relating to advertising, distribution systems, franchising, trade marks and other industrial and intellectual property rights. His clients have included many of the world's leading franchise organisations, the most notable being Pepsico, Pizza Hut, Taco Bell, McDonalds and Denny's.

He is a member of the International Franchising Committee of the Section on Business Law of International Bar

Association.

David Shannon has produced many papers and articles on marketing law topics. He has published two books - "Sales Promotion in Australia" and "Franchising in Australia". The latter, published by the Law Book Company in 1972, is the only Australian text on franchising and has received wide critical acclaim.

DR. WALTHER SKAUPY

Dr. Skaupy studied law in Geneva and Berlin and he is an Attorney-at-law in his law office which he established in Munich in 1960.

He was, from 1953 to 1959, representative of the German Government on the "Validation Board for German Dollar Bonds" (an International Commission) in New York and was Founder President of the German Franchise Association. He is a member of the International Franchising Committee of the Section on Business Law of the International Bar Association.

Dr. Skaupy has published numerous articles in the field of industrial property law, currency law, antitrust law, international law and franchise law. He is also co-author of the following books:- "Das Franchise-System" (which introduced Franchising in Germany), "Franchising in der Praxis" and "Checklist Franchising".

He has given numerous talks on franchise problems in Germany and West-European countries (France, Belgium, Netherlands, Austria, Switzerland and Italy).

PHILIP F. ZEIDMAN

Philip F. Zeidman received his law degree from the Harvard
Law School and also studied at the Harvard Graduate School
of Business Administration.

He has been a partner in the Washingtom law firm of
Brownstein, Zeidman & Schomer since 1968. Prior to entering
private practice Mr. Zeidman served in several positions
with the United States Government, including General Counsel
of the Small Business Administration and Special Assistant
to the Vice-President of the United States, Hubert H.
Humphrey. He is admitted to practice before the Supreme
Court of the United States, and in the District of Columbia,
New York, Florida and Alabama.

Mr. Zeidman served as that first Chairman of the American
Bar Association Antitrust Law Section's Committee on
Franchising, and is the Vice-Chairman of the International
Franchising Committee of the Section on Business Law of the
International Bar Association. He is contributing Editor
for antitrust and trade regulation of The Legal Times, and a
member of the Advisory Board of the Bureau of National
Affairs' Antitrust and Trade Regulation Report. He serves
as Secretary and Counsel to the American Business
Conference, and as Washington Counsel to the International
Franchise Association.

Mr. Zeidman has written and spoken widely in the fields of
financing, franchising, antitrust law and energy regulation,
and is the Editor of "Survey of Laws and Regulations
Affecting International Franchising" (published by the
American Bar Association) and of "Legal Aspects of Selling
and Buying" (published by McGraw-Hill).

INTERNATIONAL FRANCHISING – AN OVERVIEW
M. Mendelsohn (editor)
© Elsevier Science Publishers B.V. (North-Holland), 1984

CHAPTER 1

AN INTRODUCTION TO FRANCHISING
Lewis G. Rudnick

1. HISTORY AND GROWTH OF FRANCHISING IN THE UNITED STATES

Franchising as we know it today is a relatively recent phenomenon. Although franchising has long been used by governments as a means of procuring public services, not until this century was franchising widely used by privately-owned businesses as a method of distribution or expansion. In the private sector, franchising was used initially by manufacturers as a means of increasing the sales and distribution of their products. Independent wholesalers and retailers then adopted franchising as a means of remaining competitive against chain stores. Business format franchising - the licensing of a trademark in conjunction with a prescribed method of operation, as in the case of franchised fast food outlets - was not fully developed until the 1950's, and accounts for much of the explosive growth in franchising which has occurred since then.

Franchising in its most fundamental sense, that of bestowing a valuable privilege, or "franchise," for a consideration, has probably been practised since the beginning of civilization. A secular authority or ruler who had been vested with certain authority and powers found it practical to delegate some of those powers and to confer privileges on those who could provide needed services or money in return. Land rights might be granted to a person who could pledge the services of an army, or a person might be authorized to collect taxes in the name of the ruler, provided a certain portion of the revenues was remitted to the ruler.(1)

The first example of franchising in the United States was probably the legislative grant of rights to privately owned businesses, which became "public utilities" such as railroads and banks. Even though the grant of these rights typically entailed some form of public control over the operation of these utilities, an exclusive right of exploitation provided an inducement for private businesses to make substantial capital expenditures to develop those utilities. In this way, franchising by the government provided a means for public utilities to be developed relatively quickly and without public funds.

(A)   Early Franchise Systems

Franchising by private businesses began when manufacturers granted exclusive area distributorships. As early as the 1860's, Singer Sewing Machine Co. used franchised distributors to sell its goods throughout much of the United States.(2) Around the turn of the century, automobile manufacturers began to establish franchised dealerships. Lacking the capital and the trained personnel to develop and operate a large number of company-operated retail outlets, companies within the industry turned to franchising as a means of developing a network of outlets in a relatively short period of time.(3) Somewhat later, around 1930, the oil companies followed suit and began to franchise gasoline service stations. Whereas before they had relied exclusively upon company-operated outlets to sell gas, within a short period of time franchised units were their primary method of distribution.(4)

The soft drink industry also began to franchise around the turn of the century. A franchised bottler received a proprietary syrup or concentrate, or the right to produce syrup using the proprietary formula, together with the right to produce the soft drinks, identify them with the franchisor's trademark and distribute them in an exclusive area. The franchisor generally provided marketing and other support services, and required the bottler to produce the soft drinks in accordance with defined quality standards.(5) Without franchising, it would have been difficult for proprietary brands of soft drinks to achieve a wide distribution. Bottling had developed as a localised business because the finished product could not be economically shipped over long distances, and because of the use of returnable bottles. These limitation on soft drink distribution did not apply to soft drink syrups and soft drink companies were able to increase the sales and name recognition of their product by licensing the bottler-wholesaler to produce the finished product. In doing so, however, they needed to be able to maintain standardisation and control over the quality of the soft drinks produced and distributed by their franchisees. The franchised bottler's extensive role in production of the soft drink product and the franchisor's control over the franchisee's production and distribution differentiated soft drink bottling franchises from typical product distribution franchises.

Although the early use of franchising was primarily by manufacturers, independent wholesalers and retailers soon found a use for franchising. Faced with the growth of corporate chains and other competitive factors, these independents found that franchising enabled them to compete more effectively. Around 1902, the seeds of the Rexall drug store franchise were planted when a group of independent druggists formed their own private label manufacturer. This co-operative arrangement made it possible for the druggists to decrease their product costs and increase their profit margins. As the co-operative flourished, it established its own chain of Rexall stores. After World War I, however, Rexall decided to franchise independent drugstores to use the Rexall name and private label products, finding it an easier and more profitable method of expansion.(6) Other franchise chains established by independent wholesalers and retailers in the 1920's and 1930's were Western Auto, Ben Franklin, and Super Value Stores. These and other wholesaler-retailer chains also prospered, with franchised stores now numbering in the thousands. Thirty years after selling its first franchise, Western Auto had more than four thousand establishments in operation, while Ben Franklin stores totalled about twenty-four hundred by the early 1960's.(7)

Franchising was introduced to the food service industry in the 1930's, when Howard Johnson established its first franchises. Johnson had successfully established two ice cream businesses and a restaurant, but lacked the capital to open additional restaurants. However, he agreed to help a former classmate design, furnish, and supervise a restaurant and to sell him ice cream and other supplies under a Howard Johnson's franchise. When the first franchise was successful, Johnson granted other franchises and opened additional restaurants of his own. By 1940, over 100 Howard Johnson's restaurants were in operation. Many of these were owned by franchisees who had no prior experience in the restaurant business.(8) Through franchising, the restaurant owners obtained the benefit of the franchisor's expertise and guidance, and the opportunity to profit from a proven concept. In return, Howard Johnson's made a profit from the supplies it sold to its franchisees.

Franchising was not adopted by other countries to the extent of its utilisation in the United States. Franchising in such industries as motor vehicles and gasoline has been utilised in Canada and Europe for many years, but has not been widely used outside those industries. Cooperatives, which have certain attributes in common with franchising, have been extensively utilised in Scandinavia and other European countries, but modern franchising is a recent phenomenon outside the United States.

(B) Modern Franchising

Although franchising became an established business
relationship in the United States during the first half of
the century, the major growth in franchising occurred after
World War II. Several factors made the post war period ripe
for the rapid development of franchising. A booming economy
and growing population created a rapidly increasing demand
for goods and services, and an opportunity for enterprising
businessmen to provide them. Returning servicemen had
access to Veterans Administration-backed loans to finance
their business ventures.(9) Franchising enabled these
servicemen and others who were ambitious but inexperienced
in business to start their own businesses with training and
supervision from a franchisor. Businessmen who had
innovative concepts or valuable business experience found
that by franchising they could exploit their ideas and
experience without the capital required for other methods of
expansion.

An evolution in United States trademark law is also
significant in the development of modern business format
franchising. At common law, trademarks are an indicator of
source. This concept made the licensing of a trademark by
its owner to an unrelated person a questionable practice.
Use by the licensee might not be deemed use by the owner-
licensor and would not benefit the licensor in developing a
stronger mark (and might even jeopardize his mark). A
second concept of trademarks began to evolve in the 1930's:
a mark could serve as an indicator of quality. A trademark
that indicates quality could be used by its owner and others
licensed by him, as long as the owner controlled the quality
of the goods or services sold by licensees under the mark.
This concept was codified in the United States federal
trademark law in 1946 (the Lanham Act)(10) and is a

fundamental legal basis for modern business format
franchising. The recognition under United States trademark
law of the service mark as a species of trademark that
identifies a service, and has essentially equal status with
trademarks that identify goods, has also facilitated modern
business format franchising.(11) Most countries do not
recognise service marks, a factor that may inhibit
franchising.

Convenience goods and services were the basis for many of
the franchises established in the 1950's and 1960's. Fast
food franchises, such as McDonalds and Kentucky Fried
Chicken, proliferated during these years. Laundry and
cleaning services and convenience grocery stores were among
the other businesses which experienced significant growth
through franchising during that period. Hotel and motel
franchise chains and travel and recreation businesses,
such as campgrounds, catered to an increasingly mobile
population. Holiday Inns, for example, developed a
network of nearly fourteen hundred Inns in less than twenty
years.(12) Franchisors also responded to the needs of
businesses and consumers by developing temporary help
services such as Manpower, employment services and tax
preparation services, among others.

After two decades of explosive growth, units operated by
franchisors and franchisees in the United States numbered
over 400,000, generating sales of over $131 billion during
1971. Ten years later, over 440,000 units accounted for
nearly $365 billion in annual sales.(13) The number of
product franchise outlets (particularly gasoline stations
and automobile dealerships) declined significantly during
this period (though they continue to represent a large share
of the total number of franchisor owned and franchised
outlets and sales) and the increase in business format
franchise outlets and sales is thus more dramatic than
indicated by the above totals. A Franchising Fact Sheet

prepared by the International Franchise Association from the 1981-83 edition of Franchising in the Economy is attached as Appendix A.

The proliferation of franchises in the United States was not without its problems. Some franchisors focused more on the sale of franchises than on selling goods and services to the public or on providing training and support systems to their franchisees. In some cases, franchisors made misrepresentations to franchisees about the franchise in which they were investing, or failed to provide important information to prospective franchisees.

When franchises floundered and failed, the losses suffered by franchisees attracted the attention of state and local authorities, who sought ways to prevent perceived abuses by some franchisors. In some cases, legislation was addressed to problems in a particular industry, such as the automobile industry. Such regulation addressed such problems as coercive practices of franchisors and arbitrary termination of franchises. Many states passed legislation regulating pyramid sales plans, or the sale of certain kinds of business opportunitites and franchises. The problems observed in franchising in the United States during the 1960's and 1970's have been less prevalent in other countries, perhaps due in part to the slower growth of franchise systems in those countries.

Similarly, government regulation of franchising is far less pervasive outside the United States, though there are indications that some countries (e.g., Canada and Australia) may consider more comprehensive regulation.

Today, the abuses once associated with franchising appear to be far less prevalent. Franchising is a vital and growing part of the United States economy. Some segments of the franchise industry - primarily gasoline stations and auto-

mobile dealerships - are contracting in response to changes
in market conditions.   However, most types of franchise
systems are continuing to expand, with strong growth in
sales volume and number of units expected for some segments,
such as the computer product stores and health improvement
businesses.

The growth of franchising outside the United States is
rapidly accelerating.   Many American franchising companies
have successfully franchised in other countries and some are
rapidly expanding their international franchising programs.
In 1971, 156 American franchisors operated or franchised
3,365 outlets in other countries.   By 1981, 288 American
franchisors operated or franchised 21,416 outlets in other
countries.   Canada, Western Europe, Japan and Australia are
the principal markets of this expansion.   The number of
franchisors of other countries franchising outside of their
home countries is not as great, but is growing.   A
substantial number of Canadian franchisors are expanding to
the United States and a growing number of European
franchisors are eyeing the United States market.
International franchising appears to be on a fast growth
track.   Not only are franchisors seeking franchisees and
joint venture partners in foreign countries, many
individuals and companies are actively seeking franchises
from franchisors of other countries.   Overall, franchising
has grown steadily in number of units and sales volume over
the last thirty years, and the predicitons are that its
growth will continue.

(C)   Advantages of Franchising

The principal reasons of business failure are proprietor
inexperience and lack of sufficient capital.   Franchisors
generally furnish initial and continuing training, guidance
and other assistance to their franchisees, thus enabling
inexperienced businessmen to compete in the marketplace.

Many franchisors also provide capital assistance to franchisees with insufficient capital resources of their own, and to this extent, franchising helps to eliminate one of the principal causes of business failure. Franchised businesses are generally believed to experience a significantly lower failure rate than completely independent businesses, because an individual franchisee's risk of failure is reduced by his participation in a franchise system in which the franchisor provides training and tested marketing and operation programs.

Low entry barriers make franchising an attractive method of business expansion. Unlike other methods of expansion, large capital outlays are not required and start-up costs may be quickly recovered. Franchising furnishes the human and much of the capital resources necessary for rapid expansion and market penetration. Rapid expansion enables the franchisor to realize economies of scale earlier in the franchise system's life cycle and allows risks of expansion to be shared among the franchisor and its franchisees. Despite these obvious advantages, even in the aggregate they do not constitute franchising's principal advantage to the franchisor.

Probably the single most important benefit of franchising to the franchisor, and the principal reason for franchising's success as a method of business expansion, is the participation of local, highly motivated managers committed to their businesses because of their ownership interest. Franchisees are typically more highly motivated than company employees. While company employees may have at stake their future advancement and perhaps their compensation or even their present positions, franchisees put at risk their ownership interest in the franchised outlet. Superior performance of highly motivated franchisees can result in greater profitability or return on investment for the franchisor than is obtainable from company-owned outlets.

Among the frequently asserted benefits of franchising to the franchisee are the profitability of franchised businesses; the opportunity to become an independent businessman; the advantages of the franchisor's trademark, marketing and operating plans, joint advertising programs, and initial and continuing assistance; the low cost of acquiring many types of franchised businesses; and the ability to finance part of the investment in a franchised business.

A franchisee's degree of independence may be measured by the extent to which the franchisee may operate the franchised business according to his own wishes. Franchisee independence is limited by the mandatory specifications, standards and operating procedures with which the franchisee agrees to comply in the franchise agreement and the extent to which such agreement is actually enforced by the franchisor. The notion that franchisees are totally independent businessmen has been overemphasized. No businessman is totally independent and free of controls, since all businesses are subject to controls imposed by government, suppliers, creditors, employees and accounting rules. In no other method of doing business are controls more necessary than in franchising. Successful franchising depends upon the development and maintainence of uniform specifications, standards and operating procedures in the franchisee's business to ensure uniform quality throughout the franchise system. Franchisor controls, however, tend to lessen the degree of independence of the franchisee. Despite necessary franchisor controls, the franchisee operates his own business, and ultimately determines its success or failure. Profits from franchising can be large and the growth of the franchisee's realisable equity in his business substantial. In most cases, these would seem to be more significant benefits to the franchisee than greater independence.

While not without cost to the franchisee in the form of

decreased independence, franchising enables the franchisee to compete more effectively. The franchisee obtains the benefits of the franchisor's marketing and operating plans, advertising, training and guidance and assistance in establishing and operating the franchised business. Franchisor training programs typically include both classroom and on-the-job training and enable many prospective franchisees with little or no prior business experience to enter a field that they would otherwise be unable to enter. Upon joining an established franchise system, the new franchisee commences business with a recognised trademark in addition to tested marketing and operating plans. Most franchisors also provide guidance and direct assistance in connection with site selection; design and engineering of the franchisee's business facility; acquisition of operating equipment, furniture, fixtures and inventory; and general contractor services. Another form of franchisor aid frequently offered is assistance in arranging financing from other sources.

Moreover, some franchisors aid their franchisees by constructing the facilities and then leasing them to the franchisee.

Franchising is essentially a method of distribution which combines the advantages of an integrated corporate network with those advantages inherent in individual business proprietorships. A franchisor does not have to acquire and deploy the capital, manpower or organisation of a vertically integrated chain. The franchisor is able to obtain the benefits of franchisee-financed growth, local owner management and avoidance of the inefficiencies and costs of centralised management. Moreover, the franchisor is at least partially insulated from the failure of an individual outlet. The franchisee, in turn, acquires an instant public reputation, training, advertising and other support services, which enables an individual entreprenuer to

complete with large corporate chains and nationally
recognised brand-name products and services.

(D) Reasons Not to Utilise Franchising

Reasons to avoid utilizing franchising in expanding a
distribution system for the sale of goods and services will
vary from one country to another. In the United States,
asserted reasons to avoid franchising include the inadequate
control that can be maintained over franchisees (in contrast
to retail outlet managers in a vertically integrated chain),
the extensive regulation of the grant of franchises and the
franchise relationship and the alternative (and assertedly
less costly) means available to raise capital needed for
expansion of a distribution system and to motivate retail
managers. Regulatory burdens and their associated costs are
a frequently asserted reason to select other methods of
expanding a distribution system. To the extent that
avoidance of regulation is a valid reason not to utilise
franchising, it would be limited primarily to the United
States, for regulation is far less pervasive in other
countries. Regulation in the United States takes several
forms, focusing primarily on the grant of franchises (e.g.,
pre-grant disclosure and registration) or on the substantive
relationship between the franchisor and its franchisees
(e.g., antitrust law, limitations on termination and non
renewal of franchises). In international franchising,
regulation may limit the royalty and other fees that the
franchisor may charge to the franchisee or may jeopardise
the franchisor's trademark protection. Even absent specific
regulation, the law of a country may not be conducive to
effective trademark protection or enforcement of quality
control or other terms of a franchise agreement.

Regulation of franchising is most highly developed in the
United States. Franchising developed and expanded rapidly
in the United States during the 1950's and 1960's in a

laissez faire legal environment that posed few obstacles for franchisors. However, the legal climate commenced a rapid change in the late 1960's. In the following decade, the pendulum of government regulation swung far toward comprehensive regulation with widespread enactment of statutory regulation of various elements of the franchise relationship and restrictive antitrust interpretations. In the past decade the pendulum has been swinging back with respect to federal regulation (e.g., antitrust), but state legislatures have shown an increasing interest in regulating franchising and distribution relationships. The most severe regulation (e.g., prohibiting franchisor operation of retail outlets and protecting the territories of existing franchisees) has been confined to gasoline station and motor vehicle franchisees. However, there have been serious proposals to extend such regulation to other industries, and to the franchise relationship generally, and franchisors in maturing industries (e.g., fast food and lodging) have cause to be concerned that they may face such regulation in the future.(14)

Under United States Law, distribution relationships are generally either between independent contractors or master and servant (though, as discussed in footnote 14, a franchisee will frequently be deemed the franchisor's agent, and occasionally his employee, for certain purposes). This dichotomy limits the flexibility of distribution relationships in the United States. Unless a relationship is carefully structured to avoid certain controls or powers over dealers characteristic of a master servant relationship, a company could find that it has some or all of the regulatory and tax burdens and liabilities of agency and employment relationships as well as the regulatory burdens and antitrust limitations of franchising relationships. The laws of other countries may afford greater flexibility in structuring a franchise relationship and give the franchisor greater controls over outlet

Lewis G. Rudnick

management by the franchisee.

Recently, critics would add as a fourth reason to avoid franchising, the breakaway franchisee syndrome. In the United States, the incidence of attempted unilateral termination of franchise agreements by franchisees appears to be increasing. Such unilateral terminations typically follow one of two patterns. In one pattern, the franchisee simply ceases to participate in the franchisor's system and unilaterally terminates the franchise relationship. The franchisee may undertake a deidentification program, but not infrequently is casual about taking steps necessary to change his image as a franchisee. This is a particularly common problem when the premises of the franchisor's system are of distinctive design and a significant expenditure of funds is required to modify the premises sufficiently to eliminate its identity with the system. The former franchisee may intentionally seek to gain whatever advantage he can from continued identification with the franchisor's system and advertising. This form of breakaway may also occur in the context of a franchisee's attempt to sell the assets of his franchised business to a buyer who does not want the franchise, thereby taking a franchised outlet out of the system.

The second breakaway pattern involves intentional noncompliance by the franchisee in an effort to avoid restrictions of the franchise or provoke termination by the franchisor. Such noncompliance may include persistent late payment of fees and advertising fund contributions and may also extend to noncompliance with quality control and other requirements of the franchise. Noncompliance may also take the form of the franchisee's development of additional outlets outside franchisor's system, utilising to some degree confidential information acquired as a franchisee. Such franchisee expansion will frequently violate an in-term covenant not to compete or restrictions on use of trade secrets or confidential information contained in the franchise agreement. As in the case of the franchisee who simply declares the franchise terminated, the franchisee seeking to provoke termination by the franchisor will generally assert multiple breaches by the franchisor.

Franchisors have several legal remedies to deal with breakaway franchisees (e.g., damage suits, covenants not to compete, control of the franchisee's business premises, options to buy the franchisee's business, required termination payments and liquidated damages), but such remedies are expensive to enforce and frequently fail to achieve a satisfactory result. The breakaway franchisee causes multiple damage to a franchise system. In addition to a loss of revenue (e.g., from royalties, advertising contributions, sales to the franchisee), a breakaway franchisee can diminish the system by removing one or more outlets, harming the image of the franchisor and establishing another competitor. A number of breakaway franchisees have become successful franchisors. (15)

(E) Alternative Distribution Systems

(1) The Vertically Integrated Chain

The most commonly suggested alternative to franchising is a vertically integrated chain of distribution outlets. On the assumption that a company can more effectively impose controls and standards on retail outlet managers than on independent franchisees, the vertically integrated chain does have an advantage over a franchised chain in terms of maintaining quality control. A related advantage is the speed with which the chain can react to changes in its market or in its costs of doing business (e.g. higher labor or energy costs) requiring modifications in format, image products, services, equipment, pricing, or operating

procedures.   At   least   theoretically,   vertical
integration should facilitate implementation of the
requisite modifications.   There are no independent
franchisees to convince (by persuasion or contract
enforcement), merely employees to direct.

Proponents of franchising counter with the argument
that not even employees can be merely directed to
adhere to standards and procedures or to implement
changes.   Employees, like independent franchisees, must
be persuaded that they will benefit from following
directions, or policies and standards will not be
effectively implemented.   The negative reinforcement of
the threatened loss of employment is not a sufficient
motivator, particularly in a dynamic market where
innovation, change and readjustment are continual
processes.   A store manager has less motivation to
perceive and react to changing market or competitive
conditions and is less likely to conceive or advocate
corrective strategies.   A manager may make suggestions
to his immediate supervisor, but is naturally reluctant
to "go over the head" of his superivsor, who can
terminate his employment or influence his future with
the company.   A franchisee has greater motivation to go
to top management of his franchisor if he perceives
market or competitive problems for his business that
the franchisor can remedy.

Proponents of franchising further contend that controls
on franchisees can take several forms and, if
reasonable and enforced, can effectively maintain the
standards established by the franchisor for the
franchisee's business and adjust to changes in the
market for the franchise's product or service.   The
franchise agreement and operations manual typically
prescribe mandatory specifications, standards and
operating procedures relating to the franchisee's

facility, equipment, signs, maintenance, decor, supplies, personnel (e.g., training, appearance, form of dress), products and services offered, sources of supply, bookkeeping, record keeping and reporting, business hours and many other aspects of the franchisee's business. These specifications, standards and operating procedures are subject to change when change is required in the judgment of the franchisor. Failure to comply with one or more of such obligations, after notice, is generally sufficient legal ground for termination of the franchise.

There are, of course, limits on the right of the franchisor to require franchisees to comply with modified specifications, standards or operating procedures. If such modifications require a substantial capital investment by the franchisee or significantly impact on the profitability of his business, and the franchisee has not expressly agreed to such modifications in his franchise agreement, they are likely to be legally unenforceable (franchisors would usually find it impractical to seek advance agreement by franchisees to modifications involving substantial capital investments or impact on outlet profitability). However, courts have enforced franchisor requirements that the franchisee's business be open twenty-four hours each day, based on the right to specify hours of operation reserved by the franchisor in the franchise agreement, despite proof by the franchisee that he would incur operating losses during the extended hours.

Franchisors also can maintain control through ownership or lease of the franchisee's business premises (the consequences of termination of the franchise is loss, by the franchisee, of the right to occupy such premises) and by renewing franchises of, and granting

additional franchises to, only those franchisees whose
compliance record is good. Franchisors have found that
this combination of controls generally is effective,
though some enacted legislation and current regulatory
proposals may impede the effective utilisation of such
controls in the future.

Once convinced of the benefits of a given
specification, standard, procedure or modification
(generally by demonstration of its results in
franchisor or franchisee owned outlets) the franchisee
becomes a willing supporter of the policy. In fact,
franchisees are a fertile source of innovations in
franchise systems. It is not infrequently the
franchisor that must be convinced to change product,
service, format, advertising, procedures, pricing,
etc., by franchisees with a direct sense of market and
competitive conditions.

The proponents of franchising further argue that there
is no form of compensation or partial ownership that
compares to complete business ownership (and its estate
building potential) as a motivational force. As an
owner of his business, a franchisee will generally be
more highly motivated then an employed manager
notwithstanding any bonus system adopted by the chain
for compensation of managers. Of course, as
franchisees themselves have become multiple outlet and
chain owners this argument has declined in
significance. Presumably, the franchisee who owns two
or more outlets will encounter similar difficulties in
motivating managers and supervisors.

As a device for raising capital, franchising is
similarly the subject of both support and criticism.
Proponents point out that franchise chains have
attracted capital investment from a broad spectrum of

individuals seeking ownership of "their own business" and that the aggregate of this investment far exceeds what could have been raised from traditional sources of equity and debt capital. For an illustration of the capital raising potential of franchising, consider a fast food concept utilised by a company in a few successful outlets. Assume that this company has a net worth of $500,000 and good earnings. The owners decide to expand to a 200 unit chain over ten (10) year period. At an average investment of $500,000 per unit, the aggregate capital required for this expansion will be $100,000,000. Only a small fraction of this sum could be generated from cash flow. Thus, even if the company could arrange such financing (which it surely could not), the resulting equity dilution would be unacceptable.

Critics of franchising as a capital gathering device point out that capital raised by, in effect, selling ownership in retail outlets is, in the long run, more expensive than either debt or equity capital raised from traditional sources. The franchise chain may expand faster than a vertically integrated chain, but it builds no asset base. Further, proponents of ownership argue that a franchise relationship necessarily involves relinquishment of an excessive portion of the retail outlet profits.

Both the proponents and critics of franchising make valid arguments. This is perhaps best demonstrated by the growth of dual distribution (a combination of franchisor owned and franchisee owned retail outlets). Many franchise chains have from their inception expanded with a mix of owned and franchised outlets. Others chains have turned increasingly to owned outlets as they have matured and developed the financial capacity for a greater number of owned outlets. Dual distribution chains have obviously not found it impossible to motivate managers and supervisors (there is an ongoing debate on whether owned outlets are managed as well as franchised outlets). In an increasing number of retail chains, an incentive to managers of an owned outlet is the potential to acquire a franchise, sometimes at a reduced cost or on other favorable terms. The future availability of a franchise opportunity, possibly with financial assistance from the franchisor, can be a very positive motivator of outlet managers.

The franchise versus ownership debate frequently overlooks the fact that some businesses can operate successfully only with franchisee ownership (e.g., businesses with relatively low sales volume), whereas others can operate effectively with company or franchisee ownership. In actuality, the clearly evolving pattern throughout much of franchising is a combination of company and franchisee owned retail outlets. Though this approach does raise some potential legal problems in areas where the law is still developing, in many instances it results in greater franchisor profits and retention of the benefits of franchising. Many managers can be motivated by means other than an ownership interest and can and do operate retail outlets as effectively as franchises. However, most companies would find it impossible to recruit a sufficient number of such persons to fully staff all of their retail outlets.

The franchise versus ownership debate will likely continue, but it is interesting to note that companies who have the means to expand entirely or predominately with owned outlets are continuing to franchise (some are even increasing the percentage of franchised outlets). Some among these franchisors will readily

admit that many of their most successful innovations
have come from their franchisees. Thus, irrespective
of whether ownership or franchising is the optimum
system for raising capital, maintaining standards or
motivating managers, a system that relies, at least in
part, on franchising will likely have a better chance
of being innovative, a critical capability in a rapidly
changing market.

(2)   Variations on Vertical Integration

In an effort to achieve the advantages of vertical
integration (i.e., greater control over retail
operations, higher profits) and at least some of the
advantages of the franchise relationship (i.e., owner
management and capital investment at the outlet level)
a few companies have developed several hybrid systems.
The common thread found in such hybrid relationships is
minority ownership of the retail outlet by its manager,
generally ranging from 20% to 30% of the equity of the
retail business. The remainder of the equity is owned
by the system sponsor. Provisions for repurchase (at a
formula determined price) of the manager's equity, upon
his death, disability or termination of employment, are
typical.

In some systems, the retail outlet manager will also
own an equity interest (usually small) in other retail
outlets operating in the same market area. The theory
of this variation is that the outlet managers in each
market area will be motivated to "watch each other" and
that "good" managers will bring pressure on a
nonconformist manager to adhere to the policies of the
sponsor and thereby aid the sponsor in maintaining
system standards. A second rationale for manager
ownership interests in adjacent outlets is the
resulting greater willingness of outlet managers to

participate in market area promotions and marketing programs.

The best known example of this hybrid system in the United States is the now defunct Sambo's coffee shop chain. After several years of rapid expansion, this chain modified its manager equity program (known as the "fraction of the action"), reducing the equity available to managers and increasing its cost. The Company also attempted to repurchase equity acquired by managers under the original program. The minority ownership program of Sambo's was apparently an unsuccessful motivator (the decline in the chain's growth and its financial problems may be primarily attributable to other causes, but minority ownership by managers does not seem to have helped the chain meet competitive challenges).

Other examples are more positive. An article in Nations RESTAURANT NEWS (2/11/80) describes a joint venture plan of a Canadian company, Mother's Pizza Parlor and Spaghetti House. The sponsor owns 50% of the unit and the other 50% is divided between regional and unit management (20% by the unit manager and 30% by field supervisors and head office employees). Mother's Pizza asserts that it has found this a successful method of expansion, as did Weinerwald, a restaurant chain in Europe, and Chick-fil-A, a chain of chicken sandwich stores in the United States, whose programs involve a substantial outlet ownership or profit share for each manager.

(3) Joint Ventures

Joint ventures have been suggested as alternatives to franchising. Though generally recommended to be limited partnerships, they can also take general partnership and corporate form. The joint venture is utilised as a device for attracting capital investment at the retail outlet level. The joint venture partner may also function as the outlet manager. Otherwise the joint venture operates like a vertically integrated chain, the system sponsor being solely responsible for the management of each retail outlet and the joint ventures being passive investors. While they may avoid franchise regulation, the joint venture technique may be subject to more burdensome regulation under United States federal and state securities laws. (16)

A variation of the joint venture is the combination franchise-management contract. The franchisor actually grants a franchise to an investor and simultaneously enters into a second agreement providing for management of the franchisee's business by the franchisor. Though significantly different in legal structure from a joint venture, it is similar in practical application to a joint venture in which the sponsor assumes responsibility for management of each retail outlet. Franchise-management arrangements may also be subject to regulation under franchise and securities laws.

The joint venture business format has been virtually unused in the United States in retail distribution systems and there is thus little experience with the legal and practical problems that may develop in such relationships. For example, the legal problems associated with the expiration and termination of such relationships may prove even more troublesome than they have in franchise relationships. The relationship of partners is fundamentally different than the relationship between independent contractors and the greater fiduciary standards by which partners are required to deal with one another may excessively restrict the sponsor's business flexibility. In

franchise-management relationships, there are practical
and legal problems in tying together a long term
franchise and a customarily shorter term management
contract. Is the franchisee irrevocably married to the
franchisor as manager, even if the franchisor's
management is unsatisfactory? One is inclined to
speculate that the absence of more extensive
utilisation of joint ventures and franchisor management
arrangements is evidence of their drawbacks.

(4) Co-operatives

In some industries (e.g., manufacture of bedding
products, retail grocery and hardware stores)
manufacturer and retailer owned co-operatives are
common. Several major bedding product lines in the
United States are manufactured by independently owned
factories operating under patent and trade mark
licenses granted by a co-operative owned (in equal or
unequal proportions) by the licensees. Similarly,
there are a number of large retailer owned grocery and
hardware store co-operatives. The focus of a co-
operative is usually the economies to be gained from
combined purchases of goods. Some co-operatives also
furnish advertising and other services.

Co-operatives generally are formed by a group of
participating retailers, though a sponsor might induce
existing retailers and/or new investors to join a co-
operative established by the sponsor, and cause the co-
operative to enter into a management contract with the
sponsor. From the perspective of the sponsor, control
over the co-operative may be tenuous.

Well managed co-operatives have some of the advantages
of franchise systems, though co-operatives may not be
able to police system standards as well as franchisors

and generally do not furnish as much service as
franchisors. Currently in the United States there are
a large number of franchise systems in which the
franchisees were established business owners when they
elected to join a franchise program. Real estate broker
franchises are the best known (e.g., Century 21), but
this type of franchising, known as conversion or
affiliation franchising, has spread to insurance
brokers, banks, savings and loan institutions,
painters, used car dealers, accountants, home
remodelers, repair services and other businesses. Co-
operative systems might have been adopted by these
businesses as a form of organisation. Though there
have been recent press reports of retailers of common
products or services forming co-operating associations
for common advertising and the purchase of goods and
services, the incidence of such co-operative
associations appears to be dwarfed by the avalanche of
conversion franchise programs.

A major legal disadvantage of co-operatives under
United States antitrust law is the determination by the
United States Supreme Court in two landmark cases that
restrictions imposed by a co-operative on its members
are horizontal restraints (i.e., restrictive agreements
among competitors), rather than vertical restraints
(restrictions imposed by a company operating at one
level of distribution upon other companies operating at
a different distribution level). Horizontal restraints
are subject to much stricter antitrust limitations than
are vertical restraints.(17)

The substantial increase in the incidence of franchisee
associations and advisory counsels, and the expanded
role of such franchisee organisations in the planning
and operation of franchise systems, has somewhat
narrowed the differences in the operations of franchise

systems and co-operatives. Franchisees have no control over their franchisor by means of ownership, but in a growing number of franchise systems the franchisees are gaining considerable influence, both in current operations (e.g., in advertising programs) and long term planning, through associations and advisory counsels. A recent example is a new franchise agreement negotiated between Midas Muffler and its franchisee association.

Alternatives to franchising do exist and one or more alternative methods may be suitable and even appropriate for a particular company. A company planning expansion should investigate franchising merely as one of the available techniques. In examining available expansion techniques, a company should keep in mind that franchising is a well developed business relationship in the United States. The development of franchising in Canada is not far behind and it is catching on rapidly in Europe and Japan. The Middle East, South Asia, South Africa and Central and South America are also experiencing an increase in franchising. The growth of franchising during 1950-1980 has been phenomenal and by every measure has been beneficial to the economies and societies in which this growth has occurred. The extensive development and growth of franchising is one of its strongest advantages; franchising is an increasingly well understood business relationship, which facilitates it utilisation in expansion of a distribution system.

This discussion has treated franchising as if it were a single business relationship, which is not the case. Franchising relationships are quite varied, running the spectrum of simple trademark licenses with minimal supervision and assistance, authorised dealerships and comprehensive ongoing relationships with substantial franchisor assistance and service. Franchise systems also vary widely in the relative investment made by the franchisor and the franchisee in the franchisee's retail outlet. At one extreme, the investment is made solely by the franchisee. At the other, the franchisor may funish all assets other than inventory (e.g., certain convenience food store franchises) and share the gross operating profit with the franchisee. A company planning expansion must not only consider the alternatives to franchising, but also which of the variations of franchise relationships is most suitable to its type of business, objectives and human and capital resources.

2.   **FORMS OF FRANCHISE RELATIONSHIPS**

(A)   Introduction

As noted above, the concept of franchising covers a broad spectrum of distribution relationships. Variations include whether the relationship primarily involves the sale of a product manufactured by the franchisor, the relative importance of the capital needed to establish the retail outlet, the significance of the franchisor's trade or service mark, the complexity of the business, the level of services needed by the franchisee, the capabilities of the franchisor to furnish services and the exclusivity of the relationship. Defining different categories of franchise relationships is a somewhat arbitrary exercise involving generalisations. Nevertheless, certain generalised categories have been identified.

(B)   Product Franchises and Selective Distribution

The product franchise is typically a distribution system for marketing goods manufactured by the franchisor, though the

franchisor could also be a distributor or other marketer of
such goods manufactured by others and sold under the
trademark of the franchisor or the manufacturer. The
fundamental distinctions between a product franchise and an
ordinary supplier-dealer relationship are greater
identification of the dealer with the franchisor-supplier's
trademark, more extensive and comprehensive franchisor
services to franchisees and exclusive or semi-exclusive
franchisee marketing and services of the franchisor's
product line. Instead of selling to a broad range of
distributors and/or dealers, the franchisor sells its
products exclusively or primarily to selected franchised
distributors and/or dealers who deal exclusively or
concentrate their marketing and service in such products
(and typically do not sell a competitive product). The
franchised dealer may adopt the franchisor's trademark as
his exclusive or principal trade identity.

Products requiring extensive presale or postsale service and
possessing strong brand identity lend themselves to product
franchise relationships. By franchising a limited number of
dealers, and limiting or proscribing intrabrand competition
(e.g., by granting each dealer an exclusive territory and
prohibiting dealers from selling outside their territories),
the franchisor-manufacturer assures each franchisee a
sufficient market to induce the franchisee to furnish
exclusive or concentrated marketing and product service and
thereby obtain market penetration. Achieving market
penetration is a key motivation for product franchising.
Only by securing exclusive or semi-exclusive dealers can
many franchisors become effective interbrand competitors.
Automobile distribution is perhaps the best known example of
product franchising. Gasoline, automotive products,
alcoholic and non-alcoholic beverages, bicycles, hearing
aids, farm machinery and other products are distributed
through dealer networks having characteristics of product
franchising/selective distribution.

(C) Business Format Franchising

Business format franchising typically involves the license of a trade and/or service mark and a format for the retail sale of products and/or services and the use of related know-how. The business format franchisor typically manufactures no product, but may serve as a supplier of raw materials (e.g., spices, ingredients, trademarked service and packaging materials) or finished products used by the franchisee in performing a service (e.g., automotive parts, rental products, business forms). Business format franchisees typically perform services, but may sell and install a product in conjunction with such service (e.g., fast food restaurants, automotive product replacement services).

Business format franchises share certain characteristics with product franchises. The business format franchisee generally deals exclusively in the franchisor's sponsored services and typically is required to adopt the franchisor's service mark as his exclusive or predominant trade identity. There is also a similarity in the typical franchisor services, such as training, guidance and advertising. In some franchise systems the demarcation between product and business format is blurred.

(D) Manufacturing Licenses

Companies sometimes license other companies to manufacture a product that is patented or produced by means of a patented process and/or proprietary know-how. Manufacturing licenses are common in international commerce. If the relationship also involves the licensee's sale of the product identified by the licensor's trademark, it contains elements of a franchise relationship. The best known example of manufacturing license franchises in the United States are soft drink bottling franchises. The franchisor supplies a

trade secret syrup and licenses bottlers to use that syrup
to manufacture bottled soft drink beverages sold under the
franchisor's trademarks.

(E) Affiliation Relationships

Affiliation and conversion franchises, referred to above, is
a relatively new and fast growing type of franchise
relationship. Affiliation franchising commenced with real
estate broker franchise programs in the early 1970's and has
spread to a number of other services (e.g., insurance
brokers, financial service businesses, painting and
decorating services, used car dealers, home remodeling
services, accounting). Product franchising may also be
involved. A hearing aid manufacturer is currently offering
exclusive product franchises to hearing aid dealers, some of
which it has been supplying on a non-exclusive basis.

Affiliation franchising involves the organising of
independent businesses under the umbrella of a franchise
system. The franchisor gains the expertise of an
experienced, established businessman, and the former
independent gains a national identity and system of doing
business, as well as advertising, purchasing, research and
development and other services. Affiliation franchising
speeds expansion since there is little or no start-up time
or expense. The franchisee must adopt the service mark of
the franchisor as a trade identity, though in some
affiliation franchise programs the franchisee retains his
original trade name as a secondary or even predominent trade
identity. The franchisee agrees to conduct his business in
accordance with the franchisor's specifications, standards
and operating procedures and to pay fees to the franchisor.
However, affiliation franchisees may be more resistant to
franchisor control than are traditional franchisees in the
early phase of their relationship. The franchisor will
typically furnish training, purchasing and advertising

services. the economies of joint purchasing, advertising under a common trade identity and the availability of specialised services at lower cost are the usual motivations for independent businesses to become an affiliate franchisee.

Such businessmen may also have defensive reasons; for example, the need to become part of a franchise system in order to compete with national services businesses. Insurance brokerage is an example of a business with large, expanding national companies acquiring an increasing share of the market for insurance brokerage services. A number of affiliation franchise programs for insurance brokers have emphasised the needs of independent insurance brokers to join a franchise system that can furnish sophisticated services and national identity and prevent further erosion of the market share of the independent brokers. As large banks and other financial services business become national companies in the United States, thousands of small banks and savings institutions are likely to fear the loss of market share and join franchise programes.

Professional services (e.g., law, medicine, dentistry, accounting, architective, engineering) many also be the subjects of affiliation franchising programs. Formidable regulatory barriers exist in the United States. Several dental service franchise programs are currently offered in the United States, a reflection in part of an excessive number of young dentists struggling to make a living. Dental services are being marketed in commercial shopping areas through franchised dental offices in an effort to market these services to the large share of the population that does not regularly purchase them.

(F) Quasi and Other Franchise Relationships

Franchisor-franchisee management contracts, described above,

are a quasi franchise relationship. The franchisee owns the
outlet, but to the extent that the franchisee relies upon
the franchisor's management, the franchisee is in reality a
passive investor in a security. Certain hotel management
relationships have attributes of franchising. The investor
furnishes the capital to develop the hotel and the hotel
operators furnishes a trade identity and development and
management services. These relationships differ from
franchisor-franchisee management arrangements in one
fundamental respect. If the hotel management agreement is
terminate, the hotel operator's trade identity is withdrawn.
However, the franchisor's management agreement can terminate
without termination of the franchise, leaving the franchisee
in the position of a traditional franchisee.

Usually in response to deteriorating system performance,
some franchisors have sought to renegotiate their franchise
relationships to provide for substantial reduction or
complete elimination of franchisor services and
corresponding reduction in the franchisee's fee obligations.
The system in essence becomes a series of trademark licenses
with minimal quality control. The inadequate managerial and
financial resources of the franchisor are likely to result
in wide variations in format and quality among franchisees
and erosion of the essential attributes and benefits of a
franchise system.

Certain franchise systems, notably gasoline service stations
and catalog stores of Sears and Wards, though purporting to
be independent contractor franchise relationships, contain
elements of employment relationships and are at most quasi
franchise systems. The franchisee makes a minimal
investment. In a gasoline station, the real estate, tanks,
pumps and other equipment is typicaly owned by the
franchisor. The franchisee may own a tow truck and
automotive repair equipment and tools and some inventory of
tires, batteries and accessories. The franchisee

customarily does not pay for gasoline until it is sold. Until recently, the lease and dealer agreements were terminable on short notice without cause. Longer term agreements, terminable only for cause, are now common (and gasoline station franchises are now regulated by federal law). Gasoline station and certain other types of franchisees do have a variable income, related to sales, but little or no investment risk. The substantial investment in fixed assets and inventory is made by the franchisor.

Bonanza, a budget steakhouse franchisor, has recently announced a hybrid franchise arrangement with its largest franchisee. The two companies will divide the several functions of franchisor, with Bonanza responsible for site selection and financing and the franchisee responsible for restaurant development and opening and franchisee training. The franchisee has developed several food concepts for shopping malls, which it operates in addition to its Bonanza steakhouse franchises. To develop and expand these concepts more rapidly, the franchisee turned to its franchisor, Bonanza, to furnish financial resources and site selection expertise. Bonanza and its franchisee will jointly franchise these concepts and share the revenue from these franchising programs.

(G)   Types of Franchise Systems

(1)   Individual and Area Franchises

Franchise relationships can be somewhat arbitrarily classified into two classes and several subclasses. The two primary classes are individual franchises and area franchises. An individual franchise is simply a franchise for a single business outlet and is historically the most common form of franchise. The individual franchisee may acquire rights to establish additional franchised business, in the form of options

or rights of first refusal, or merely as a reward for
co-operation and successful operation of his initial
franchise, and may thereby move into the second class
of franchise. The area franchise takes many forms,
generally resembling one of the following.

(2) Multiple Outlet Franchise

The multiple outlet franchise may evolve from an
individual franchise, as discussed above, or may be
contemplated and documented at the inception of the
relationship. In the latter case, the franchisor and
franchisee typically enter into an area development
agreement that grants the franchisee the right to open
franchised businesses in an identified area and
prescribes the development responsibilities of the
franchisee and a development schedule. Each business
outlet is usually governed by a separate franchise
agreement. The franchisee must generally own a
controlling interest in each franchise, but is
frequently permitted to have minority investors (e.g.,
equity owing managers) in individual franchised
outlets.

(3) Subfranchising

A second type of area franchise permits the area
franchisee to grant subfranchises. The true
subfranchise involves two distinct contractual
relationships: one between the franchisor and the
franchisee and a second between the franchisee
(subfranchisor) and the subfranchisee. There is
generally no privity of contract between the franchisor
and the subfranchisee, though the franchisor may
reserve final approval of the subfranchisee and/or the
location of his business. Typically, the
franchisee/subfranchisor will own and operate some

franchised outlets. The right to grant subfranchises reduces the capital requirements of the area franchisee, who can look to subfranchisees for much of the capital required to develop the territory.

Subfranchising raises significant legal questions (e.g., the delegability under United States trademark law of the obligation to police the subfranchisee's use of the franchisor's trademark; the extent to which the franchisor can control the economic relationship between the franchisee and the subfranchisee) and potentially troublesome legal problems under disclosure regulation and when the area franchisee becomes insolvent or is terminated. Loss of franchisor control and evolution of significant variations in operations among different areas are serious potential problems of subfranchising. Subfranchising has been successfully utilised by franchisors in the United States, but has been a cause of difficulties when subfranchisors have been granted, or have acquired by default, excessive control over the operation of the system in their respective territories.

(4)   Three Party Relationships

The third form of area franchising is a hybrid of the first two forms. This form is a three party relationship and involves a development agreement between the franchisor and the area franchisee, which delegates to the latter the obligation to secure, train, assist and/or supervise franchisees. However, the franchisor grants the franchise directly to and has privity to contract with the franchisee (the area franchisee may or may not be a party to the agreement). Fees paid by franchisees are shared by the franchisor and the area franchisee.

The three party relationship eliminates certain legal
and business problems of subfranchising attributable to
the absence of contractual privity between the
franchisor and the subfranchisee (e.g., enforcement of
qulaity control, control of the economics of the
franchised business and a proclivity for power to to
disperse from a single source (i.e., the franchisor) to
multiple sources (i.e., area franchisees). As in the
subfranchises relationship, the area franchisee may
also own and operate one or more franchised outlets.

(5) Area Franchising Considerations

With respect to all forms of area franchising, certain
considerations are important in formulating the
relationship, including a precise definition of the
area for which the franchise is granted, the nature of
the exclusivity that the franchisee will enjoy therein
and the conditions for maintaining that exclusivity. A
development schedule is essential to avoid
underdevelopment of a territory. It is important to
prescribe a realistic schedule and to anticipate
external forces that may delay development (e.g., high
interest rates, unavailability of credit) and formulate
a procedure for stretching out the development
schedule. Consideration must also be given to the
consequences of the franchisee's failure to meet the
development schedules. Will such failure result only
in the loss of exclusivity or in the termination of the
area franchise in order to facilitate refranchising the
territory on an exclusive basis? Will the franchisor
have a claim for damages against an area franchisee
that fails to fulfill its development obligations?

Both subfranchising and three party relationships
reduce the franchisor's administrative burdens, as many
of a franchisor's customary obligations are delegated

to the area franchisee. Area franchising (particularly of multiple unit franchises) will result in fewer franchisees with whom the franchisor must deal. This may simplify the introduction of new concepts and other system modifications and may facilitate the reacquisition of franchised outlets through purchase of an entire area from a single franchisee and retention of its management team. Area franchising attracts franchisees with greater financial resources and business experience and can facilitate rapid and self-sustaining growth of a franchise system. However, it also creates large, sophisticated franchisees with vested interests that may not always coincide with those of the franchisor. Such area franchisees are likely to insist on negotiating a greater range of issues both at the inception of the relationship and as it evolves, which can impede a quick response to changing market conditions. Area franchisees will typically demand a greater voice in the development and implementation of advertising and other franchisor programs. An excessive shift of power to area franchisees can ultimately impede the growth and performance of a franchise system.

3. **FRANCHISING AS A DISTRIBUTION RELATIONSHIP**

(A) Economic and Financial Characteristics of Franchising

The economic and financial characteristics of franchising vary widely depending on the type of franchise, the type of franchise system, the investment required in the franchisee's outlet, the type of product or service and other factors. In a product franchise, the primary economic and financial characteristics relate to the sale of the franchisor's product line to the franchisee and the prices charged to the franchisee and the terms of payment. Warranty service and co-operative advertising reimbursements

to the franchised dealer may also be significant. If the
product sold is expensive and customarily financed (e.g.,
automobiles) the franchisor may furnish consumer finance
services. If the product requires on going service and
parts replacements, the franchisor is likely to be a
supplier of parts. The product franchisor usually does not
finance the development of the dealer's business facility,
though United States automobile manufacturers have
dealership financing programs.

The business format franchisor generally charges an initial
fee for the grant of the franchise. This may be a single
fee or broken down into separate fees for the franchise,
training, site selection, outlet development and/or other
services. The business format franchisee also generally
pays a continuing fee. This fee is usually a percentage of
gross sales or revenues (excluding sales taxes), but may be
measured by unit sales, equipment used, products purchased
or the franchisee's gross or net profit, or a fixed periodic
fee. Business format franchisees are also typically
required to contribute to a franchisor administered
advertising fund that pays the cost of creation of
advertising materials and advertising programs. The
business format franchisor may lease real property or
operating assets, offer financing and serve as a supplier to
its franchisees.

(B)   The Franchisee as a Source of Capital

Traditionally, franchisees have performed two significant
functions in the franchise relationship. They have
furnished the capital to develop the franchised outlet and
they have furnished the management of that outlet. The
role of the franchisee as a source of capital is an
obviously significant element of the franchise relationship
and a subject that has generated much discussion with the
advent of an era of scarce capital and high interest rates.

Many industries in which franchise systems are prevalent are characterised by capital-intensive retail outlets (e.g., fast food, lodging, motor vehicle rental, automative services and convenience stores).

The last few years have been difficult ones for franchisors dependent upon franchisee capital for expansion. Only franchise systems requiring relatively little capital to establish each outlet, those few that are able to tap the equity capital market and those that are generating sufficient internal cash flow to finance expansion have been unaffected by the scarcity and high price of capital. This period has challenged a fundamental precept of franchising, namely, the combination of the know-how of the franchisor with capital supplied by the franchisee. The traditional method of financing utilised by franchisees is a combination of their own resources and direct or indirect (e.g., a second mortgage on the franchisee's home) bank loans. For many franchised businesses, this method continues to be adequate. However, for other franchises the capital requirements far exceed the personal resources of most individuals. Franchises for such businesses continue to be available to such individuals only if the franchisor intervenes to establish or assist in the development of programs to make nontraditional financing available. Faced with high capital requirements and increasing capital scarcity and cost, franchisors have been forced to look to a different kind of franchisee and beyond the franchisee to other sources of capital.

Franchisors have always assisted their franchisees in various ways to raise needed capital. Frequently the predominant capital requirement of retail outlets is the purchase cost of land and the business facility erected or remodelled thereon. This is particularly true where the retail outlet is a free standing structure (though even an in-line facility can require extensive leasehold

improvements). Considerable effort has consequently been
made by both franchisors and other distribution system
sponsors to attract capital from private investors for the
real estate portion of the retail outlet investment. These
efforts have been successful and enormous aggregates of
private capital have been attracted by this means to retail
distribution systems.

Typically, the system sponsor will package one or more
sites, purchase and resell the sites to a private investor
or investor syndicate (or arrange for direct purchase); the
investor improves the sites in accordance with the sponsor's
plans and specifications; and the sponsor then leases the
improved sites for operation of retail outlets or sublease
to franchisees. There are several variations on such "build
to suit" arrangements, including extending the investment to
include equipment and fixtures. Frequently, the real estate
owner leases to the franchisor for sublease to the
franchisee, thus incorporating a credit guarantee by the
franchisor, in exchange for which the franchisor acquires
control of the outlet and additional revenue.

Other franchisors have given partial or full guarantees for
lease and conventional financing granted to their
franchisees. A few franchisors offer to directly finance or
guarantee part or all of the financing required by expanding
franchisees. Such financing may be offered at commercial
rates or subsidised rates. Some franchisors have extended
financing guarantees in the form of formal or informal
inventory repurchase agreements, which are assignable by the
franchisee to his lender, thereby assuring the lender that
if the franchisee defaults, the franchisor's repurchase of
qualified merchandise will generate funds for loan
repayment, a more effective type of security than
traditional security interests.

Increasing dependence on outside lenders has confronted

franchisors with the obligation to negotiate various modifications to franchise agreements for the protection of the lender. Lenders typically want notice of and an opportunity to cure defaults by the franchisee, subordination of royalty payments to debt service, or a moratorium on royalty payments if interest or principal are in arrears, and the right to assign the franchise without the approval of the franchisor in the event the franchisee defaults. Obviously, franchisors resist such demands, but they do frequently negotiate significant modifications.

In the United States, many franchisors have encouraged utilisation of Small Business Administration (SBA) guaranteed loans and have assisted their franchisees in securing them. SBA guaranteed loans have played a major role in franchising franchisee expansion. A second capital source, adopted by a few franchisors, is the formation of a Small Business Investment Company (SBIC) or a Minority Enterprise Small Business Investment Company (MESBIC). SBICs and MESBICs that meet certain capital and other requirements, and are certified by the Small Business Administration, are authorised to borrow up to three (SBIC) or four (MESBIC) times their capital from the SBA at interest rates substantially below prevailing market rates for comparable loans. SCIBs and MESBICs can make loans to, and equity investments in, eligible small business (MESBICs can only grant loans and can only deal with small businesses owned by persons who are members of certain minority groups). A substantial mark-up is permitted in the interest rate charged by the SBIC or MESBIC over its borrowing rate. When a franchisor sponsors an SBIC or MESBIC, it is subject to certain restrictions on loans to franchisees of the sponsoring franchisor (e.g., the percentage of the loan that the franchisee may use for purchases of goods and services from the franchisor; an SBIC sponsored by a franchisor generally may not make equity investments in its franchisees).

A third capital-raising technique that has recently emerged is the publicly offered limited partnership in a pool of outlets to be developed for lease to franchisees. The traditional sale and leaseback investor makes a large investment in one or a few outlets. The publicly offered limited partnership is an effort to tap the vast pool of small investors, a variation of the real estate investment trust. Franchisors have not been the promoters of these public offerings, but have approved them and may themselves be the lessee for some of the outlets developed with the proceeds of the offering. Franchisors ordinarily co-operate with the underwriters, but do not own any interest in the limited partnership. In most instances, the franchisor does not guarantee the franchisee's indebtedness. Occasionally, the franchisor may manage the real estate owned by the partnership and/or will agree to take over the operations of terminated franchisees. Such public offerings have been utilised by fast food franchise systems, but, if successful over a long period, this capital raising technique may spread to other types of franchise systems.

Financing the development of franchisee outlets is unlikely to become easier in economies where capital is chronically in short supply, subject to fierce competition, and expensive. In addition to the techniques discussed herein, franchisors may be required to develop other approaches to and sources of financing.

In addition to efforts to develop new sources of financing franchisee outlets, there is a discernable trend by many franchisors to a new kind of franchisee. Instead of a person of limited means and experience, but a strong desire to learn and progress, franchises are frequently being granted to existing franchisees (of the same or another system) with proven records and available capital or sources of capital and to investment groups, who commit to develop multiple outlets in a defined territory. Some area franchisees are medium size or even large companies that successfully operate another business and are seeking diversification (some are franchisors or operators of other business concepts). The public sale of equity securities by area franchisees is increasing significantly. Others are wealthy individuals attracted to the opportunity to establish a chain of outlets in a protected territory. Such an area franchisee satisfies the traditional capital contribution function of the franchisee more effectively than the individual franchisee. Area franchising appears to be rapidly expanding and a growing number of franchisors will only grant multiple outlet franchises.

(C) The Franchisee as a Motivated Business Owner

The significance of the franchisee as a highly motivated business owner is discussed above. The franchisee has much to gain if his business is successful and much to lose if it is not. As the nature of franchise relationships evolves, and many franchisees become large, multiple outlet operators, the problem of manager motivation shifts from the franchisor to the franchisee. This evolution may ultimately result in some franchise systems acquiring characteristics of a vertically integrated distribution system. There will be a level of owner-management (the franchisee) closer to the retail outlets than in many vertically integrated chains, but outlet managers will be employees, not owners.

(D) The Different Roles of a Franchisor

As noted above, the franchisor may serve multiple roles in a franchise system. As the licensor of a trade or service mark, and a format for conducting business, the franchisor furnishes the trade identity and basic business plan of the franchisee. The franchisor furnishes know-how, operating experience and problem solving guidance to its franchisees. The franchisor may be the supplier of the principal product line sold by the franchisee or ingredients and supplies that the franchisee uses in producing products or services. Franchisors administer centralised advertising and marketing programs. The franchisor may be a direct or indirect source of financing to its franchisees or administer programs to assist them in securing financing. The franchisor will frequently serve as a product and market research and development resource for its franchisees and develop programs and format changes to maintain or enhance the competitive performance of its franchisees.

(E)   Sources of Franchisor Revenue

The franchisor typically derives revenue from several of the multiple sources found in franchise relationships. Initial fees and continuing fees are a primary source of revenue. The franchisor may also derive revenue by leasing real estate or equipment to its franchisee, directly or indirectly loaning capital to them and in selling goods and services to them. The purchase and resale of franchised businesses is also a source of revenue to a franchisor.

(F)   Analysis of Franchising From Perspective of Franchisee

The basis of the appeal of a franchise to a franchisee is discussed above. For many prospective franchisees, due to lack of experience and financial resources, a franchise is the only realistic means to become a business owner and such individuals are generally unable to conduct a thorough analysis of a franchise and are frequently disinclined to hire professionals to do it for them. Only the more sophisticated prospective franchisee is likely to thoroughly analyse the economics, advantages and disadvantages of a franchise. However, an increasing number of large companies are acquiring area franchises, particularly fast food restaurant franchises, presumably after just such analyses.

A franchise confers a variety of benefits and imposes certain costs upon the franchisee. Those benefits and costs are discussed above. The key economic issues are the probable value of the benefits of a given franchise and the relationship of that value to those costs. If the franchisor furnishes some or all of a strong trade identity and consumer good will; valuable know-how and experience; effective training, outlet development and start-up assistance; financing; procurement programs; advertising programs; research and development and continuing guidance, the value of the franchise is likely to exceed the costs that the franchisee will incur. If the franchisor's services are focused primarily on the opening of the franchisee's business, the franchisee is likely to conclude that the costs associated with the franchise will in the long run exceed the value of its benefits. The analysis involves a good deal of prediction and projection of the past operating history of the franchisor into the future. There are many potential events which could change the performance of the franchisor, causing the costs of the franchise to exceed its value. For example, as a result of illness, death, retirement or acquisition of the franchisor, its management could change, resulting in the introduction of new operating philosophies. Acquisition of franchisors by companies that have not previously operated a franchising business is an increasing phenomenon. For the franchisee entering into a ten to twenty-five year relationship, the predictions inherent in the cost-benefit analysis of a franchise become rather speculative.

In addition to the economic cost benefit analysis, a prospective franchisee should conduct an introspective analysis of his own personality and temperament in the context of a franchise relationship. Most franchises involve extensive and comprehensive restrictions and franchisor control over the operation of the franchisee's business. Not all persons are suited by personality or goals to this type of business enviroment (well managed franchisors attempt to determine the suitability of prospective franchisees to the franchise relationship, generally seeking a delicate balance of innovativeness, diligence and acceptance of instruction, guidance and operating rules).

Finally, the prospective franchisee should analyse his ability to expand within the franchise system in accordance with the goals, and whether he will be restricted by contract from developing in the same or competitive businesses outside of the franchise system. He should anticipate the possibility that the franchisor will become less competitive, the cost benefit analysis of the franchise will change or expansion within the franchise system will be barred by unavailability of additional franchises or the expansion of other franchisees or franchisor owned outlets. In any of these situations, the prospective franchisee should also consider the extent to which obligations and restrictions of the franchise will preclude business activity outside the franchise system.

CONCLUSION

The franchise relationship has changed considerably in the last three decades. These changes were due in part to criticism of early abuses, litigation, full disclosure and other regulation. Much change has also resulted from experience and increased knowledge. Franchisors understand far better today what does and does not work in the franchise relationship. Franchisees also have a better understanding of the franchise relationship. Franchisors and franchisees view each other differently today than they once did. They regard each other less as protagonists and are more will to recognise that they are engaged in a common enterprise in which both or neither will be successful.

The new breed of franchisee is radically different from his predecessor of the 1950-1970 era. He is frequently a trained and well-financed businessman or company, with a good understanding of the franchise relationship and his role in it. An increasing number of multiple outlet franchisees are developing different types of restaurant or other business under area franchises of two or more different franchisors. A number of multiple outlet franchisees have become franchisors of separate business concepts. Such franchisees are quick to perceive the advantages of franchisee associations, collective bargaining and vigorous assertion of the rights of franchisees. In some respects, it may be more difficult for franchisors to deal with this new breed of franchisee, but in other respects it may be easier. Enhanced knowledge and appreciation of the essential interests of both franchisor and franchisee may enable both franchisor and franchisee to effectively protect their separate interests and simultaneously enhance their joint interests. The franchise relationship in many systems may be evolving towards an effective partnership, composed of relative equals, rather than a dominant franchisor and a dependent franchisee.

FOOTNOTES

1.   C. ROSENFELD, <u>THE LAW OF FRANCHISING,</u> CH. 1 para 1-4
     (1970).

2.   R. ROSENBERG, <u>PROFITS FROM FRANCHISING</u> (1970) at 9
     (1969).

3.   Id. at 10.

4.   Id.

5.   C. VAUGHN, <u>FRANCHISING</u> (1974) at 12-13.

6.   H. KURSH, <u>THE FRANCHISE BOOM</u> (1968) at 5.

7.   C. VAUGHN, <u>FRANCHISING</u> (1974) at 15.

8.   Id. at 16-17.

9.   H. KURSH, <u>THE FRANCHISE BOOM</u> (1968) at 6.

10. The Lanham Act, 15 U.S.C 1051 et. seq. (1946).

11. The Lanham Act, 15 U.S.C. 1053.

12. C. VAUGHN, <u>FRANCHISING</u> (1974) at 17-21.

13. All statistics on franchising are derived from U.S.
     Dept. of Commerce, <u>Franchising in the Economy</u> 1969-71
     and 1981-83 editions.

14. The following is a summary of regulation of franchising
     in the United States:

(1) State and Federal Regulation

State governments began the enactment of statutes regulating the termination and renewal of dealers with a 1965 Puerto Rican statute and 1969 Delaware law. In 1970 California enacted its Franchise Investment Law, the first of 15 state disclosure and registration laws governing the sale of franchises. State legislatures have established a patchwork of over one hundred industry specific laws, including laws regulating manufacturer-dealer relationships in such industries as motor vehicles, petroleum products, alcoholic beverages and farm implements. The states also have enacted more than twenty laws regulating the relationship between franchisors and franchisees, focusing on the franchise relationship rather than a specific industry. Some of this substantive regulation is incorporated in disclosure statutes.

Franchise disclosure laws typically require the registration of the franchise (and in some states the independent registration of franchise salesmen) and the use of an offering circular in the sale of franchises. State administrators have authority to deny or suspend registration in certain cases (e.g., insufficient financial resources to implement a franchise program); to require franchisors to escrow initial franchise fees and other franchisee payments until the franchisor has performed its obligations relating to the development and opening of the franchisee's business; and to prohibit deceptive or misleading advertising for prospective franchisees. Disclosure statutes require the franchisor's offering circular to contain certain specified information regarding the recent business history and litigation and bankruptcy experience of the franchisor and its directors and officers; financial statements of the franchisor or its parent company; and a description of the terms of the franchise, the investment which the franchisee is required to make, the recent history of the franchise system and any actual or projected financial results of the operation of franchisee or franchisor owned outlets which the franchisor proposes to use in the sale of franchises. In addition, state laws require disclosure of all other material facts relevant to the franchise offered and all facts necessary to make the disclosures not misleading. The specified disclosures are fairly uniform among the states and have been made more uniform by the universal adoption of the Uniform Franchise Offering Circular rules and guidelines, recommended by the North American Securities Administrators' Associaton. Sales must be suspended and offering circulars and registrations amended in the event of a material change in the information contained in the offering circular. Most state laws require only disclosure, financial responsibility and compliance with registration requirements. A few state laws permit a limited merit review of franchise offerings and Michigan has implemented its limited statutory authority to impose a rather arbitrary review of the fairness of franchise agreement terms. Several years ago the California administrator unsuccessfully sought merit review authority from the California legislature.

State laws regulating the franchise relationship generally apply primarily to the termination and renewal of franchises, requiring good cause for termination and, in some cases for nonrenewal, prior notice (from 30 to 90 days) to the franchisee of his failures to comply with the terms of his franchise that are the grounds for termination or nonrenewal, and usually an opportunity for the franchisee to cure his breaches. Some of these laws also regulate the transfer of the franchise by the franchisee, competition by the franchisor in the exclusive territory of its franchisee, and discrimination among franchisees.

State laws regulating the relationship among manufacturers, distributors and dealers in a specific industry are typically more comprehensive, covering in addition to termination, renewal and transfer, such aspects of the franchise relationship as disposition of the franchise upon death of the franchised dealer, compensaton to the dealer for warranty service, the sale of goods and parts by the franchisor to the dealer and the grant of additional franchises in the market of the dealer, referred to as zone flooding or encroachment. Regulation of encroachment is relatively recent, has imposed severe restrictions and so far has been limited to the motor vehicle industry.

In a large number of judicial decisions in the past decade the courts have consistently held that these statutes (both industry specific and general franchise relationship statutes) may not be made retroactive so as to apply to franchise relationships that commenced prior to the effective date of the statute. These decisions have been highly significant. Contrary ruling would have drastically changed the rules applicable to several hundred thousand franchise relationships and might have induced wider enactment of such legislation.

More recently, the states have enacted business opportunity laws aimed at promoters of a wide variety of dealerships, vending machine and rack jobbing businesses, home manufacturing ventures and other "business opportunities," many of which are fraudulent or of marginal value. Such business opportunities typically require low investments and are promoted to the uneducated and unsophisticated. While the definitions of "franchise" in franchise disclosure laws focus primarily on business format franchises, the definitions of "business opportunity" are far less uniform and generally are broad enough to include most distribution relationships. Though state legislatures readily perceive a distinction between franchising and the class of business opportunity ventures at which this his new legislation is aimed, excluding franchising from these statutes in defining "business opportunities" has proven to be exceedingly difficult.

Some business opportunity laws require registration, all require disclosure and some require the seller to obtain a surety bond in certain circumstances. Of the twenty business opportunity laws enacted so far, five are in states that already have franchise disclosure laws. When a state has both a franchise disclosure law and a business opportunity law, regulation under the franchise law constitutes an exemption from the business opportunity law. This exemption will not, however, aid a manufacturer whose distribution relationship is exempt from the state's franchise disclosure law, but fall within the broader definition of its business opportunity law.

United States federal regulation of franchising is far less comprehensive. There are two federal statutes regulating franchise relationships in specific industries, the Automobile Dealers Day in Court Act and Petroleum Marketing Practices Act. The former was enacted in the mid 1950's and focuses primarily on coercion of dealers by manufacturers. Though automobile dealers have prevailed in some cases, this statute has not proven very beneficial to automobile dealers, one reason for the extensive state regulation of the franchise relationship in the distribution of motor vehicles.

Congress did not act again to regulate franchising until the late 1970's this time focusing on franchise relationships in petroleum products distribution, a field in which the great majority of states had already enacted regulation. Petroleum refiners initially resisted this legislation, the Petroleum Marketing Practices Act (PMPA), but then negotiated its terms. An interesting aspect of these negotiations was industry acceptance of tougher regulations in exchange for federal preemption of inconsistent state regulation, a rare instance of federal preemption. The PMPA is far more comprehensive than the Automobile Dealers Day in Court Act, dealing extensively with termination and renewal of franchises in various circumstances and with other aspects of petroleum products franchises. This statute is an even-handed approach to the regulation of vertical distribution relationships. There has already been extensive litigation under the PMPA and petroleum products franchisors have fared better than might have been expected.

The sole federal regulation of franchising as a business relationship (as distinct from a specific industry) is a trade regulation rule concisely titled "Disclosure Requirements and Prohibitions Concerning Franchising and Business Opportunity Ventures," adopted by the Federal Trade Commission in 1978, effective in October, 1979 (the "Franchise Rule"). This trade regulation rule requires disclosure of specified information to prospective franchisees and buyers of business opportunities in advance of the sale of a franchise. Its definition of a "franchise" differs from state law definitions in terminology but encompasses essentially the same types of business franchises, primarily the business format variety. "Business opportunities" are separately defined, more narrowly than in most state business opportunity laws. Provisions exempting product franchisors were adopted by the Commission in its interpretive guides, as a result of considerable business opposition to the broad coverage of the Franchise Rule's definition of a "franchise" adopted by the Commission. The Franchise Rule does not require registration of franchises. Notwithstanding an attempt by the Commission to afford franchisees a private cause of action to enforce the Franchise Rule, private enforcement has been rejected by the courts. However, state disclosure laws do afford franchisees the right to sue for damages and rescission if a franchisor fails to comply with registration, disclosure or other obligations of the law. Other state laws may authorise franchisee suits based on a failure to comply with the Franchise Rule of the Federal Trade Commission. See generally the BUSINESS FRANCHISE GUIDE , Commerce Clearing House.

(2)   Regulation Under Securities Laws

Both before and since the advent of franchise disclosure laws in the United States, disenchanted franchisees, and occasionally government agencies, have asserted that certain franchises are securities. Whether a franchise constitutes a "security" (in the form of an "investment contract" or a "profit-sharing arrangement") for purposes of federal and state securities regulation is ultimately determined by the legal and factual context peculiar to a given situation. The definition of the term "security" under federal securities laws includes, among other things, "investment contracts." An investment contract has been judicially defined as (a) an investment (b) in a common enterprise (c) with the reasonable expectation of profit to be derived from the entrepeneurial or managerial efforts of others. This formulation is the so-called Howey test, the name of the defendant in a landmark Supreme Court decision. SEC v. W.J. Howey, Co., 328 U.S. 293 (1945). As originally stated. the third element of the test read that an investor "is led to expect profits solely from the efforts of the promoter or a third party." Subsequent court decisions have not maintained a restrictive reading of that language, but rather have deemed it sufficient if the efforts made by those other than the investor are the undeniably significant ones, those essential managerial efforts which affect the success or failure of the enterprise. Although the Supreme Court has expressly withheld comment as to this interpretation of its Howey opinion, it appears to be the prevailing formulation of the Howey rule among the lower federal courts.

In applying this interpretation of the Howey test, the courts look to the economic reality of the relationship of the parties. Since, in the context of a franchise, there usually is an investment (the franchise fee) by the franchisee and both the franchisor and the franchisee are participants in a common enterprise (the franchise), the focus in the case law has been upon the third element of the test, that is, whether there is a reasonable expectation by the franchisee that he will derive profits from the entrepeneurial or managerial efforts of others.

In the relatively few cases that have applied the test to franchise relationships, the courts have examined the quality of the franchisee's contributions to the success or failure of his business and have determined whether the franchisee or the franchisor has control over those factors essential to success of the enterprise. Thus, it appears that if a franchisee has control over such factors, a security does not exist.

However, if the franchisor retains control over the
essential areas of management of the franchisee's
business, or couples the offer of a franchise with an
offer to manage the franchisee's business, the third
element of the Howey test may be satisfied, and a
security could exist.

The definition of an investment contract form of
security under state securities or "blue sky" laws is
usually consistent with that under federal law.
However, a number of states have also adopted a "risk
capital" test (or some variation thereof) whereby an
investment contract form of security will be deemed to
exist if the franchisor is thinly capitalised and is
dependent upon initial franchise fees paid by its
franchisees to provide the working capital essential to
the continued operation of the franchisor. Under this
definition of a security it is not significant that a
franchisee actively participates in the operation and
management of his franchise, for the underlying
rationale of the risk capital test is that the
franchisee is, in effect, required to invest in two
distinct businesses: (1) the franchisee's business,
which may be self-managed and (2) the thinly-
capitalised franchisor's business, which is managed
solely by the franchisor. The latter investment by the
franchisee of "risk capital" is deemed a security.

In a recent decision of the Oklahoma Securities
Commission, the franchisees of a company engaged in the
business of franchising a nationwide network of trade
exchanges were deemed securities under the Oklahoma
Securities Act through application of the risk capital
test. Opinion of Oklahoma Securities Commission,
Department of Securities re Barter Systems, Inc.,
(December, 1981). The definition of a security under
the "risk capital test" in the Oklahoma statute has

four parts: (1) an investment of money or money's worth; (2) in the risk capital of a venture; (3) with the expectation of some benefit; (4) where the investor has no direct control in the venture. In its opinion, the Oklahoma Securities Commisssion reasoned that the first, third, and fourth elements of the test were unquestioningly met. There was no question that franchisees were investing money with the franchisor for the right to obtain a franchise. In addition, a franchisee could reasonably expect some benefit from the venture over and above the initial license, equipment and assistance in establishing the franchise and the profits to be obtained from his efforts, specifically, future benefit from the use of the franchisor's name and continued availability of the franchisor for consultation as provided in the agreement. The Commission noted that the statutory test requires only the expectation of some benefit, not necessarily economic benefit or profit. Finally, while a franchisee would control his trade exchange business, he would have no voice in the franchisor's business venture as a whole and would be dependent upon the managerial ability of the franchisor for the success of the overall program.

Therefore, the only issue in deciding whether the franchise arrangement was a security was whether the investment made by the franchisee was in the risk capital of the venture. The Commission noted that the original risk capital test has been expanded to include continuing risk capital, i.e., it applies to "schemes" to raise money for existing but unproven businesses. Because the franchisor derived approximately 83-84% of its income from the sale of franchises, and therefore would fail if it were not for money paid by its franchisees, the Commission concluded that the investment of the franchisee was indeed in the risk capital of the venture. In light of this opinion, companies starting a new franchising company in the United States that could be deemed to be undercapitalised (i.e., dependent upon revenue from the grant of franchises for continued operations) should pay attention to the risk capital concept.

To the extent that the definition of a "franchise" under state franchise disclosure laws does not include the full gamut of arrangements which may fall within the concept of "franchise," there may well be regulation under state securities law (the California franchise disclosure law expressly exempts franchises within its coverage from regulation under California Securities Law; no other franchise disclosure law contains this exemption). Similarly, in the absence of specific franchise legislation, the applicability of the state's securities law may be more likely. Through there has been little apparent effort to date to apply state securities laws to franchises under a risk capital analysis, this may be attributable in large part to the focus of attention on franchise disclosure laws and the relative obscurity of the risk capital theory in American jurisprudence. If a franchise is deemed to be a security, its offer and sale will be subject to the registration and disclosure requirements, broker/dealer regulation, anti-fraud provisions and civil and criminal remedies of the applicable federal and/or state securities laws.

(3) Antitrust Law

Antitrust and trade regulation of the franchise relationship has also fluctuated during the past three decades. Vertical distribution (the relationship between business entities at different levels of the chain of distribution; e.g., manufacturer and dealer

and franchisor and franchisee)provoked scant antitrust
attention until the mid-1950's, though vertical price
fixing had earlier been held per se unlawful. The
United States Justice Department began a sustained
attack on vertical territorial and customer
restrictions in the mid-1950's, which culminated in a
1967 Supreme Court ruling, in the Schwinn case, United
States v. Arnold, Schwinn & Co., 388 U.S. 365
(1967)) that such restrictions were per se unlawful if
applied to the resale of goods to which title has
passed to the dealer.

It took the Supreme Court ten years to reverse the
Schwinn decision and firmly establish that all vertical
territorial and customer restrictions are to be judged
under a rule of reason analysis (which requires an
evaluation of the purposes and effects of the
restriction and its probable impact on competition).
Continental TV, Inc. v. GTE Sylvania, Inc., 433 U.S. 36
(1977). The court gave little guidance to lower courts
with respect to their application of the rule of reason
standard to such business practices. These courts have
responded by establishing what is, in effect, a rule of
presumptive legality. A dealer or competitor of a
franchisor who challenges the legality of a vertical
territorial or customer restriction bears a difficult
burden of proof that the restriction is, on balance,
anticompetitive. Few challengers have prevailed, even
in a series of recent decisions where the challenge was
predicted on the fact that the franchisor engaged in
dual distribution (i.e., distributed its own goods in
some geographic or customer markets) and was therefore
a potential competitor of its dealers, whose
territories or customers it restricted. The lower
federal courts have held that if a territorial or
customer restriction is imposed by a franchisor
primarily to regulate its distribution network, it will

be judged under the rule of reason (not the per se
standard applied to agreements among competing sellers
to allocate territories or customers), notwithstanding
that the franchisor is also a dealer in its own goods.

Allegedly unlawful tying practices have generated the
most private litigation in franchising. Commencing in
the late 1960's, hundreds of antitrust suits were filed
by franchisees against franchisors, predicted primarily
on allegations that the franchisor had forced its
franchisees to buy equipment, suplies or other goods,
lease real property or buy other services as a
condition of acquiring or retaining their franchises.
In most of these cases, the plaintiff franchisee(s)
sought to bring their suit as a class action on behalf
of all franchisees of the defendant franchisor with
similar claims. The history of this litigation is
voluminous and replete with issues with which the
federal courts wrestled for a decade. A series of
judicial decisions since the late 1970's have
significantly restricted the antitrust theory of
unlawful tying arrangements. There now appear to be
circumstances in franchising relationships where the
franchise and the lease for the premises at which the
franchisee conducts business or the principal product
sold by the franchisee, will not be deemed separate
products. The franchisee now bears a more difficult
burden of demonstrating that the franchisor has
sufficient power in the market for his franchise to
impose an unlawful tie. Finally, even if an unlawful
tie would otherwise exist, the franchisee may be unable
to prove that he was damaged as a result of the tie.

A fair summary of this era of franchise litigation is
that franchisees accomplished relatively little in the
many settlements reached before the courts began to
generally reject franchisee class actions against

franchisors. Nevertheless, franchisor practices changed significantly under the joint influence of potential antitrust liability; the very high cost of defending an antitrust case; the advent of disclosure regulation (which required franchisors to describe dealings with their franchisees, the basis for unlawful tying claims); greater franchisor ability and willingness to derive revenue from royalties, selling to franchisees on a competitive basis and financing franchisees (e.g., by leasing real property to them on a profitable basis for the franchisor); and greater reliance on franchisor owned outlets as a source of revenue.

Allegations of unlawful price fixing have been relatively uncommon as the principal basis of antitrust claims against franchisors, but have not infrequently been added as an additional claim n a tying or territorial restriction suit. There have been few significant damage recoveries by franchisees predicated on price fixing by their franchisors. However, the per se unlawful status of vertical price fixing can impact on a franchisee termination if the terminated franchisee can prove that termination resulted from a conspiracy between the franchisor and another franchisee to eliminate the terminated franchisee because he was a price discounter.

Franchisors rarely attempt to control by contract the prices charged by their franchisees, but may indirectly attempt to influence such prices by discussions with franchisees and price advertising. Canadian antitrust law permits a franchisor to establish the maximum price its franchisees may charge. United States antitrust law permits neither maximum nor minimum price fixing, declaring either practice to be per se unlawful. This rule has come under a sustained attack by antitrust commentators since the Supreme Court ruled that all other vertical distribution restrictions are to be judged under the rule of reason. Even the federal antitrust enforcement agencies have become hostile to the per se rule in vertical price fixing and it is now predicted by some that at least maximum price fixing, and possibly all vertical price fixing, may ultimately be judged under the rule of reason. In the meantime, franchisors appear to have achieved sufficient control over the prices charged by their franchisees by means that are not readily susceptible to antitrust challenge.

The antitrust laws have other applications to franchising. Giving franchisees a veto over the grant of additional franchises within the market of existing franchisees has been held unlawful, a decision that is difficult to reconcile with the legality of the exclusive territory (the franchisor's promise to its franchisee not to grant an additional franchise in a specified territory). American Motor Inns, Inc., v. Holiday Inns, Inc., 521 F.2d 1230 (3d Cir. 1975). It is also noteworthy that such veto power by existing franchisees is the result achieved by some state regulation of encroachment in automobile distribution. Though existing dealers usually do not have the power to permanently veto the establishment of a new dealer, their power to temporarily block a new dealership will often effectively preclude its establishment. The antitrust laws have also been applied to a franchisor that opened multiple outlets in close proximity to a franchisee's outlets for the purpose of depressing the value of the franchisee's business and acquiring it at a reduced cost. Photovest, Inc. v. Fotomat, Inc., 606 F.2d 704 (7th Cir. 1979), cert. denied, 445 U.S. 917 (1980). Finally, the federal price discrimination statute applies to a franchise relationship if it involves the sale of goods. There have been few price discrimination damage recoveries by franchisees in the past decade and a recent Supreme Court decision will significantly increase a franchisee's burden of proving damages as a result of discriminatory prices paid to its franchisor.

Throughout most of the past three decades of rapid development and expansion of franchising in the United States, antitrust enforcement, governmental and private, has been predicated principally on federal antitrust law. State antitrust law dates as far back as federal, but has rarely been utilized by state governments or private plaintiffs. In the last several years there has been a dramatic change in the dormancy of state antitrust enforcement. Both state enforcement agencies and private plaintiffs have discovered state antitrust law. State antitrust litigation has generally resulted in decisions that are consistent with prevailing interpretations of federal antitrust law. However, a number of state antitrust decisions have interpreted state antitrust law differently than federal law. It is also significant that only a few state courts have adopted the more liberal application of antitrust law to vertical distribution relationships that is now commonplace in federal court decisions applying federal antitrust law. There appears to be considerable hostility to the "new antitrust" among state attorneys general, who had been expanding their antitrust enforcements efforts on the basis of the "old antitrust" when federal law began its rather abrupt change. New Jersey v. Lawn King., Inc., 417 A.2d 1025 (N.J.1980).

(4)   The Legal Status of the Franchise Relationship

The franchise relationship is fundamentally one of

private contract. What, if any, status does a franchisee have beyond that conferred by the terms of his franchise agreement. I have previously discussed legislation that gives franchisees such status (e.g., by limiting the rights that the franchisor may reserve by contract to end the relationship), but does the franchisee have any such status at common law? The first case to test whether a franchisor has fiduciary obligations to its franchisee was a Canadian case involving the Mr. Donut franchise, the Jirna case. Jirna, Ltd. v. Mr. Donut of Canada, Ltd., (1975) 1 S.C.R. 2, affg. (1 O.R. 251 (C.A.), revg. (1970)3 O.R. 629. The trial court held that the franchisor did have such obligations and breached them by withholding the information that it received payments from the franchisee's suppliers. The appellate court reversed this decision and its decision was affirmed by the Ontario Supreme Court. The holdings of these courts is that unless the disparity between franchisor and franchisee in bargaining power, knowledge and experience is so great as to render the franchisee dependent upon the franchisor, the franchise relationship is one of independent business entities and neither is trustee for the other.

Several United States courts have held that a fiduciary relationship could exist in a franchise, Arnott v. American Oil Co., 609 F. 2d 873 (8th Cir. 1979) cert, denied, 446 U.S. 918 (1980), but most courts have rejected the concept of fiduciary obligations in franchise relationships. However, several courts have ruled that a franchisor does have a duty of good faith and fair dealing. It is unclear if this is a general obligation of all contracting parties or is to any degree unique to the franchise relationship.

Application of fiduciary concepts to the franchise

relationships would, of course, radically alter the
relationship as it currently exists. In addition to
impacting on a variety of business dealings between
franchisors, franchisees and third parties, wherein
each seeks to maximise its profit, fiduciary duties
would encompass disclosure obligations of uncertain
dimensions, but certainly beyond the scope of those
that currently prevail. I think it is doubtful that
the courts will engraft the elements of traditional
fiduciary obligations onto the franchise relationship.
We may well see opinions that discuss a duty of good
faith and fair dealing, but that is not a particularly
troubling prospect. With few exceptions, franchise
relationships are not oppressive or unfair to the
franchisee (they could hardly be so popular if they
were). A duty of good faith and fair dealing should
not obligate a franchisor to do more than faithfully
perform its franchise agreements, comply with
commitments expressed or implied in its offering
circular and advertising and deal fairly with its
franchisees.

(5) Vicarious Liability

The courts have wrestled for decades with the issue of
a franchisor's responsibility for the conduct of its
franchisees. Early cases involved mainly suits against
gasoline refiners for injuries sustained on the
premises of their franchised stations. In recent years
these issues have surfaced in a wide variety of
franchise systems. The courts have identified several
theories on which a franchisor can be held liable.
These include the apparent or actual authority of the
franchisee and negligence of the franchisor. Apparent
authority arises out of the uniform appearance of
franchisee and franchisor operated outlets and the
absence of any notice to the public that the outlet is

operated by anyone other than the company whose trademark is prominently displayed there. Actual authority is found when the franchisor has imposed restrictions on, or reserved sufficient controls over, the operation of the franchisee's business of sufficient magnitude that the franchisor is deemed to control day-to-day operations. Negligence (and, in some circumstances, strict liability) can exist as a basis for liability (direct liability) when injury is caused by the design of a product or facility, or as a result of a method of operation, over which the franchisor had actual control or a right of control.

These theories of vicarious liability have applied to both tort and contract claims. Though franchisors have often prevailed as a matter of law on the issue of actual authority, the application of each of these theories is frequently decided by a jury. It is a common belief that a franchisor has an uphill battle to convince a jury that it should not be held liable, particularly if there is any doubt whether the franchisee has sufficient insurance or resources to satisfy a judgment. Franchisors have reacted to potential vicarious liability by requiring franchisees to carry adequate insurance and indemnify the franchisor against damages incurred and costs of defense in suits arising out of the operation of the franchisee's business. Franchisors also carry their own insurance that extends to vicarious liability claims. Many franchisors reserve the right to require their franchisees to carry expanded insurance coverage (in terms of amounts and nature of claims insured against) during the term of the franchise. Insurance coverage generally does not extend to contract claims. However, the relatively few vicarious contract claims that have been successfully asserted against franchisors have usually involved either apparently intentional franchisor conduct or substantial franchisor negligence, situations within the franchisor's control. Indemnification provisions are common to franchise agreements, but are of doubtful value.

A variation of vicarious tort and contract liability is franchisor liability as an employer under various labor and tax laws. A number of administrative and a few judicial proceedings have dealt with these issues. In most cases, franchisees have been found not to be employees, and therefore are not entitled to the benefits of federal labor law and franchisors have been found not to be employers, and therefore not to be obligated to make payroll tax deposits or unemployment compensation contributions on behalf of their franchisees. A few decisions have reached the opposite conclusion. The Wisconsin Supreme Court has ruled that franchised catalog store operators of Ward and Sears are employees for puposes of the Wisconsin unemployment compensation law. Sears, Roebuck and Co. v. Dept. of Industry, Labor and Human Relations, 280 N.W. 2d 240 (1979). The National Labor Relations Board and several courts have found certain franchisees to be employees, with the right to bargain collectively and the United States Department of Labor has issued but apparently never enforced guidelines as to the types of controls that will cause a franchisor to be deemed an employer under the Fair Labor Standards Act, which covers such aspects of employment as overtime compensation. A franchisor is particularly vulnerable to a finding that its franchisees are employees for purposes of labor law if it was formerly an integrated claim that converted to a franchise system to avoid existing collective bargaining agreements. NLRB v. Big Bear Supermarkets No. 3, 88 LC Sec. 11,998 (9th Cir.) cert. denied, 89 LC Sec. 12,368 (1980.

A federal court has recently ruled that a class of distributors of Standard Oil Company that had been found to be employees under federal labor law could nevertheless assert that they were independent contractors for purposes of the Petroleum Marketing Practices Act. Neff v. Standard Oil Company, No. C-3-80-229 (S.D. Ohio November 4, 1981). This case underscores the fact that a franchisee may be classified differently for different purposes. As in vicarious tort and contract law, the degree of the franchisor's control over its franchisees will be highly significant in determining the franchisors status under such regulatory laws. An additional factor of importance will be the significance of the franchisee's investment in his franchised business. If the franchisor furnishes the outlet and other fixed assets and the franchisee's investment is but a small portion of the aggregate investment in the outlet, the relationship will have more of the appearance of employment.

Vicarious liability law will continue to develop and generate a significant amount of litigation. Such claims against franchisors are inherent in the franchise relationship and the establishment of a chain of uniform outlets. The case law does suggest means by which franchisors can reduce their exposure.

15. For a discussion of the breakaway franchisee issue, see THE BREAKAWAY FRANCHISEE, RUDNICK, Fifth Annual National Franchise Law Institute, University of Missouri at Kansas City and Kansas City Bar Association, 14th September 1983 (Institute materials).

16. ALTERNATIVES TO FRANCHISING, ROLLINSON, Arizona State Law Journal, 1980, page 505.

17. For a comparison of franchises and co-operatives, see FRANCHISE OR CO-OPERATIVE: WHITHER THOU GOEST, ALDRICH, Fifth Annual National Franchise Law Institute, University of Missouri at Kansas City and Kansas City Bar Association, September 14, 1983 (Institute Materials).

APPENDIX A
FRANCHISING FACT SHEET*

Franchised sales of goods and services reached an estimated
$386 billion in 1982 and are expected to reach $436 billion
in 1983.

Retail sales from franchised establishments comprise 31
percent of all U.S. retail sales.

Franchising directly employed some 4.9 million people in
1981, and is expected to employ more than 5.2 million by the
end of 1983.

The majority of business format franchise companies are
small, with more than two-thirds of these companies
operating 50 units or fewer in 1981.

The success rate for businesses owned by franchisees is
significantly better than the rate for other independently
owned small businesses:

-   The Small Business Administration has estimated that
    65% of business start-up fail within five years.

-   By contrast, each year since 1971, the Department of
    Commerce has reported less than five percent of
    franchisee-owned outlets being discontinued. (In 1981,
    the last year for which actual data are available, only
    about 3.8% of franchisee-owned outlets were
    discontinued, many for reasons other than business
    failure.)

*NOTE: Unless otherwise stated, the source for these facts
is Franchising In The Economy 1981-83, U.S. Department of
Commerce, Bureau of Industrial Economics.

- According to a 1982 Congressional committee report, there is "an average failure range of 2 to 6 percent for all franchises."

- According to a 1980 survey of IFA member companies, in 1979 only 175 (of a survey total 26,581) franchised outlets closed as a result of business failure - about seven-tenths of one percent of the existing number of units of respondents to the survey.)

Background

"The concept of modern franchising, particularly in its evolution since the late 1960s, has opened a remarkable door of opportunity for many of our country's prospective small businessmen."

> 97th U.S. Congress,
> 2nd Session (1982)
> House Report No. 97-916

Franchising is not an industry but a method of distribution used by more than 1800 companies in some 40 different industries.

The U.S. Department of Commerce calls franchising "a significant part of the U.S. economy," and reports that franchising "continues to prove its validity as a marketing method adaptable to an ever widening array of industries and professions while providing immediate identity and recognition for prospective enterpreneurs joining the system." The Commerce Department reports established companies turning to franchising for expansion and cites a 5.6 percent increase in the net number of companies entering the franchise system in 1982 over the previous year - a trend expected to continue at about 5 percent annually.

Essentially, there are two types of franchising arrangements product/tradename franchising and business format franchising.

Typical of product tradename franchises are automobile and truck dealerships, gasoline service stations, and soft drink bottlers. These three industries account for 74% of all franchise sales estimated for 1983.

While the number of establishments in this category is expected to decline in 1983 to 168,000 from 174,000 in 1982 (due mainly to closings of gasoline stations and auto and truck dealerships,) the total sales by product and tradename franchisors are expected to reach an estimated $324 billion in 1983, up from $276 billion in 1981.

In business format franchising, the franchisor establishes a fully integrated relationship with the franchise owner, governing the product or service, trademark, marketing strategy and plan, operating manual and standards, quality control, and a communications system between the franchisor and the franchise owner.

Business format franchising - represented by the newer types of franchises ranging from fast food restaurants and hotels to muffler shops and real estate services - is expected to increase to $111 billion in 1983 compared with $99 billion in 1982 and $89 billion in 1981. The number of business format establishments is expected to increase to almost 297,000 in 1983 from about 261,000 units in 1981

Franchise Contract Renewal Rate High - Few Terminations

The overall strength of the franchise system is particularly evident in the high renewal rate of contracts and the low number of contract terminations.

Of the 11,515 franchise contracts up for renewal in 1981, 98% were renewed; of those not renewed, 80% were at the initiative of the franchisee or by mutual consent.

In 1981 there were 356,513 franchisee-owned outlets, yet only 7,181 terminations of franchise agreements (2.0%). A majority of those contracts terminated - 57% - were at the initiative of the franchisee or by mutual consent.

Ninety-seven percent of the franchisees who sought permission to sell their franchise to another business person (2,878 out of 2,978) were permitted to do so.

Franchisee-owned vs. company-owned outlets

Long range trends indicate a decrease in the number of business format franchised units being repurchased for company ownership and an increase in the number of such company-owned units being converted to franchisee-ownership. In 1981, just 760 business format franchises were repurchased for company onwership, while 1,068 were converted to franchisee ownership. Given the pool of some 261,000 business format units in 1981, both figures add up to less than one percent of the total number.

The average yearly sales for franchisee-owned outlets was $881,000 in 1981, predicted to rise to $996,000 per outlet by 1983. For franchisees the mean average annual sales per outlet in 1981 ranged from a low of $31,000 (tax preparation franchises) to a high of $8,118,000 (soft drink bottlers).

International Franchising

Expansion of American franchising overseas is growing. In 1971, there were 156 franchising companies operating 3,365 outlets in foreign countries. By the end of 1981, the numbers jumped to 288 companies with 21,416 units in the

foreign markets - an 85% increase in franchisors and a
sixfold increase in outlets.

IFA's 1980 survey of member companies underscored the trend
in international franchising, with 42 percent reporting that
they already franchise internationally and an additional 21
percent reporting that they intend to do so in the near
future.

CHAPTER 2

FRANCHISING: TRADE MARK PRACTITIONER'S PERSPECTIVE
Iain C. Baillie

The international trade mark attorney will not regard
franchising as presenting a series of unique problems - the
problems are found in other aspects of practice - but the
nature of a franchise does require concentration on certain
aspects of international practice and certain issues are
more significant and troublesome than when dealing with
other types of trading. A key issue in franchising is that
the use is primarily by other than the trade mark owner.
Trade marks are historically intended as identifiers of
origin for a manufacturer. Licensing is a late development
resulting in inconsistencies in the law and conceptual
problems.   Franchising is therefore in an area of practice
which has certain particular difficulties.

Franchising also has a high service content. Here again the
protection for trade marks for services (sometimes called
service marks) is a relatively new development in the law
and the law is not always consistent or as well developed as
one would desire.

These special features of franchising have to be considered
whether one is in the initial stages of securing protection
for a trade mark, or terminating the right of one who has at
some stage legitimately used a trade mark.

It is also desirable never to isolate consideration of trade
marks from other aspects of intellectual property.
Generally the practice of trade marks is only part of an

intellectual property practice, whether as an individual or as part of a firm. Again the precise relationship of the trade mark in franchising to the other aspects of the franchising rights will vary from country to country and the possibility of such variation must always be borne in mind.

The difficulty of the cost of multiple registration in a number of countries is of course well known. One can take advantage of such situations as the Benelux Treaty to cover Belgium, the Netherlands and Luxembourg which is indeed the only vehicle for trade mark registration in that area. The international trade mark registration (Madrid Union) does cover a number of European countries, particularly France and Germany but not at the present time the United States and Great Britain. There is also a proposed Trade Mark Registration Treaty but this has hardly any adherents at the present time. The disadvantage of the Madrid Union is that it requires the registration to be by a company having significant trading in one of the member countries and thus one must either trade as such in one of these countries (not merely through a licensee) or transfer ownership to a local entity. Therefore an international programme is expensive and, if not carefully managed a great deal of money could be spent for an inherently weak mark.

The significance of use and the general liklihood that, in franchising, such use is by other than the registered owner of the mark, will have greater or lesser significance depending on those countries where use is important in determining distinctiveness. In discussing trade marks in general, we will place the emphasis on word marks rather than logos or designs. While designs or logos have certain marketing advantages in that they are international without the problem of language and have, from the legal viewpoint, the advantage of being easier to establish as distinctive, nevertheless in practical marketing terms words do seem to be more effective. Experience seems to indicate that for a mark to become internationally well-known it must be a short word or combination of one or two short words and one which is acceptable commercially in a large number of countries. Finally, it should carry some suggestion of the products without being descriptive and this, of course, is where the problem usually arises. For the purpose of this discussion we are ignoring the possibility of conflict with another registered trade mark except in the situation where there may be some element of misappropriation.

Completely invented words e.g. Kodak or Exxon are, of course, perhaps the most legally desirable but do have the disadvantage of requiring a considerable marketing effort to establish their relationship to the product. On the other hand, in attempting to balance the inventiveness of the word as against its descriptiveness, one may come too close to the descriptive aspect. Assuming that one does not go to the point of being completely descriptive, one may then require evidence that the word is capable of distinctiveness in the public mind or had acquired it. The problem also arises that, by the time the trade mark practitioner is consulted on the trade marks to be used in the business, the owner has already developed extensive use of the marks and cannot afford to re-select marks in line with the necessary legal characteristics. There may be situations where one has to advise a client that he inherently cannot secure protection in at least some jurisdictions. Extremely geographic marks e.g. London or New York would be unregisterable in a country such as Britain and registerable only with difficulty in many other countries. Similarly common surnames have problems. The most usual problem is descriptiveness e.g. Windowcare for a service for repairing windows. One should also bear in mind however, apart from legal considerations, that what is descriptive in one language may not be descriptive in another.

Assuming, however, that the mark while certainly descriptive

to some degree nevertheless does have some distinctiveness
then one will have to try and persuade a Trade Mark Office
that it is capable of distinguishing the client's service or
product and, indeed, has come in the public mind to provide
such distinction.

One here runs into the difference between the two principal
legal systems in the world in respect of the rights acquired
by registration.

There is a distinction between those countries, particularly
civil law countries, in which filing followed by
registration confers a property right in a mark (in French
"depot attributif de propriete") and those were it is merely
declaratory of a pre-existing property right created
essentially by use (depot declaratif de propriete). Thus,
in so called common-law countries in general the right to a
mark is acquired primarily through use. In most systems it
is possible to apply for a mark on the basis of proposed use
but use is still necessary to consolidate the right. The
onus of proving use will be upon the user. As already
indicated in the other countries only the registration will
create the right e.g. France or Benelux. Thus in France
Article 4 of the law of December 31st, 1964 provides:

> "ownership of a mark is acquired through the
> first filing validly effected according to
> the provisions of the present law"

The applicant then becomes proprietor of the mark as from
the date of application although the right is not completed
and invocable against others until the actual date of
registration.

The opposite extreme of this right by registration is in
countries, such as the U.S.A. or Canada, where the right to
register can only come into existence after there has been

some use. In the case of the United States that use must be in international or interstate trading as distinct from use within one of the states of the United States. Thus an applicant in the United States must provide not merely an illustration of the mark but an illustration of the mark as actually used in trading e.g. labels or photographs of the product. A foreign applicant who has, either, an application and applies within six months of the foreign application date, or a foreign registration can rely on use outside the United States at least for the purpose of applying for his U.S. trade mark rights. Again, however, if his original country does not give protection for service marks, this possibility may not be open to the foreign applicant if a service mark is desired in the U.S.A. Similarly the law in Canada requires that a mark to be registerable must have been so used as to be distinctive of the applicant; evidence of use of the mark is required.

One can in Canada rely by statute on use by the owner in another country, but, what if the use in that country is only by the franchisee? Does that use enure to the owner for Canadian purposes? One way round this problem which is being tried is to register the mark for providing franchise services - an activity which the owner undoubtedly undertakes.

It is true that Article 6 bis of the Paris Convention does give protection for "well known marks" even in those countries where registration is a prime condition of protection. Unfortunately the decisions in the courts as to what constitutes a well known mark make it clear that the mark must be one of the relatively few marks which are internationally recognised e.g. Coca Cola, Kodak etc. The average mark even through relatively extensively used in its home country, will not have acquired sufficient significant international reputation and will not benefit from this provision. That is apart from the problems as to whether the provision is effective in many countries where statutory enactment is required for each provision of the Convention.

Another problem which is particularly relevant to franchising is whether the nature of the use by the owner is in fact trade mark use as distinct from use as a trading name. The boundary between these two concepts is never of the clearest and this is particularly so in many service-type franchises. For example Southpaw Knife Sharpeners, a chain of cutlery sharpening shops could be held to be using Southpaw primarily as a trading name. If, however, they supply the sharpening devices called the Southpaw sharpening devices then this would clearly be trade mark use. In those countries giving service mark protection the distinction is probably more subtle but, again one might have to talk about the Southpaw service as distinct from the service provided by the Southpaw shop. This distinction can be important in two ways:

1.   In countries such as the U.S.A. where use has to be domonstrated in the application one must be careful that the type of evidence available for registration of the franchise or mark demonstrates trade mark use or a use of a service mark rather than a trading name.

2.   At least theoretically a trading name should be protectable without specific registration (Article 8 of the International Convention).

Therefore it could be possible that trading under a name in one country could create rights in a country where there has been no trading. This was the so-called Eskimo pie case in Germany (through later discussions qualified that decision). On the other hand, despite the Convention, France has held that a name must be used in France for it to be protectable and this would also be the law in the United Kingdom and countries such as the United States and Canada.

On the question of trade name protection, one must emphasise that generally registration of trade names does not give protection but is usually a requirement for the protection of the public. Various countries require registration of artificial names which are used in the course of business. Equally formation of a company may require some form of clearance of the name before registration. Only rarely do these registration statutes actually provide protection for the name and they do not create the degree of exclusivity and protection against infringement which would be created by trade mark statutes, for example in the civil law countries. Thus in the United States various state registration statutes do not provide name protection and may in fact disclaim such protection. In a few states for example California, Michigan, Oregon before a name may be approved for incorporation or qualification it must be investigated as to whether it is deceptively similar to other corporate names. A somewhat similar situation existed under the old British Business Names Registration Act, in that a business name registration did not confer any rights in the name.

It is traditional for an International Trade Mark Attorney to warn that in allowing franchisees to use a trade mark they should not be permitted to incorporate the trade mark into their corporate name. There are a number of reasons:

1.   The difficulty of amending a company name once the relationship breaks.

2.   The possibility that rights will be created by way of trading name which are not explicitly set out in the Licence Agreement and which will not therefore so easily be recoverable on termination of that agreement.

3. The question as to whether the licensed use is as a
    trade name or as a trade mark. Thus in the Canadian
    "Cheerio" case (Dubiner -v- Cheerio Toys and Games
    (1965) 1 Ex. C.R. 524 etc.) the trade mark Cheerio was
    invalidated on the basis that it was not distinctive
    because the defendent had used the name as a trade name
    and part of its corporate name where it had no
    registered user status.

To return to the problem of the mark where at least some
argument will be necessary to convince a registry that,
although suggestive of goods or services, the mark is not
descriptive, the question arises, how will one demonstrate
that in fact it does fall on the right side of the border
line? In those countries where registration is the prime
source of protection one is usually dependent on argument
with the examiner and the extent of the use will not in
itself be of great assistance, although one must be careful
to warn that this is a very general comment. In other
countries, such as Britain, evidence of actual use and the
resultant effect on the public mind may become extremely
important. One may have to undertake surveys of the trade
providing appropriate questionnaires to demonstrate the
manner in which the mark has acquired distinctiveness.

Can one use for such evidence, use by other parties?
Generally opinion was that, since use by a properly
constituted licensee enures to the benefit of the licensor,
the use by such licensee is a valuable part of the necessary
evidence. Consternation was created in the British trade
mark profession when it appeared for a time that the
Registrar was construing the Act and Rules as indicating
that use by a licensee was not sufficient to assist in
proving distinctiveness in the mark. Though the Registrar
has retreated from this extreme position the practice still
is not as clear as one would desire. One suggestion in
regard to securing use to support a descriptive mark is for

the licensee/franchisee to undertake the use and then when the mark is registered to assign back to the franchisor. This has two dangers:

1. It then rests some of the property right in the franchisee, and

2. In some countries, particularly in Latin America the so called "grant-back' clause may be struck down; this is particularly true in Mexico.

In some instances you may be able to apply in a register having less requirement for distinctiveness (the Part B Register of the U.K. Register is an example) but of course this does provide weaker protection.

A further problem in having to demonstrate actual use to evidence distinctiveness is that one may have to demonstrate this nationwide. Again drawing on British experience one may have to demonstrate use of the mark in a wide variety of parts of the United Kingdom. Where a franchise is growing by extending outlets slowly from a central major city, such as London, this can be extremely difficult.

This problem of nationwide use brings us to the problem of concurrent user, again a problem primarily of the use-based countries as distinct from the registration countries. Clearly in a country such as France or Germany where registration is the prime source of rights, the registration automatically extends to the whole of the jurisdiction and slight use in one part of the jurisdiction by a small entity will not be a problem if he has not registered his rights. In the other extreme of the United States it is perfectly possible that there could be innocent concurrent use creating concurrent rights. Under U.S. law a trader who used a mark in a small area in ignorance of the use by another of the same mark will have rights. The allocation of the respective areas will be determined by:

1.   Who registers first;

2.   Who had most extensive use;

3.   The area of use and the extent to which that use might
      be extended to other areas legitimately.

An example would be the case of Weiner King Corporation in
the Court of Customs and Patent Appeals.   In this case
Weiner King Inc. opened a hot dog restaurant in Flemington,
New Jersey in 1962, another in the same town in 1967,
another in Beach Heaven, New Jersey in 1973 and yet another
in Flemington in 1975. Weiner King Corporation intended to
launch a nationwide chain of franchised hot dog restaurants
and opened its first restaurant, innocently, in North
Carolina in 1970. By May 1972 Weiner King Corporation was
the owner of a Federally registered mark, owning 11
restaurants.   In July 1972 Weiner King Corporation first
learned of Weiner King Inc.   Weiner King Corporation
continued to expand reaching 100 locations in 20 States by
1975.   Weiner King Inc. subsequently opened shops in
Warminster, Pennsylvania and White House, New Jersey. The
Court held that concurrent use issues must be resolved by a
comprehensive factual analysis that weighed equities, good
faith and policy of encouraging prompt Federal registration
by rewarding it.   The Court refused to rule that a
subsequent user, at least one who first registered, had to
curtail expansion when they learned of the prior user (since
the subsequent user simply continued previous, good faith
expansion plans) or that the prior user could not expand
from one town to the other side of the of the State after
the second had registered. In balancing the equities the
Court then upheld the right of expansion of the first
company Weiner King Inc. to Beach Haven was considered to
be in Weiner King Inc's "natural zone" of expansion from

Flemington where it had operated for 11 years. The eventual outcome was that by concurrent registrations Weiner King Corporation obtained the entire United States except for districts within a 15 mile radius of Fleminton, White House and Beach Haven all in New Jersey.

The franchisor may consider that his reputation is such, that inherently all over the world his mark will be famous, even though he has not yet operated outside his own particular country. In the first instance this is not inherently likely. Secondly, for the registration countries it is quite clear that it is the registration which will create the right and it will be difficult to rely on international reputation except in the most usual of situations. Thirdly, even for common law countries the tendency of the Courts seems to be to require some actual activity in the country before any rights will be recognised. In Hong Kong the Weinerwald chain was prevented from franchising the name in Hong King by reason of an earlier reservation of the Weinerwald name on behalf of "undisclosed principals in Singapore". The Court in Hong Kong held that there was no significant segment of the Hong Kong population who had knowledge of the Weinerwald name. The British type countries seemed to be coming to the conclusion that, although goodwill does not stop at a frontier, it does not mean that goodwill has no frontiers. If you are going to support your franchise name in another country which has this type of law you have to demonstrate creation of goodwill which means actual customers in that country and even a "significant segment" of that country.

In South Africa where a local Wimpy company attempted to register Burger King the Court rejected the registration primarily on the basis of evidence that the applicants had known of the Burger King as being the property of another rather than on the basis of Burger King's reputation in South Africa which was relatively slight. In Kenya

McDonald's were able to stop registration of Gold Arches
again on the basis of international reputation and confusion
to the public and the element of bad faith. There are cases
in Australia which have said that foreign reputation is not
enough but there is a Ringling Circus/Barnum & Bailey circus
case where the Court did appear to look favourably on the
argument of international reputation even without actual
business activity. In Britain Maxims Restauant were able to
prevent a Maxims restaurant opening in Norwich, England but
here the judge appeared to be swayed partly by EEC
considerations and partly by the evidence that a significant
number of people in Britain had had meals in the Maxims
Restaurant in Paris. Decisions of a similar type exist in
the United States where Pruniers were able to prevent a
Prunier Restaurant opening in New York and there is also a
Maxims case in the United States and another more recent
decision against in Hong Kong. Cases in other jurisdictions
such as Taiwan, Colombia and Panama have gone both ways.

In Britain the cases seem to have gone both ways with at
least one decision, the Athletes Foot case being against the
U.S. franchisor even though there had been some activity in
Britain at least in terms of seeking out a master
franchisee.

The possible complexities of concurrent use situations are
however illustrated by the L"AMY case in the United Kingdom
((1983) R.P.C. 137) which was an opposition by the owner of
a registered mark against an application for registration
where there had been extensive use. The hearing officer
held that a concurrent use provision would have been
appropriate in the application for registration except that,
ironically, the owner of the registered mark had not used
his mark. Since a concurrent use provision was necessary
for registration, the application was then rejected.

The problem of relying on international reputation has again

been emphasised in the Irish case, Adidas -v- O'Neill
((1983) Fleet Street Reports 76) where the Irish Supreme
Court held that "neither the copying of a design, nor the
anticipation of a fashion, nor the taking advantage of a
market or demand created by another's advertising was
sufficient to support an action for passing off, providing
that the trader against whom the camplaint is made has
sufficiently distinguished his goods so as to distinguish
confusion arising". There was reference to the so-called
Pub Squash case a Privy Council case in the United Kingdom
on appeal from Australia (Cadbury Schweppes -v- Pub Squash
(1981) 1 All E.R. 213). In particular Lord Scarman on page
218 was quoted "but competition must remain free; and
competition is safeguarded by the necessity for the
plaintiff to prove that he has built up an intangible
property right in the advertised descriptions of his proper
product, or, in other words, that he has succeeded by such
methods in giving his product a distinctive character
accepted by the market".

Though this language appears to support the possibility that
one can rely on goodwill from mere advertising as distinct
from actual sales nevertheless current opinion, at least in
the U.K. is that actual U.K. sales are required.

The Irish Courts, however, did prevent a company in Ireland
opening under the name C & A which is the name of a well
known large chain of stores in Britain, holding that it
would not permit incorporation of a company with a name
which was likely to give the impression to the public in
Ireland that it was a subsidiary branch or associate of a
company with established goodwill. Here it does appear
though that there was at least goodwill in the sense of
customers of the British C & A stores in Ireland and not
merely international reputation.

A further problem which has less significance in franchising is the question of the common field of protection. A franchisor is usually primarily concerned with persons who are attempting to use his marks and other rights in a business which will compete with his own. He may not like a competitor in a somewhat different industry using his trade mark but it will not be commercially significant unless there is possibility of expansion. It would seem that the cases recognise a reasonably broad scope in protection so that a franchisor with registration of trade marks in say the hamburger area could prevent somebody who tried to retail market goods bearing his most famous trade marks even if they were not ones sold in his store. Nevertheless it is again advisable to note in international protection that the scope of protection of a trade mark does vary from country to country. Thus in Great Britain the classification and specification of goods for a trade mark is very significant with regard to its enforceability against goods which differ somewhat from those within the classification. In other countries e.g. the United States the classification is more a matter of information rather than a definition of rights and certainly suits for infringement have been successfully brought against goods which fall well outside the strict terms of the specification of goods in the actual registration. Nevertheless attempts by franchisors to secure registration of unduly broad definitions of goods can be prejudicial for two reasons:

1. The marks are open to the possibility of attack for non-use for at least part of the mark.

2. The mark may be less effective as a means of preventing others registering simply because the specification is too vague and those national offices which do carry out searches for conflicting marks may not appreciate that a later application is in fact for a substantially similar scope of goods.

To summarise the position, therefore, the more that a mark requires verification of use to demonstrate its distinctiveness the more the franchisor may have problems since he may have to rest on use by others. Such use should be acceptable but there has been some tendency not to accept such use.

Similarly, one cannot rest on one's international reputation or one's use of the trade mark as a "trading name". Even for relatively notorious marks there have been major difficulties in preventing attempts by others to use them or register rights in so-called use countries such as the Common Law countries.

In the case of the civil law countries where registration is the source of the right it becomes imperative to secure one's registration as soon as possible otherwise the mark is continually at risk. It is perhaps no longer true that there are pirates who regularly attempt the registration of famous marks in countries in which they have not been registered, or, for goods for which registration has been omitted. Such attempts have been limited by treating them as criminal offences where a pattern of piracy has been demonstrated. On the other hand the Courts are somewhat reluctant to prevent a legitimate trader from using an attractive mark or device even when it is the property of another party in another country.

One should at this point perhaps remember, however, that there are other means of protecting certain types of trade marks besides actual registration. Although the value of designs or logos was depreciated as commercially significant marks, nevertheless their commercial value cannot be denied and they have one other major value and that is the possible copyright protection. There is at least one British case which indicated that the copyright in the distinctive design could prevent another party securing trade mark protection.

There are some U.S. cases which seem to indicate that a simple trade mark style device cannot be registered for copyright, which registration is of course mandatory for litigation. On the other hand a more complex device or label including for example some descriptive material would be registrable. There does not seem to be very much jurisprudence on this question but it would certainly be worthwhile adding to any distinctive design, logo, style of presentation of a name etc. the well known international copyright symbol capital C in a circle, year of first publication of sale, copyright owner. It is worth emphasising at this point, however, that one must own the copyright. Too often when investigating this particular problem, one finds that the symbol was created under somewhat obscure circumstances perhaps by an advertising agent and the copyright ownership is not of the clearest. It is imperative that there be a written transfer of copyright ownership and one should particularly insist on this from advertising or other design agents. Assuming that again one has a distinct mark and has decided to go international with the franchise, the immediate question is the potential owner of the mark. Should the mark be retained in a single owning entity, the master franchisor in the original country? Should it be transferred to some form of international holding company where there might be tax advantages? Could there be advantages in having local national ownership? It is the automatic reaction of most trade mark attorneys under modern circumstances to recommend against diversification of ownership of marks. In practical terms the problems that arise when more than one entity owns a mark become very considerable. This is not the place for the discussion of the EEC problems which arise from different ownership in different countries but the Cafe Hag case amply demonstrated these problems. The existence of multiple owners internationally can also weaken arguments that there is international recognition of a single "origin" for goods or services. Particularly if one of the owners is

not 100 per cent owned by the original franchisor, apart
from the commercial risk that the ownership may then pass
out of his control, there are always problems which can
arise such as parallel imports etc. and in addition problems
can arise as to quality control. Since in most trade mark
jurisdictions the mark is supposed to indicate a source of
origin there is always a problem when multiple owners
exist.

It is sometimes argued that at least in the United States
ownership of a mark is desirably placed in a U.S. entity
rather than being retained in a foreign entity. In this
connection reference has been made to the various Tariff Act
procedures which tend to protect U.S. corporations and not
foreign entities. On the whole this appears to be of less
significance in the franchising field where one is perhaps
less concerned with parallel imports and more concerned with
local competition. On balance the factors in favour of
maintaining single ownership of the important international
mark would tend to prevail.

In addition sometimes the suggested tax arrangements can
include a holding company in a tax haven. Many of these tax
havens are not members of the International Convention.
Weak as is the protection which arises from the Convention
(since it is primarily a governing treaty establishing
standards for national laws rather than creating positive
rights) nevertheless there are some features such as the
trading name protection which could be advantageous. It may
not be possible to exercise these rights from a holding
entity in a country which is not a member of a convention.
In addition some countries such as Germany and Switzerland
either deprecate or do not permit holding companies to own
marks for licensing to others. It is important therefore
that the ownership of the mark should reside in a single
entity which has some trading aspects and that preferably
such a country should be located in a member country of the

Paris Convention.

In this area of tax it is always worthwhile remembering that
at least as far as Britain is concerned permitting another
party to file a mark in another country which you presently
own in Great Britain may in itself create capital transfer
problems and thus tax problems even though in fact there has
been no assignment of an actual mark in that country.

We have already discussed the problems which arise because
of the differences between common law countries and civil
law countries in delaying registration of rights. It must
equally be recognised, however, that securing a registration
either by simple registration or, in the case of the United
States, by a nominal series of transactions which cannot
support the application for registration, does not entitle
one to a trade mark for the rest of time. Most countries
have some form of actual use provision. Again we run into
the problem as to whether such use can be satisfied by a
licensee i.e. franchisee. In the case of a country such as
Britain when the only possibility of application is under a
registered user type provision in which a licensee must
exist at the time the application for protection is
undertaken. For most franchises the commercial procedure
which is most likely to succeed is by some form of joint
venture or even the first store as a company owned store
although this is perhaps an opinion which is not shared by
all franchisors. From a legal viewpoint such a "company
store" has the great advantage that it satisfies the
requirements of those countries where use has to be by the
owner of the actual trade mark i.e. the original foreign
franchisor.

Let us assume that the franchisor has undertaken a worldwide
registration of a mark to protect himself against possible
loss of rights. However, his financial resources and the
potential commercial interest does not develop as quickly as

he would like leaving him in the situation that there are a number of countries where there has been little or perhaps even no use whatsoever. As you will have gathered commercial use is necessary to protect a mark. For example, in the United States it has been held that although nominal use may be sufficient to support an application, early actual commercial use is also necessary. In the Instant Spring case which was a Trade Mark Trial and Appeal Board case application for cancellation of the registration was granted. Although the registration was only 15 months old and had been the subject of approximately four shipments each month to four different locations in four different states. The court stated that "to provide bona fide usage, the respondent must demonstrate that its use of the mark has been deliberate and continuous with an intention to create a commercial impact on the market, and not sporadic, casual or transitory". The Weiner King mark, however was held not to be lost or abandoned in a seaside resort where the store owner lost his lease for a season. Here, the U.S. court held that resort business was seasonal and the loss of the lease was beyond the lessee's control and one year was not too long a hiatus.

An analogous situation in Great Britain the Nerit/Merit cigarette case demonstrates that even a sale of several millions of cigarettes could be held insufficient to support a mark where the evidence was that the sales were only nominal for the purpose of attempting to control a situation where the word Merit itself was not registrable and the registration of Nerit was therefore not a registration of the mark of interest.

Most other countries will specify a period, for example five years, during which the mark must be used sufficiently to prevent a successful attack on it for non-use. Here a distinction must be drawn between countries, such as Britain or France, where until an application for cancellation for registration for non-use is brought, the mark continues in force, and other countries where there must be actual positive use. For instance, in the United States one must submit an affidavit within 6 years of registration to demonstrate use of the mark within the United States, while in other countries proof of use will be required at the time of renewal or renewal will not be permitted.

Accordingly therefore, in so far as franchising is concerned, a franchisor in one country has to accept that in extending his operation to other countries, he must proceed:

A. In many instances only after he has use of a franchisor/ franchisee set up in that country (particularly the common law countries).

B. Even where he is able to receive secure registration without existing use or licensee, then there must be use within a relatively short time or the registration which he has obtained will lapse.

With an operation in existence and with a valid registration of trade marks and other rights the next question must be the continued control of these rights. Where a master franchisee has been appointed for a country it may not be possible to pass through him all the rights under the franchise. In particular many countries, one example would be Britain, do not permit "sub-licensing" of trade marks. A licence must run directly from the trade mark owner to the licensee. This may sound like an argument in favour of permitting ownership in a master franchisee. My own view is that it is very easy to write the sub-franchise agreements in a given country so as to include a clause by which the master franchisee acts as an agent of the franchisor and undertakes to secure a trade mark licence. The master franchisee can then be given the authority to sign such licences on and behalf of the franchisor.

In most countries which have a system for recording licensees officially the question must arise as to how far one should register all the franchisees in a given country. In the United States it is not usual to record licenses and indeed there is no specific provision for such recordal. The issue will be whether the licence in question satisfactorily controls the behaviour of a licensee (i.e. franchisee) so that a court could properly hold that his use enures to the benefit of the original owner of the mark and does not confuse the public as to such ownership. This raises one question which is, of course, appropriate marking of the goods bearing the trade mark. It is one principle of much business format franchising that one tries to create as far as possible the relationship with the consumer such that he believes he is only dealing with one business in its various branches rather than with a series of independent business. Clearly it is contrary to this concept to have goods marked in such a way as to suggest that there is a distancing between the franchisee and the owner or some other entity. On the other hand it does seem desirable that at least some of the trade mark and goods bear the basic franchisor's name and some legend indicating licensing by the owner. In commercial practice such markings have little significance although they have a major significance when the issue is raised in court and one has to demonstrate that the paper cups bearing the mark bear the appropriate trade mark and licence notices.

In the U.K. the law appears to be that existence of an unregistered licence which licence is otherwise satisfactory does not affect the validity of the registration but a recent South African case indicates that one cannot rely on use by such an unregistered licence for the purpose of demonstrating sufficient use to maintain the mark.

Where there are a large number of franchisees in a country such as Britain, one does not recommend registering all of them. Apart from the possible redundancy of such multiple registrations and their limited value, one can introduce problems by the sheer number of licenses since one then has a constant possibility of adding to and removing from the register these registrations. Even when carefully controlled this can result in omissions and errors.

At least in Canada, however, it has been held that where there is a proper registered user agreement then packaging which refers only to the licensee's identification is quite appropriate (S.C. Johnson Ltd. -v- Marketing International (1979) 44 C SCPR (2d) 16). However this was a case where there was a single licensee and such licensee was registered. Whether such a case would be so clear where there were multiple licensees i.e. franchisees is not clear. Certainly it seems safer to require that all material bearing the trade mark bears the name of the trade mark owner.

In the recent "Friday's" case (Herman Lindy -v- Registrar of Trade Marks discussed Patent and Trade Mark Institute of Canada, Bulletin, Series 8, Volume 11, January 1982, page 637) the use was not by the owner but by his company and his company had not been indicated as a registered user. The court held that, although use could be demonstrated, nevertheless as it was not by the registered owner nor by a registered user and it was not use of the mark as required by Section 44(1).

One cannot overstress the necessity of maintaining quality control. Probably in franchising this is inherent in the nature of a good franchising operation so that one has fewer of the problems found in other types of trade mark licensing, but nevertheless the maintenance of not only quality control but records of such control is vitally

important.   Yet curiously enough, however, the consequence
of failure of quality control is not completely certain.
The recent MacGregor series of cases in Britain appears to
indicate that, although failure of quality control can lead
to mark being removed from the register, that does not
necessarily mean that the licensee acquires the possibility
of registering in his own name the mark in question.

Some concern was recently expressed whether the so called
Holly Hobbie decision (High Court: 1983 Fleet Street Reports
138; Court of Appeal April 28th 1983 not yet reported).
That case involved character merchandising and the question
of trafficking.   Essentially the question was whether a
number of registered users could be registered for different
classes of goods in the light of the prohibition in Section
28 against a licensing practice which would facilitate
trafficking.   Mr. Justice Whitford (page 146) stated "If, as
is the case here, the Registrar becomes aware that what is
afoot is not merely the grant of a right to some associated
organisation or the grant of a right in a name which has
acquired fame elsewhere to a trader whose use of a name is
subject to adequate supervision, but an application for a
trade mark, ------- with at the same time registered user
applications, the intention being that thereafter the marks
will be licensed, albeit on terms and subject to the
provisions of the registered user agreements, to <u>any number
of trades,</u> (emphasis added) the Register can, in my view,
only sensibly conclude that the grant of any one such
application, <u>a fortiori</u> the grant of all of them, would tend
to facilitate a trade in the relevant mark, or, as it is put
in sub-section (6), trafficking".

He commented unfavourably on the multiple usage of a mark
leading to confusion and deception.   This broad language in
the decision appeared to relate as much to the multiple
licensing found in franchising as it did to character

merchandising. In the Court of Appeal* Lord Justice Dillon
appeared to approve, however, of at least franchising. In
specifying a case where the granting of a registered user
licenses would be convenient and proper he gave in one
example as "where a proprietor grants franchises to local
distributors to market the proprietor's goods under the
proprietor's mark or to make up and market under the marked
goods according to the proprietor's formula or patent".
Here Lord Justice Dillon found an obvious trade connection
between the licensor and the goods of the licensee. Perhaps
significantly, however, the discussion was very much in the
context of the "trade connection". It is therefore still
possible that some risk could exist under this problem of
"trafficking" in Britain where the franchise involves a
relatively high service content with a provision of only
very limited types of articles. For this type of franchise
it is important that the quality control be specific as to
those goods which are supplied to the customer and that the
franchisor or his agent i.e. master franchisee be provided
with actual samples of these goods. An example of a problem
solution might be where the franchisee uses conventional
market spares as the only goods which are supplied through
the franchise and the franchise might indicate that it is
merely sufficient to buy from recognised dealers. Clearly
where a pure service is involved then, as indicated earlier,
there is virtually no possibility at the present time of
securing adequate trade mark protection in the United
Kingdom.

A further point on registered users may be the possibility
of licensing suppliers under the trade marks used in the
franchise where one would not otherwise wish to control the

---

* The Holly Hobbie case was taken by the applicants to the
House of Lords who have dismissed the appeal thus upholding
the Registrar's decision which had been confirmed by
Whitford J. and the Court of Appeal - Editor

provision of goods to the franchisee. In some countries the actual application of the trade mark to goods (even when intended for export) may be an infringement. It is therefore useful to consider trade mark agreements by any party who is involved with the use of a trade mark in any way.

In the drafting of the franchise agreement and the relationship with the franchisee, one sometimes finds in the master agreement simple and rather cursory broad language stating that the franchisee will, in all ways, protect the mark and will, if required, sign a registered user agreement. It is important that one analyse the requirements of a registered user agreement in the specific country in question and that these requirements be at least outlined in the franchise agreement. This avoids any possibility that the franchise agreement, which usually contains an overriding clause in respect of any other agreement, will not be held to be in conflict or derogate from the registered user agreement. In many instances for example in Great Britain the Registrar will want to see the basic franchise agreement at least to ensure that it is not in conflict with the agreement as registered. It seems preferable to incorporate virtually in total the provisions of such registered user agreement into the master agreement.

Particularly important is the correlation of the termination conditions in the registered user agreement with those of the master franchise as there should be no discrepancy in this area.

It is important to note that it is not merely the existence of a quality control provision but it is the enforcement which will have to be demonstrated to the court. Thus in a U.S. case Alligator -v- Robert Bruce (176 F. Supp. 377 (1959)), the court emphasised the language in the statute "any person who ...... is controlled by the registrant" (emphasis by the court). This is more than merely the right to control. The U.S. courts have certainly placed on the franchisor the affirmative requirement of control to avoid confusion to the public.

Part of the quality control is of course use of the mark as registered. A franchisor who has established an international trade mark programme as part of his quality control certainly must constantly police the manner in which a trade mark is represented. This is perhaps less of a problem in franchising where such policing is almost inherent in the nature of a franchise, but the franchisor must himself constantly be aware of the possibility of drift away from what is registered and realise that up-dating of a marker symbol might involve very major legal costs in up-dating the registration.

Another problem which does arise in some instances in franchising is the possibility that the franchisee may himself develop property rights and this is particularly true of master franchisors who will be developing property and products and services specific to the country in which they are operating. Generally one would prefer to see clauses which obligate such franchisee to assign the rights in the developed trade marks back to the franchisor. This may have competition law problems since grant-back clauses are generally not favoured by the enforcement authorities particularly the EEC. If one adds the appropriate additional explanation for example that these marks are to be developed in consultation with the basic franchisor and are so closely associated with the overall nature of the franchise so that it would lead to public confusion if they were separately owned, this should minimise competition law questions.

This brings us generally to the question of termination

clauses and to the extent that they are specific to the franchise area. Clearly it is important that the change from authorised use to unauthorised use be made explicit in the franchise agreement. Generally it will be true that once the licence agreement ceases then any continued use of the trade mark not only is a breach of contract but is also an infringement of the rights in the mark under trade mark law. There seems to be no harm, however, in emphasising this point in the actual agreement. In some instances it might be possible by reason of the effects of copyright law to enhance the damages which could be available from such unauthorised use. Similarly the provision in a franchise agreement that the use of a mark on unauthorised products produced by the franchisee is trade mark infringement provides another method of controlling the activities of the franchisee.

Use by a licensee, even when authorised and registered, is always weaker than use by the actual owner of the mark and leaves open a possibility, however slight, that an attack may be brought against the mark in the basis of confusion of the public by reason of multiple "entities". It is important that the franchisee be prevented as far as possible from being able to attack the registration of the mark so as to weaken the franchisor's property.

Again there is a problem of competition law under both U.S. and EEC law. In the EEC, at least in patent law, one can no longer generally prevent a licensee from attacking the rights under which he is licensed. Decisions by the EEC Commission (e.g. the Penney's case (1978) 2 C.M.L.R. 100 and Toltecs/Dorset (1983) 1 C.M.L.R. 390 where a fine was imposed for a no-challenge clause) apply the same rules to trade marks. However, it does seem likely that one could devise a clause which at least prevents the licensee from using his own authorised use within the agreement as a basis for attempting to overturn the mark. How far and what precise wording for such a clause can be successful must still be regarded as speculative.

In contrast to the tendency of the EEC commission to regard licensee estoppel clauses as invalid not only for patents but for trade marks, the U.S. courts have distinguished between patent and trade mark licenses. Thus decisions such as Lear -v- Adkins 295 U.S. 653 (1969) have been held as not applying to trade mark licences (Beer Nuts -v- King Nut 477 F.2d 326 (1973)). Thus in an infringement action against a terminated licensee who refuses to stop using the mark, the licensee may not challenge the licensor's ownership or claim abandonment on facts which occured before the agreement was terminated (Professional Golfers Association of America -v- Bankers Life 514 F.2v 665 (1975)).

As an inverse of the comment above in regard to infringement being available as well as breach of contract as a remedy against a former franchisee. It is also worthwhile bearing in mind that one should have in the contractual terms agreement not to use marks so that use of such mark would be a breach of contract as well as an infringement under the trade mark law.

Another area in which the Trade Mark Attorney has become increasingly involved is the problem of product liability arising from trade mark licensing. This is of course particularly a problem in franchising. Clearly the actual seller of goods in the United States and indeed in most countries has liability under various product liability laws because of the manufacturer of goods, even though the manufacturer may try and distance himself from the customer by intervening corporate distributors. U.S. law has certainly extended the jurisdiction of the State Courts very broadly as against actual manufacturers including foreign manufacturers. In this connection one must always bear in mind the various enforcement conventions which are coming into existence.

How far does licensing, however, create liability? A trade mark owner must have quality control to have a valid trade mark licence arrangement. Thus in a franchise, a U.S. court has held that the licensor franchisor was strictly liable on the basis of the legal responsibility arising from the quality control which amounted to a guarantee of a roofing product. Similarly a woman burned by a dress bearing the licensor's fabric certification label was successful against the Licensor and a Pennsylvenia Court held that, for the purpose of the statute, the licensors were "sellers" under the law of Pennsylvenia. There seems little doubt therefore that a franchisor will be held liable under a trade mark licence for a defect in the product distributed by his franchisee which bears his trade mark upon it and this must be borne in mind by any foreign franchisor in relation to U.S. liability. Similarly as the laws of other jurisdictions become tougher, the same problems will raise, for example in the EEC countries. This type of liability might also be created by know-how and other intellectual property licensing where the licensor takes responsibility for the nature of the product being produced. Probably the only adequate protection a licensor or franchisor has in this type of situation is to provide adequate insurance.

A Trade Mark Attorney advising his franchisor client may also become involved in associated areas when that franchisor or his franchisees wish to take advantage of personality marketing. The whole law of personality and character merchandising is fraught with problems. A franchisor who decides to use, as part of a campaign, a personality or a character must be sure that the property which he is purchasing through an international organisation can be used in all the countries. For example, character development rights secured in the United States may not be available or enforceable in European countries. The

franchisor must therefore make sure (a) he has the rights
and (b) that they are worth something in various countries
in terms of being enforceable against possible imitators.

Summary

In creating an intellectual property packaging for
international franchising, the necessity of a "strong" trade
mark package including marks which are inherently
registrable even though they may have certain suggestive
aspects becomes even more important than in the initial
national phase. Particularly in civil law countries, one
may have to depend on registration to create rights and one
cannot rely then on a development of a right by use, which
can be brought to the attention of the Registrar to
demonstrate distinctiveness. Also the careful initial use
of a strong mark can enhance the international position
bearing in mind the problems of international registration
before the franchisor is in fact ready to effect and
demonstrate actual use in each of the countries in which he
has sought protection. The lack of service mark protection
still in many countries may suggest a slight restructuring
of the franchise to provide at least some provision of
product to support a trade mark programme. Careful use of
designs and symbols may enhance the possibility of
protection by copyright where trade mark protection is not
initially available. However desirable certain taxation
schemes may appear to be, they should always be analysed,
not merely in terms of their tax advantages, but against the
possible effect on the intellectual property rights which
might result from "absentee" ownership.

More than most of fields of commercial activity, franchising
is the trading in a bundle of intellectual property rights.
This discussion has been primarily directed to the trade
mark aspects since indeed, of the intellectual property
rights, it is often the trade mark which is by far the most

important.   Nevertheless the careful management and inter-
relation of all the rights is imperative as has been
demonstrated for example in relation to copyright.   The
international intellectual property lawyer should therefore
be an integral member of the franchising team, if possible
from the inception of the franchise.   One can only advise
against attempting to build an international franchise
organisation on the shifting and unstable foundation of a
virtually unregistrable or very weak trade mark.

CHAPTER 3

CHARACTER MERCHANDISING

Nicholas Fyfe

The "character" which is the subject matter of the business now known as character merchandising appears to be an image. In the hands of the merchandiser, the image is perceived as being a property right, while in the hands of a licensee, the image is perceived as having value in that the licensee may use the image in association with his products to commercial advantage in the sense that the image will enhance the saleability of those products.

Typically, a merchandisable character will, for reasons wholly related to the business of the licensee, have in some manner already acquired an established reputation because it is the reputation that attaches to the character or image that provides for the user a marketing advantage. This paper deals primarily with fictional characters of the type that may have been featured in a successful comic strip, television show, or movie. Examples include Mickey Mouse (the Walt Disney organisation probably originated character merchandising), The Muppet characters,E.T. and the various personalities depicted in the Star Wars series of films.

An apparent exception to the requirement that a merchandisable fictional character be well known is shown by the successful merchandising of Strawberry Shortcake. This character differs from the foregoing types in that, although the character had been used on greeting cards, it was apparently selected for the express purpose of character merchandising and was successfully merchandised in the

absence of a pre-established reputation. It is my
understanding that this occurred in part because of the
intrinsic attention-getting value attributable to the
Strawberry Shortcake character (research had shown that the
particular character would prove attractive, especially to
young females), but primarily because the merchandiser, as
well as conferring the right to use the character, also bound
itself extensively to promote the character, thereby
providing the image with an "instant" reputation. The
success of Strawberry Shortcake has not been ignored, and I
believe that there are a number of other characters or
images now being created (as opposed to having been
previously established) for the sole purpose of
merchandising.

The Federal Court has recently recognised the value of
character merchandising as a business in a judgement of
Walsh J. in Universal City Studios Inc. et al v. Zellers
Inc. (1) where he granted an interlocutory injunction
restraining the distribution of unauthorised E.T. dolls. The
following statements appear at pages 3,4 and 7:

> "The motion picture (E.T. The Extra-Terrestrial)
> was first exhibited to the public on or about June
> 11, 1982 and became an enormous box office
> success, becoming the most successful motion
> picture of all time as disclosed by its box office
> gross. As of February 17, 1983, the box office
> gross in the United States for the motion picture
> has been in excess of $293,241,000. It is
> estimated that there has been in excess of
> 104,365,000 admissions in the United States. As
> of the same date Universal had spent in excess of
> U.S. $6,300,000 in the United States advertising
> the motion picture, by media advertising, press
> kits and the like and some of such advertising has
> spilled over into Canada. The motion picture has

also been extremely successful in Canada and has received substantial publicity in Canadian press and in U.S. newspapers and magazines which have substantial Canadian circulation. As a result of this the copyrights have become extremely valuable property. Plaintiff Universal has granted a number of licences authorising manufacturers to manufacture and sell various goods representing or relating to the E.T."

"It is not unusual for spinoff rights for merchandise of all sorts such as dolls, keychains, T-shirts, posters, and so forth, originating from a motion picture which has captured the public imagination such as "E.T. The Extra-Terrestrial" to be of immense value to the creators of the motion picture and of the designs of the merchandise originating from it. One has only to look at the Walt Disney characters such as Mickey Mouse and Donald Duck to realize the potential for such distribution and also the temptation to counterfeit, which is also frequently attempted with puzzles or toys such as Rubik's Cube, the original frisbees, yo-yos and so forth. It is trite to state that such attempts at counterfeiting, whether they result from copyrights, trademarks, industrial design or patents must be dealt with severely by the Court so as to protect the valuable rights of the creators."

Although there may be an overlap, the property right that is the subject matter of character merchandising operations seems to differ from that which is normally the subject matter of more conventional franchise arrangements where a

series of licensees all market products (eg. COCA-COLA) or
services (eg. HOLIDAY INNS) which have common
characteristics and which are identified and distinguished
from the products and services of others through use of a
common trade mark or trade name. Thus, the licensees in
typical franchising situations are all in the same business.
In contrast, licensees in a character merchandising
situation are almost always deliberately selected so that
each is in a different line of business.

An ordinary franchisee is protected from competition arising
through the activities of his co-licensees through the grant
of, for example, exclusive territorial rights. Although a
character licensee may seek similar protection, he is more
often than not granted exclusivity as to product or service
and his co-licensees, although operating in the same
territory, are required to be in different lines of
business. Thus, with character licensing we have a wide
range of goods, each being put out by a different licensee,
and all bearing a common image.

The manner in which the image is used by the character
licensee also appears to differ from the manner in which the
conventional franchisee uses the trade mark that forms part
of the subject matter of his licence. A franchisee proudly
advertises and uses the trade mark so as to tell the public
that he is one source of a particular kind and quality of
goods or services. The character licensee, on the other
hand, seldom uses the character image for this purpose.
Instead, he decorates his product with the licensed image,
thereby placing into the marketplace his own TIMEX brand
Mickey Mouse watches, his own KENNER brand Strawberry
Shortcake dolls, or his own JOCKEY brand t-shirts emblazoned
with the image of E.T.

It appears that successful merchandisers percive that they
are marketing something in the nature of a trade mark. In

the 5th April 1982 edition of Newsweek Magazine, there was an article entitled "The Selling of the Smurfs". In that article, a merchandiser is quoted as stating that character licensing is advertising that makes money instead of costing money; that the licensor lends the right to an image for a certain percentage of sales, and that in return, the licensee receives "a recognisable brand name and national marketing assistance". It is submitted that, to the extent that it is suggested that the licensed character is equivalent to a brand name, this is seldom the case, at least in accordance with Canadian law as it now stands. Thus, although use of the image undoubtedly creates demand for the product, it does not do so in the conventional trade mark sense. Rather, perhaps because of the "hype" that is associated with the reputation of the image per se, the consumer is induced to buy because of a psychological desire somehow to publicly associate himself with the image.

It is the essence of a character merchandising program that the merchandiser has enforceable property rights in the character because it is axiomatic that if unauthorised use of the character cannot be restrained, the licensing program must fail.

In the case of fictional characters of the type discussed in this paper, the copyright laws provide a powerful remedy with respect to the appearance of the character, but no remedy at all in respect of the character's name:

".... there is no copyright in the mere name of a fictional character" per Dillon L.J. in In Re Holly Hobbie .(2)

If the merchandiser can prove his title to the copyright character and if the Court can be persuaded that the character was copied by the defendant, whether in two or three-dimensional form, both injunctive and monetary relief

is available. Thus, in the E.T. case (supra), the
plaintiff's cause of action was founded on both copyright in
the dramatic and artistic work comprising the motion
picture.

In American Greetings Corporation et al -v- Oshawa Group
Limited et al (3), interlocutory relief was also obtained,
with copyright in the greeting card character there being
successfully asserted by the merchandiser and one of its
licensees who was selling Strawberry Shortcase dolls.

It is important to recognise, however, that if copying,
whether direct or indirect,(4) cannot be proven or inferred,
an action for copyright infringement must fail. Consider
the now well-known and successfully merchandised Smurf
characters. These characters find their origins in an
illustrated children's book. If pirated through copying,
the merchandiser's rights appear clear. If, on the other
hand, the alleged infringer can show that he has derived a
similar character by copying a drawing of a third party who
had independently created his drawing, then no matter how
much the elfin figures of the defendant may resemble the
Smurf character, the cause of action will fail. This would
also be true if the alleged infringer had copied from
drawings of the original character if the copyright in those
drawings had expired (this is a problem that the Walt Disney
people will soon have to face).

Even if it can be shown that the idea and spirit of the
defendant's character was inspired by the plaintiff's work,
the cause of action may fail if a Court is prepared to find
that the defendant's character is a new work of art.(5) This
could be the result if the defendant, rather than pirating
the plaintiff's character, has used the character as an idea
in order to create perhaps an uncomplimentary parody of the
character in such a manner as to produce an original work.
In this type of situation the copyright laws may not provide

a remedy, even though it is quite possible that the use of the defendant's character may effectively diminish the goodwill necessary to support a character merchandising scheme.

A further word of warning: fictional characters such as E.T. and Strawberry Shortcake have economic value to the merchandiser in part because potential sources of licensing revenue include manufacture of dolls, wallpaper and textiles such as bed sheets. A combined reading of Section 46 of the Copyright Act and Rule 11 of the Industrial Design Rules operates to prevent the acquisition of copyright in works as applied to such goods if, at the time the character was first created, the author intended the character to be used as a model or pattern to be multiplied by an industrial process. In such case the author obtains only a right to secure the protection of industrial design registration. The danger today is that character merchandising appears to have become sufficiently sophisticated as a business that it could be argued that the creator of, for example, the E.T. character, had every intention of creating a character that would not only be successful in the movie, but that would also become a merchandising vehicle. Industrial design registrations, although federal in scope, provide a term of protection for only ten years, and are limited to the particular articles of commerce in respect of which protection is obtained. Thus, although it may be possible to secure an industrial design registration extending to the ornamenting of a doll so as to have the appearance of E.T. or Strawberry Shortcake, that registration will be of no value whatsoever in respect of an infringer who uses the images in association with, for example board games or t-shirts. In Canada, there are also strict rules as to when industrial design protection must be secured (registration must be obtained within one year of publication in Canada) and as to who is the proper person to secure registration. In the E.T. and Strawberry Shortcake Federal Court decisions

referred to above, Section 46 defences were raised, but
because the matters have not yet proceeded beyond the
interlocutory stage, they have not yet been resolved. The
dangers are, however, obvious: If the Court should find
that there is no copyright, it will be too late to secure
industrial design protection.

The Trade Marks Act may provide a vehicle for protecting
both the image of the character and its name. If the
character merchandiser can organise his affairs in such a
way as to secure valid trade mark registrations extending to
his character, he will acquire rights in the character that
are in many respects superior to those conferred through the
copyright laws. A valid trade mark registration is
infringed by a defendant who uses the same or a confusing
trade mark (the issue is an objective one; copying need not
be shown). Furthermore, as opposed to industrial design
protection, identity as to product is not required. The
Trade Marks Act does not provide for a classification system
of wares and services, and infringement will be found if the
Court is satisfied that there is a likelihood of confusion
as defined by Section 6 of the Act, i.e. that the
concurrent use of the trade marks in the same area would be
likely to lead to the inference that the wares or services
associated with such marks are manufactured, sold, leased,
hired or performed by the same person, "whether or not such
wares or services are of the same general class".

The recent decisions of the Federal Court suggest that
Section 6(2) may be construed so as to find confusion if the
evidence tends to support findings of "sponsorship" or
"authorisation".(6)

Even if the defendant is using the character (a) otherwise
than as a trade mark, or (b) in a non-confusing manner, the
Federal Court, notwithstanding an earlier decision which
appeared to limit the scope of the Section,(7) now appears

willing to invoke Section 22 of the Trade Marks Act to restrain a defendant from using that which is the subject matter of a trade mark registration in such a manner as to depreciate the goodwill associated therewith. Thus, in Source Perrier S.A. -v- Fira- less Marketing Co. Ltd., (8) Mr. Justice Dube granted an interlocutory injunction restraining the defendant from selling ordinary tap water in a green bottle bearing the words "Pierre eh ", even though the defendant's product clearly indicated that it was marked by the defendant and contained a disclaimer that it was not to be confused with the plaintiff's PERRIER product. In granting the injunction, it was held that the defendant was attempting to cash in on the well-established reputation of PERRIER, thereby diluting the quality of the plaintiff's trade mark, impairing its business integrity established over the years, and causing injury to its goodwill. The Court went on to say that the cause of action under Section 22 does "not necessarily flow from deception and that it may result without deception being present.(9)

Like the rights conferred by both copyright and industrial design registrations, a cause of action founded upon a registered trade mark may be brought in the Federal Court, thereby securing for the successful plaintiff an injunction having effect all across Canada. Furthermore, trade mark registrations, so long as they are properly renewed, may continue to have effect indefinitely, whereas protection conferred by the copyright laws and the industrial design laws is limited as to time. Unlike the interplay as between copyright and industrial design, the trade mark route may also be pursued in parallel with the cause of action founded in copyright.

As noted above, it seems to be typical of character merchandising situations that the merchandiser is not himself involved, at least in the conventional sense, in the sale of goods and services. Rather, all use of the character is through a licensee. Prior to passage of the current Trade Marks Act in 1953, this fact alone would have precluded the merchandiser from securing trade mark protection since it was then fairly well established by cases such as Bowden Wire (10) that the distinctiveness of a registered trade mark, and hence its validity, is destroyed in consequence of licensing.

In 1953 Trade Marks Act gave statutory recognition to the possibility of licensing through the registered user provisions defined in Section 49. Although the registered user provisions are invaluable in the case of the more conventional franchising situation, they pose serious difficulties when applied to character merchandising. As noted above, although the parties to a character merchandising agreement seem to believe that the subject matter of the licence has trade mark significance, it is at least my thesis that in most situations the character, rather than being used as a trade mark, is being used in a decorative sense. This gives rise to serious difficulty in that the Courts have indicated that the permitted use of a trade mark by a licensee must be as a trade mark (11) and that in this and all other respects, the registered user provisions are to be strictly construed (12). Another difficulty is created in that the registered user provisions apply only to registered trade marks. The only exception to this rule is provided through a combined reading of Section 49(7) and Section 39(2), which specify that in the case of a proposed trade mark (which cannot proceed to registration until evidence of use has been filed), the use that may be relied upon can be use by a person approved as a registered user, rather than by the trade mark owner.

It seems that the promotion and "hype" surrounding modern-day character merchandising gives rise to a situation where, from a practical point of view, the character merchandiser will seek a series of licensees on a contemporaneous basis and that, to the extent that the licensees are obtained, all will wish to commence use of the character forming the subject matter of their licence as soon as possible. In particular, prospective licensees wish to ride the crest of popularity associated with the character and are for this reason unwilling to wait for what may be a fairly considerable period of time pending completion of administrative procedures within the Trade Marks Office. Since it is the Registrar's practice not even to consider a registered user application until such time as the trade mark application to which it relates has been allowed (i.e. has successfully gone through the opposition period), it appears that from a practical point of view the licensee will in all likelihood have commenced his use of the licensed character prior to his approval as a permitted user. In such situations, it is currently the registrar's practice, in the event that the application has been opposed on lack of distinctiveness grounds, to conclude that he must refuse the trade mark application if evidence as to use by the licensee should come to his attention. This particular issue is now the subject matter of an appeal to the Federal Court (13). However, should the Registrar's decision be sustained, a character merchandiser who wants to protect his property pursuant to the Trade Marks Act should prevent his licensees from using the mark until they have been approved as registered users thereof.

It had previously been thought that in the event that a trade mark application could successfully be prosecuted through to registration, the fact that there may have been licensed use without benefit of the registered user provisions prior to registration could be overcome following registration through the passage of time. This view was based upon the fact that Section 49(3) of the Act specifically provides that the permitted use of a trade mark "has the same effect for all purposes of the Act as a use thereof by the registered owner" and because, with respect

to attacks on the validity of a registered trade mark, the
Act, to the extent that it refers to distinctiveness, says
that the registration of a trade mark is invalid if the
trade mark is not distinctive "at the time proceedings
bringing the validity of the registration in question are
commenced" (Section 18(1)(b)). In other words, it was felt
that, although the trade mark may not have been distinctive
while it was pending before the Registrar, it would become
distinctive following its registration.   Unfortunately, a
recent decision of the Federal Court of Appeal has cast
doubt upon this theory in that there is language in that
decision which suggests that if it can be shown that a trade
mark was not distinctive as of its date of registration, it
will be held invalid on the grounds that it was not
registrable at that date (14).   Lack of registability at the
date of registration is a specific ground of invalidity
pursuant to Section 18(1)(a) of the Act.

As noted above, the registered user provisions only apply to
use of a trade mark as a trade mark.   A practical
application of that rule was demonstrated when McDonald's
Corporation sought to register the image of their RONALD
MCDONALD character for use in association with various
articles of clothing.   It appears that it was McDonald's
Corporation's intention to generate income through the grant
of licenses to use their RONALD MCDONALD character and their
application to register the mark for use in association with
clothing was based upon proposed use supported by registered
user applications in favour of various licensees.   The
application was not opposed and the Registrar in due course
called for the filing of evidence to the effect that use of
the mark had commenced in Canada by McDonald's Corporation
or an approved registered user.   In order to comply with the
Registrar's requirement, articles of clothing, which for the
purpose of this paper may be treated as t-shirts, were filed
which prominently displayed the RONALD MCDONALD character on
the front thereof.   The Registrar rejected the evidence

holding that it demonstrated a decorative, rather than a trade mark, use and ultimately refused the trade mark application (15).

The difficulties inherent in distinguishing as between decorative and trade mark use as described in the clothing field example above become almost insurmountable in the case where the licensee is to be permitted to use the image as, for example, a doll. It is submitted that in such cases, the only hope of securing valid trade mark protection would be to persuade the authorities that the get-up of the doll comprised a distinguishing guise. However, a distinguishing guise can only be registered if it can be shown that the mark has been used in Canada by the applicant so as to become distinctive as of the date of the filing of the application (16). Since the only use of te distinguishing guise will have been by the licensee, rather than by the character merchandiser, the latter will not be able to secure such a registration.

The registered user provisions of the Trade Marks Act also contemplate the quality control must be exercised by the licensor and although subjection 49(10) has never been judically construed, it provides that if the licensee can be shown to have used the mark other than by way of the permitted use, or in such a way as to cause deception or confusion, the registered user entry may be cancelled, once again giving rise to a risk of loss of distinctiveness.

The British Court of Appeal in the recent HOLLY HOBBIE case referred to above has to all intents and purposes held that a character merchandiser, as opposed to a franchisor, may not take advantage of the British registered user provisions so as to secure trade mark protection in the character. The decision was founded on an express provision contained in the registered user section of the British Act to the effect that the Registrar may refuse a registered user application

if it appears to the Registrar that by approving the licence
it "would tend to facilitate trafficking" in the mark.
HOLLY HOBBIE is the name of a character who was first used
on greeting cards and who then became the subject matter of
a merchandising program. The merchandiser applied to
register the name as a trade mark in respect of a wide range
of goods and supported its application with a series of
registered user applications in favour of its licensees. In
the HOLLY HOBBIE case, the Court upheld the Registrar's view
that the registered user applications should be refused on
the basis that character merchandising in the sense
discussed in this paper did indeed constitute "trafficking".
Lord Justice Dillon, in the main opinion rendered by the
Court of Appeal, held that "trafficking" was a common law
objection* to trade mark validity and relied upon the
Bowden Wire case (supra) as exemplifying the objectionable
conduct. In essence, the Court of Appeal appeared to find
that, although the rule against licensing as set forth in
Bowden Wire had been relaxed in consequence of the
enactment of registered user provisions, a finding of
trafficking could probably be made if the applicant for
trade mark registration was shown to be disposing of the
mark or the reputation in the name as a marketable commodity
per se in circumstances where there is no trade connection
between the proprietor of the mark and the goods or business
of the licensee. (17) It was argued that because of the
quality control provisions as set forth in the registered
user applications, the Court ought to find a trade
connection. These arguments were rejected on the basis that
the control provisions appeared in the agreements "not to
preserve the appellant's business in greeting cards, but to
protect the character whom the appellants are marketing,
i.e. to protect the mark as of itself a marketable

---

* This does not appear to be a common law point as S. 28 of
the U.K. Trade Mark Act expressly prohibits trafficking in
Trade Marks - Editor

commodity" (18). The Canadian Act makes no reference to
trafficking and for this reason the case may have not
application here in Canada. On the other hand, as noted
above, the Court of Appeal in HOLLY HOBBIE found that
trafficking was a "sin" recognised at common law and since
49(7) of the Canadian Trade Marks Act does provide that the
Registrar may refuse a registered user application if he
feels that approval thereof would be contrary to the public
interest, I am of the view that if the Court of Appeal was
right in HOLLY HOBBIE, the principle may well have
application here in Canada. If so, the merchandiser may be
unable to rely upon the Trade Marks Act to create
enforceable rights in the fictional character.

Leave to appeal has been granted in HOLLY HOBBIE by the
House of Lords. From the character merchandiser's point of
view, one can only hope * that the decision will be
reversed.

Although this paper deals primarily with fictional
characters as exemplified by Strawberry Shortcake and her
friends, it will be noted from the RONALD MCDONALD example
above that there are fictional characters who have found
their roots in and developed their fame as trade marks.
Although such characters may be perceived as having
significant value as merchandisable properties, it is
submitted that because of the very fame attributed to the
mark, it may, in respect of the merchandiser's ordinary line
of goods, represent an asset of such considerable value
that, because of the dangers referred to above, the owner
would be well advised to forego the potential income arising

---

* Nicholas Fyfe's hopes for character merchandisers in the
Holly Hobbie case have not been realised since the House of
Lords upheld the previous decisions. The Holly Hobbie case
is also referred to in Ian Baillie's paper which comprises
Chapter 2 of this work - Editor

in consequence of a licensing program on the sole basis that
the risks inherent in such a program may irrevocably
diminish the distinctiveness of his mark. Such a
consequence would tend to flow if the registration of the
character as a trade mark in respect of various sundry items
should be struck down since, if the registration had been
obtained based upon use by licensees, their use would then
prevent the owner of the mark from taking the position that
his mark had acquired such a degree of fame through his own
extensive and exclusive user that he could prevent its
unauthorised use on wholly unrelated lines of goods and
services.

If neither copyright infringement nor trade mark
infringement is available as a cause of action for the
character merchandiser, there remains the possibility of
founding an action in passing off. It now appears that such
an action may only be brought in the Provincial Courts.
(19)

One requirement for success in an action for passing off is
that, at least until recently, such actions have been
restricted to situations where the conflicting parties have
been competing in a common trade or sector in the commercial
world. In the character merchandising field, this is not
the case in that the merchandiser's licensing business is in
reality quite different from the business of the individual
manufacturer of goods bearing the infringing image. It
appears that this hurdle may now have been overcome since
the decision of the House of Lords in the Advocaat case
(20) and the subsequent English decision in Lego Systems
A/S et al -v- Lego M. Lemelstrich Ltd. (21) In the latter
case, the following statement appears (22):

> "However, it is to the law as stated in the
> Advocaat case that we now have to look and, in
> Lord Diplock's formulation of the characteristics

that are necessary ingredients to found a cause of action in passing off, there is no limitation as to the relation of the field of activity of the defendant to that of the plaintiff. Moreover, I have already drawn attention to the passage in his speech at p. 93, lines 8-14, in which <u>Lord Diplock specifically recognises that a cause of action for passing off may lie in a case where the plaintiff and the defendant are not competing traders in the same line of business.</u>"

There is a further difficulty: it is the very essence of an action for passing off that the plaintiff establish that he has adopted a peculiar or novel character as a distinguishing feature of his goods or business and that <u>his</u> goods or business have established a reputation in the market by reason of that distinguishing feature. Failure to establish either of these points will bar the plaintiff from obtaining relief (23). In a licensing situation, the character, rather than being used by the licensor in the conventional sense, is being used by a number of licensees, each with a view to somehow distinguishing their goods. In principle, it therefore seems that the licensor will be unable to succeed because the basic requirement of distinctiveness in his hands cannot be established.

Perhaps in recognition of the character merchandising situation, the Courts have indicated that they may be prepared to permit a licensee to prove that the character identifies no particular goods, but the merchandising business itself. Thus, in <u>Tavner Rutledge -v- Trexapalm</u> (24), even though the Court was prepared to concede that the requirement for a showing of confusion as to origin of goods or services might include confusion as to the endorsement, sponsorship or approval of the goods or services, interlocutory relief was refused on evidentiary grounds. In order to succeed, Walton J. stated that it would have to be shown:

(1) That the public believed that the user of a character
     had the right to use the character by virtue of a
     licence;

(2) That the public believed that in such situation, the
     licensor exercised quality control over the product in
     the sense that he guaranteed its quality.

In the case of fictional characters, I suspect that the
evidentiary burden suggested by Walton J. will be very
difficult to establish.

There remains the possibility of a character licensee itself
successfully asserting a cause of action for passing off.
However, the more successful the licensing program, the more
difficult it will be to establish that the goods bearing the
character as they originate from one licensee are
distinguishable from the goods bearing the character as they
originate from other licensees. Thus, in such cases, unless
a joint venture can be established, an action for passing
off will fail. Although the Advocaat case (25) clearly
leaves open the possibility that a group of traders may
successfully join in asserting a cause of action founded in
passing off, it should be recognised that, for practical
purposes, the principle ennunciated in Advocaat would have
to be expanded if it is going to be held to apply to
character merchandising situations. In this connection, the
Advocaat principle is, I believe, founded on the
proposition that it had been established that there were a
group of people, all of whom marketed a product that in
itself had common characteristics which were in themselves
recognisable and distinctive. It seems to be inherent to a
character merchandising program that none of the licensees
sell products that have anything in common, apart from the
application of the character to the product. For this

reason, I think that it may be difficult to adapt the Advocaat principle in order to support a joint cause of action in the hands of the licensor and its licensees.

Notwithstanding what may appear to be a rather pessimistic view as to the scope of a character merchandiser's rights in his fictional character, it should be borne in mind that at least the Federal Court has recognised that the character merchandiser is possessed of something that is recognised as having a very substantial monetary value which has been obtained at least in part in consequence of business activity attributable to the merchandiser. (26) It can nearly always be shown that the "infringer" is endeavouring to obtain commercial advantage at the expense of the merchandiser's investment. Thus, given an arguable case on the merits, it is submitted that an aura of dishonesty can usually be demonstrated in respect of the defendant's activities and that, in such cases, this is usually sufficient to enable the Court to make a finding in interlocutory injunction proceedings that the balance of convenience should favour the plaintiff. For practical purposes, this will in most cases effectively terminate the matter.

FOOTNOTES

1. Court No. T-617-83 in the Federal Court of Canada, Trial Division, 4th July 1983, unreported as yet.

2. English Court of Appeal decision dated 28th April 1983, unreported as yet, at page 3.

3. (1983), 69 C.P.R. (2d) 238 (F.C.T.D.)

4. See Fox, The Canadian Law of Copyright and Industrial Design, Second Edition, pages 329, 330, 355.

5. Bauman -v- Fussell (1978) R.P.C. 485 (English Court of Appeal decision dated 18th May 1953)

    Merchandising Corporation of America Inc. et al -v- Harpbond Ltd. et al (1983) F.S.R. 32 (English Court of Appeal)

6. Berry Bros. & Rudd Ltd. -v- Planta Tabak - Manufactur Dr. Manfred Oberman (1980) 53 C.P.R. (2d) 130

    Conde Nast Publications Inc. -v- Gozlan Borthers Ltd. (1980) 49 C.P.R. (2d) 250

7. Clairol International Corporation et al -v- Thomas Supply & Equipment Co. Ltd. (1968) 38 Fox P.C. 176

8. (1983) 70 C.P.R. (2d) 61

9. Ibid. p 65

10. Bowden Wire Ltd. -v- Bowden Brake Company Ltd. (1914) 31 R.P.C. 385

11. Samuel Dubiner -v- Cheerio Toys & Games Ltd. (1964) 44
     C.P.R. 134

12. Motel 6, Inc. -v- No. 6 Motel Ltd. et al (1981) 56
     C.P.R. (2d) 44 at 62-63 (F.C.T.D.)

13. IN THE MATTER OF Oppositions by Imperial Oil Limited to
     Application No. 376,697 for the trade mark THE IMPERIAL
     GROUP & Design, Application no. 376.698 for the trade
     mark THE IMPERIAL GROUP and Application No. 376,699 for
     the trade mark A MEMBER OF THE IMPERIAL GROUP OF
     COMPANIES, all filed by Imperial Developments Ltd. -
     decision of the Registrar of Trade Marks dated 21st
     July 1982 (unreported)

14. Chalet Bar BOQ (Canada) Inc et al -v- Foodcorp Ltd.
     (1983) 66 C.P.R. (2d) 56 at 68

15. Judicial authority for the proposition (albeit in a
     different context) can be found in British Petroleum
     Co. Ltd. -v- Bombardier Ltd. (1971) 4 C.P.R. (2d) 204;
     affirmed Federal Court of Appeal (1973), 10 C.P.R. (2d)
     21.

16. Section 13, Trade Marks Act

17. supra, footnote 2 at p 13-15

18. supra, footnote 2 at p 14

19. MacDonald -v- Vapor (1976) 22 C.P.R. (2d) 1 (S.C.C.)

     Motel 6, inc. -v- No. 6 Motel Ltd., et al (supra)

20. Erven Warnink B.V. -v- J. Townend & Sons (Hull) Ltd.
     (1980) R.P.C. 31 (H.L.)

21. (1983) F.S.R. 155

22. Ibid p 187

23. Williams -v- Bronnley (1909) 26 R.P.C. 275

     Oxford Pendaflex Canada Ltd. -v- Korr Marketing Ltd. et
     al (1982), 64 C.P.R. (2d) 1 (S.C.C.)

24. (1977) R.P.C. 275

25. supra, footnote 18

26. See the E.T. case, supra, footnote 1

CHAPTER 4

REGULATION OF FRANCHISING IN THE UNITED STATES:
IMPLICATIONS FOR INTERNATIONAL FRANCHISING
By Philip F. Zeidman *

Introduction

Franchising, simply and somewhat simplistically stated, is a
method of distributing goods or services under a common name
or mark by numerous persons who are otherwise not related.
Although the origins of franchising can be traced back
several centuries,(1) its greatest growth has occurred
within the last thirty years or so -- principally in the
United States, where "business format" franchising has
changed the face of the entire land.(2)

Franchising law has grown along with franchising itself,
especially in the United States, where franchising is
regulated to a degree unequalled elsewhere in the world.(3)
As other countries begin to experience the franchising
explosion, their laws and legal systems will surely respond
to it -- perhaps in ways similar to the U.S. legal response,
perhaps in new and different ways. After examining the
types of regulation which have been formulated in the United
States, where franchising law is relatively mature, it may
prove instructive to compare and contrast laws affecting
franchising in other countries, and to extrapolate from that
analysis a "life cycle" of franchising regulation. From
that perspective, it may be easier for persons in other

* Mr. Zeidman gratefully acknowledges the assistance of
Anita K. Blair, of Brownstein Zeidman and Schomer,
Washington, D.C., in the preparation of this article.

countries to judge whether the franchising regulations which
they have, or plan to adopt, are truly necessary and likely
to be effective.(4)

Franchising Regulation in the United States

Several traditional areas of law form the basis for both
statutory and non-statutory regulation of franchising in the
United States.   As an ordinary contract evidencing a
business arrangement, a franchise agreement is subject to
all applicable business regulation statutes and common law
principles.   Laws which are of general applicability to
business usually are not interpreted differently for
franchises.   U.S. federal and state antitrust laws, albeit
of decreasing importance in recent years, remain the single
largest area of legal concern for franchisors in part
because of the exposure to treble damages.(5) To some
extent, however, franchising is beginning to be treated as a
special case under those laws.(6)

A franchise is typically a trade mark license, combined with
the right (frequently exclusive) to distribute goods or
services over a long period of time, using the marketing
methods (often proprietary) developed and constantly
improved by the franchisor. It is immediately apparent that
many traditional disciplines -- including intellectual
property law, competition law, and commercial law
(encompassing the basic law of contracts) -- are very
important in franchising. Corporate, securities and tax
laws are also significant in franchising because the parties
are typically separate, unrelated entities, and because the
relationship begins with an investment by the franchisee and
usually involves a continuing flow of payments to the
franchisor. Moreover, in the United States at least, the
franchisor may be deemed responsible, by virtue of the
controls it imposes, for certain acts of the franchisee.(7)
Hence, tort and agency law also play a role in franchising

law in the United States.

In addition to the laws described above, the United States has a number of statutory laws, both federal and state, which specifically govern franchising. These laws take several different forms, depending upon the particular class of persons being protected and the particular practices being restricted. For example, special laws have been enacted to protect from unjust termination franchisees or dealers in specific industries (e.g., automobile and petroleum dealers, beverage distributors) typically but not always those whose businesses require a large capital investment for facilities or high priced inventory.(8) Other laws aim to protect the general public from possible abuses in connection with sales of franchises or dealerships considered to be high-risk ventures (e.g., "pyramid" schemes, "business opportunities").(9)

But the vast majority of franchises in the United States fall into none of the above special categories; rather, they are subject to broad regulation based on similar theories. While the term "franchise" has been used over the years in a non-legal sense (e.g., a right to vote; a special commercial "niche"), and is frequently used even today interchangeably with a "licence" or a "distributorship," it becomes important to define the term precisely for purposes of determining coverage under Federal and state law. For purposes of these laws, a "franchise" is generally defined as including the basic elements of:

(i) association with a trademark,

(ii) payment of a fee, and

(iii) a degree of control exercised by the franchisor over the franchisee's operations.

Most commercial relationships which fit that definition are subject to both federal and state requirements governing the offer and sale of the franchise, as well as the ongoing conduct of the parties. it is essential to realise, though, that each of these definitions has been the subject of quite expansive interpretation, bringing within the ambit of those laws relationships which would not on their face appear to be covered. (10)

U.S. Regulation of the offer and Sale of Franchisees.

The U.S. Federal Trade Commission ("FTC") in 1978 adopted a rule requiring that every offer for the sale of a franchise be accompanied by a document drawn up in a standardised format, disclosing certain information to prospective franchisees.(11) The FTC rule applies in all states. Both before and since 1978, several states have adopted similar, but not identical, disclosure requirements, coupled with a requirement of registration with a state agency prior to offering franchises for sale within a particular state.(12) Either the FTC rule format (which is slightly less detailed) or the Uniform Franchise Offering Circular (UFOC) format may be used by a franchisor, but only the UFOC format qualifies for all state registration requirements.

Both formats provide for disclosure of certain basic information pertaining to the franchisor and to the franchise being offered. The franchisor's business history and financial statements must be included. The terms of the agreement are summarised in non-legal language, and the document must contain specific information about the total investment which will be required of the franchisee. Earnings claims which state or suggest a specific level of sales, income or profits from the franchised business are strictly regulated under both federal and state rules.

In states where prior registration of the franchise offering is required, a state administrator examines the UFOC document, including the franchise agreement, and he may require changes in the UFOC or the agreement before granting registration. Franchisors who are under-capitalised may be subject to other requirements, such as depositing franchise fees in escrow until the franchisee opens for business. State agencies also license franchise brokers and salesmen and review all advertisements for the offer of a franchise prior to this publication.

U.S. Regulation of Franchise Relationships.

Most of the states which require registration, and some states which do not, also impose standards and restrictions on the substantive aspects of the franchise relationship. For the most part, these types of laws address problems involved in termination (including non-renewal) of a franchise agreement. For purposes of the substantive laws, the term "franchise" may encompass a very broad range of continuing commercial relationships. Termination laws (13) may combine some or all of the following requirements:

(i) prior written notice of termination;

(ii) opportunity to cure within a stated period;

(iii) "good cause" for termination;

(iv) repurchase of inventory or items bearing the franchisor's mark;

(v) availability of injunctive relief or other formal procedures.

Other regulated aspects of the franchise relationship include activities or practices which historically have been governed by antitrust or unfair competition laws. Various

states (14) have statutes which specifically prohibit
franchisors from engaging in conduct which would take undue
advantage of franchisees, such as the following:

(i) discriminating among similarly situated
franchisees,

(ii) requiring purchases from certain sources,

(iii) obtaining "kickbacks" from suppliers, and
establishing franchisor-owned units in the
exclusive territory of a franchisee.

Some statutes establish a standard, such as reasonableness
or good faith, for judging a franchisor's conduct.

Jurisdiction.

The FTC rule applies throughout the United States, and it is
interpreted by the FTC to apply to any offer or sale of a
franchise if there is a nexus with U.S. interstate commerce.
Thus, the FTC might well assert that its rule applies even
if a U.S. franchisor offered a franchise to a foreign
person, as well as if a foreign franchisor offered a
franchise in the United States.(15) The practical likelihood
that the FTC would use its limited resources to enforce its
rule against international sales of franchises is rather
small, and no private right of action is afforded under the
FTC rule.

Most state laws apply only to transactions which occur
within the boundaries of each particular state, although
each state law must be examined - to determine, for example,
whether it reaches a transaction in which only the
franchisor, or only the franchisee, or only the franchised
business, is to be located within that state. State laws,
however, apply without regard to the citizenship of the
franchisee. Moreover, many state laws provide private

citizens a right of enforcement;(16) hence, the risk of exposure is somewhat greater if a franchisor conducts negotiations in certain states, even if the franchise will be located in another country.

A Comparative Analysis

Very few countries have laws which specifically refer to franchising in any way. A handful have adopted laws prohibiting "pyramid" schemes, which may be viewed as a species of franchising.(17) Australia has a federal law regulating franchise relationships in the retail sale of motor vehicle fuels generally (18) and from time to time, legislation concerning franchising generally has been proposed in both Australia and Canada.(19) Other countries, notably Japan and France, have witnessed keen governmental interest in the franchising "industry."(20) No specific legislative proposals comparable to U.S. laws have resulted so far, but it seems likely that, there and elsewhere, pressure will build for additional legislation aimed at equalising the perceived disparity of bargaining position of franchisors and franchisees, (21) either through prior disclosure or through regulation of the substantive relationship.

Disclosure Requirements.

Currently, only three other countries have laws or regulations which specifically regulate disclosure in connection with the sale of franchises. In Canada, the province of Alberta has adopted a system of franchise disclosure and registration which is essentially comparable to that in the United States.(22) In Japan, a very limited disclosure obligation arises only if the franchisor desires to help its franchisees receive certain preferential treatment offered by the government for small and medium-size businesses.(23) Recently, the Japan Franchise

Association has co-operated with the Japanese Ministry of International Trade and Industry in developing a plan for voluntary disclosure and registration by franchisors.(24)

In Australia, the National Companies and Securities Commission ("NCSC"), which administers corporate and securities laws on the federal level there, recently issued a policy statement concerning conditions for exempting franchisors from compliance with certain provisions of the Australian Companies Act and Codes relating to "prescribed interests" which previously had been found to cover franchises.(25) In order to offer franchises to the public, a franchisor must be a public company must issue a form of prospectus, and must comply with applicable requirements for broker licenses. However, if the franchisor meets the standards described in the NCSC release dated 29th August 1983, it may be exempt from the trust deed and registration requirements normally imposed on offerors of prescribed interests under the Act.(26)

To qualify for the exemption from the trust deed requirement, a franchisor must enter into a written agreement with each franchisee containing certain provisions. The franchisor also must maintain a separate trust ledger for each franchisee and hold all fees paid by the franchisee in trust until they are expended for the particular purpose for which they were paid. The agreement must be given to the franchisee at least three days before execution, with a seven-day cooling-off period after execution.

To qualify for exemption from the registration requirement, the franchise prospectus must include certain specified information. The facts required to be disclosed -- business and financial history of the franchisor, terms of the agreement, financial statements, supportable earnings claims, and other material facts -- are very similar, but not identical, to the items required to be disclosed under the U.S. FTC Rule. It is too early to tell whether the new NCSC policy will be regarded as adequate protection for franchisees or whether, as in the United States, additional legislation or regulation will be called for by various interests.(27)

Restrictions on Various Distribution Relationships.

a.   Antitrust and Competition Laws.

Although no disclosure laws exist outside the United States, Canada, Japan and Australia, there are a variety of laws in many countries which are similar to the substantive franchise regulation adopted in many states (and, in the case of automobile and petroleum dealers, at the federal level) in the United States. Like the United States, many countries restrict anti-competitive practices such as price-fixing, tying, covenants not to compete, and limitations on customers and territories. Most developed countries and some regional associations such as the European Community have some form of antitrust or anti-monopoly laws which impose requirements similar to those embodied in the U.S. antitrust laws and in some state franchising statutes.(28)

Many less-developed countries address such competitive concerns through technology transfer laws, which are common in Latin America and in some developing countries in the Far East.(29) Technology transfer laws usually apply to foreign franchisors who seek to licence local franchisees. The typical standards for approval of a franchise agreement under such laws are quite comparable to the rules governing competition referred to above. (30)

In Japan, the Japanese Fair Trade Commission ("JFTC") recently issued a report which specifically considers franchising in relation to competition laws. The report, published on 20th September 1983, contains no formal rules, but instead described the factors which the JFTC will consider in evaluating the legality of various franchise practices.(31)

The JFTC considers it necessary for franchisors to disclose certain minimal information to prospective franchisees, including fees and royalties, training requirements, compensation (if any) for losses, and termination and renewal of the agreement. In addition, and in contrast to U.S. regulation, the JFTC considers sales and earnings forecasts a vital component of the disclosure given to franchisees. In reviewing other practices under the Antimonopoly Law, the JFTC would look at several factors, including market conditions, the relevant market, and the actual competitive effects -- an approach somewhat comparable to the U.S. "rule of reason" analysis.

The JFTC report culminates several years of study, including a comprehensive study of U.S. laws and practices.(32) It is interesting to note that the JFTC generally adopted the least intrusive methods of regulating franchising and, in some instances, specifically recognised economic forces and values which U.S. laws have yet to acknowledge.(33)

b.   Termination Laws.

The term "franchise" remains undefined -- and generally ignored in the laws of most countries; however, a number of countries protect by law the rights of agents, dealers or distributors engaged in a continuing relationship with a manufacturer or other supplier. In developing countries, such laws were enacted as a means to protect local citizens from unfair treatment by foreign suppliers who might otherwise take advantage of the local dealers' relative lack of sophistication or money, or the less developed legal system of the country.(34) Most Central American countries, for example, have laws which require good cause for the termination of a local dealer by a foreign supplier.(35) If the supplier terminates or refuses to renew its agreement with the dealer without having good cause to do so, the supplier may be liable for an indemnity, usually calculated as a multiple of the dealer's past earnings. Some countries impose fines and other administrative penalties as well.

Several European countries also impose a "good cause" standard upon dealership terminations,(36) but with motives which are less protectionist. European laws typically do not apply only to foreign suppliers, nor do they usually impose administrative sanctions. A wrongfully terminated dealer may be entitled to receive an amount of money reflecting the damages arising out of the termination, based upon expected profits or actual losses. In common law countries, whether or not a similar statute exists, the familiar principle of contract law requiring good faith in the performance of agreements often leads to a like result. (37)

An Evaluation of Franchising Regulation

From a review of the history of franchising regulation in the United States and a comparison of pertinent laws in other countries, two conclusions are inescapable: First, franchising (by whatever name) clearly poses a unique combination of legal issues, whether primarily viewed as an investment offered to the public or as a long-term commercial relationship between two parties of unequal bargaining power. Second, in the United States, which is the only country where franchising has thus far permeated business methods and popular culture, the urge to regulate franchising has proven a powerful lure to elected and appointed officials who are seeking votes, publicity, or a sense of having righted real or perceived abuses. Thus, the question arises: Has the body of franchising laws and regulations in the United States successfully addressed the unique issues presented by franchising?

Regarding franchising as an <u>investment opportunity,</u> the U.S. disclosure and registration laws were intended to apprise the franchisee of all material risks and obligations before he enters the franchise agreement. The FTC has recently instituted a study to determine the efficacy of such laws.(38) Meanwhile, it is apparent that compliance with disclosure and registration requirements is burdensome and expensive for franchisors. It could be argued that disclosure neither enhances the position of the reasonably sophisticated small businessman nor prevents the truly naive or incompetent person from investing in a franchise. For the franchisee who falls into neither category, however, the laws probably have been of some benefit.

Regarding franchising as a <u>commercial relationship,</u> U.S. substantive relation of franchising has been designed to ensure that the franchisees are not ousted without good cause and that they are treated reasonably during the term of the agreement. It is important to remember that termination laws in the United States have not resulted (as the Central American dealership laws may have) from widespread abuses by U.S. franchisors. Nearly all franchisees who are eligible for renewal actually are granted renewal at the end of the initial term of the agreement. Of the remainder, slightly more than half of all non-renewals are at the instance of the franchisee.(39) These statistics suggest that most franchise relationships are profitable ones, in which both parties have an incentive to continue dealing with each other. The statistics also suggest that the risks in an ordinary franchise agreement are probably fairly apportioned, since it is equally likely that either party may desire to terminate the relationship.

In the U.S. experience, most termination laws have emerged

from the desire of franchisees (who represent a more numerous political constituency) to alter the allocation of risk in a franchise agreement. Termination laws, in fact, may be viewed as a type of insurance, protecting franchisees against loss beyond their original expectations. Whether termination laws are appropriate is, therefore, less an economic or legal than a political decision.

As for substantive requirements not related to termination and non-renewal, most such laws are enforced either through the franchise registration process (in which a state administrator may disapprove certain provisions in an agreement) or as claims by terminated franchisees. In part because of the lack of uniformity of such laws, there is inadequate evidence to date to demonstrate whether the laws are "justified " or "successful."

A Life Cycle of Franchising Regulation

Without making a judgment whether the scheme of U.S. franchising regulation has been necessary or sufficient, it may be possible to sketch a "life cycle" of franchise regulation based upon the U.S. experience.(40) The life cycle seems to consist of five stages, of which some may be concurrent.

The early stage is marked by limited protection within particular industries that are strategically important and often subject to broader regulations as well (such as automobile manufacturers or petroleum producers). Typically such laws protect small dealers who have large capital investments and depend upon the products (and goodwill) of their far larger suppliers.

The second stage sees legislation to counteract specific dishonest practices, such as pyramid selling. This stage reflects the novelty of alternative distribution systems,

their attraction to marketers interested in maximum "yield"
or "leverage," and the problem of keeping the public well
informed.

The third stage is characterised by a more general impetus
to help small entities which may be cheated or victimised by
larger ones. At first, protection may be quite limited --
for example, existing principles of commercial or antitrust
law may be applied in a way that prevents terminations
without good cause or the prevents the franchisor from
applying his generally superior bargaining power in a
socially or economically unacceptable way.

The fourth stage occurs when franchising itself is a more
mature phenomenon in the country, and the number of
franchisees has increased enough to give them extra
political weight. Very broad franchise regulation may
result at this stage, where protection of franchisees has
come to be viewed as imperative for social harmony. The
regulation may take the form of disclosure and registration
laws, or substantive legislation, or both.

Finally, the market may reach a point at which the
advantages and disadvantages of franchising are widely
known, where franchisors are numerous and competitive, where
fringe operators have been either removed by the forces of
the marketplace or regulated out of existence, and where
only the truly naive and credulous invest improvidently in a
franchise. At that point, the costs of regulation may
exceed the benefits, and the pendulum may swing back to a
more laissez-faire type of regulation. Simultaneously, the
judicial system of the country may have come to recognise
franchising as a special case and may treat it in a more
realistic fashion.

Conclusion

In the United States, the regulation of franchising has not quite reached the fifth stage described above but is still growing and changing. At this point, it is not clear that the fifth stage is in fact the final one, and it is impossible to say that it is either legislation or market forces alone which have made franchising respectable in the United States today. It is clear, however, that other countries may be informed by the experience in the United States, and they may determine that a different route is more appropriate for them. All over the world, franchisors themselves are now quite aware of the possibility of burdensome regulation; in the future, franchisors may be more than willing to regulate their own conduct so as to avoid being regulated by others who are less interested in the welfare of the franchisors' businesses and in the continued vigor of the franchising system.

FOOTNOTES

1. A "franchise" was originally a royal privilege granted
    to a subject. As described in 1769, a franchise might
    consist of the power to act as a corporation, to
    acquire treasure trove or royal fish, or to conduct a
    fair or market. See 2 Blackstone's Commentaries at 37-
    38 (4th ed.)

2. In the United States today, there are over 1,800
    franchisors with about 465,000 outlets (franchised and
    franchisor owned), having annual sales of approximately
    $436 billion.   Of those totals, business-format
    franchises account for about 297,000 of the units and
    $111 billion of the sales.   U.S. Dep't of Commerce,
    Franchising in the Economy: 1981-1983, at 1-3.

3. To provide a comparative view of franchising regulation
    in various countries, the Franchising Committee of the
    Section of Antitrust Law of the American Bar
    Association recently published a compendium of laws
    affecting franchising in 21 countries and the European
    Economic Community.   See generally Survey of Foreign
    Laws and Regulations Affecting International
    Franchising (P. Zeidman Ed. 1982).

4. See Franchising: Who Needs It?, address by Philip F.
    Zeidman, inaugural convocation of the European
    University of Franchising, in Paris, France (8th
    November 1983)

5. See e.g., Zeidman and Ausbrook, Will the Answers Be
    Different if the Seller-Buyer Relationship is a
    Franchise? in Legal Aspects of Selling and Buying ss
    9.39-9.61 (P. Zeidman ed. 1983).

6. For example, in several recent cases concerning claims of forced purchasing, U.S. courts have recognised the defense that a business-format franchise may be properly viewed as a "bundle of rights" or a single produce. See, e.g., Krehl v. Baskin-Robbins Ice Cream Co., 664 F.2d 1348 (9th Cir. 1982); Principe v. McDonald's Corp., 631 F.2d 303 (4th Cir.1080), Cert. denied, 451 U.S. 970 (1981).

7. See e.g., Germain, Tort Liability of Trademark Licensors in an Era of "Accountability": A Tale of Three Cases, 69 Trademark Rep. 129 (1979); Zeidman & Austbrook, supra note 4, s 9.64

8. In the United States federal legislation protects motor vehicle dealers, 15 U.S.C. ss 2801-2806 (1982). In addition, state laws protect dealers and distributors in a variety of industries, ranging from beer and wine to office equipment.

9. In the United States, a "business opportunity" is the right (for which a fee is paid) to sell goods or services provided by a supplier who also secures retail outlets, locations or accounts for such sales. Business opportunities are subject to federal and state disclosure and registration requirements similar to franchises. See e.g., 16 C.F.R. s 436.1-3 (1982)

10. The breadth of definitional coverage is mitigated somewhat by the availability of several categories of exemptions, most of which are based on the size or sophistication of the potential franchisee or on the existence of a parallel scheme of regulation (e.g., securities registration). See P. Zeidman, P. Ausbrook & H. Lowell, Franchising: Regulation of Buying and Selling a Franchise A-39 to A-50 (Bureau of National Affairs Corporate Practice Series No. 34) (1983).

11. Disclosure Requirements and Prohibitions Concerning
     Franchising and Business Opportunity Ventures, 16.
     C.F.R.   Part 436 (1982).

12. The following states require registration prior to
     offering franchises: California, Illinois, Indiana,
     Maryland, Michigan, Minnesota, New York, North Dakota,
     Rhode Island, South Dakota, Virginia, Wisconsin and
     Washington.   In addition, Hawaii requires that an
     offering circular be placed on file with a state
     agency, and Oregon requires that a state offering
     circular be delivered to prospective franchisees.

13. The following states regulate termination (often
     including non-renewal) of franchises: Arkansas,
     California, Connecticut, Delaware, Hawaii, Illinois,
     Indiana, Michigan, Minnesota, Mississippi, Missouri,
     Nebraska, New Jersey, Virginia, Washington and
     Wisconsin.

14. Such provisions may be found in the laws of the states
     listed in notes 12-13 _supra._   In addition, Florida,
     Puerto Rico, and the U.S. Virgin Islands prohibit
     misrepresentation by franchisors.

15. See 15 U.S.C. 45, 53 (1982).   As a result of recent
     amendments, the extraterritorial jurisdiction of the
     FTC with regard to unfair methods of competition is
     limited to conduct which has a direct, substantial and
     reasonably foreseeable effect on U.S. commerce.   Id.
     45 (a) (3) (Supp.I 1983).   However, the franchise
     disclosure rule was adopted under the FTC's authority
     to regulate "unfair or deceptive acts or practices" and
     thus apparently is not affected by the new amendment.

16. Some of the state laws used as a basis for such
     enforcement are known as "Little FTC Acts" and were

modelled directly on the FTC Act but, unlike the federal law, need not bar private actions.

17. See, e.g., Trade Practices Act 1974 (C'th) s.61 (Australia); Combines Investigation Act, R.S.C. 1970, c. C-23 (Canada); Commerce Act 1975, ss 31-32 (New Zealand).

18. Petroleum Retail Marketing Franchise Act 1980 (C'th).

19. From time to time since 1976 in Australia, various committees and commentators have recommended the adoption of franchise legislation, either in the existing Trade Practices Act or in separate legislation. See D. Shannon, Franchising in Australia 7.6 (1982). Early in 1983, the Labour Party expressly called for legislation to protect all franchisees from termination or nonrenewal without compensation. Letter to International Franchise Association, Washington, D.C., from Michael C. Ahrens, Esq., Sydney, Australia (10th May 1983).

In Canada the Province of Alberta has enacted a franchise registration law similar to U.S. state laws. The Franchises Act SA 1971 c 38 as amended. The Province of Quebec has passed a bill relating to franchises as securities but has promulgated no regulations to implement that bill. The Provinces of British Columbia and Ontario also have considered regulating franchising, but have not yet enacted any bills. See e.g., Bill 88, 2d Sess., 32 Legis. (Ont. 1982).

20. The Japanese Fair Trade Commission has been studying franchising for several years and has reviewed U.S. antitrust laws as part of its study. See memorandum to Japan Franchise Chain Association from Philip F.

Zeidman, Esq. (10th November 1980), and discussion
below.

In France, the Ministry of Interior Commerce is
currently organising a work committee to study
franchising in France. The committee's eventual
recommendations could form a basis for some regulation
there.

21. Ironically, in many international franchise
    transactions, the non-U.S. franchisee has bargaining
    power superior to that of the U.S. franchisor, owing to
    the difficulties inherent in doing business in the
    franchisee's country, which the franchisee is better
    able to master, or owing to the tendency to franchise
    much larger territories internationally, leading to the
    selection of franchisees who are typically well
    financed and perhaps financially stronger than the
    franchisor.

22. See generally Shapiro, Legislation and Regulation
    affecting franchising in Canada: An overview (IBA
    section on Business Law Committee X programme 6-7
    October 1983 and incorporated in this work.

23. Law Concerning Development of Middle and Small Scale
    Retailers (Law No. 101, 29th September 1973).

24. As reporting in the Yomiuri Press in April, 1983,
    franchisors in Japan are encouraged to register with
    the Japan Franchise Association (JFA) and, in return,
    are recognised by the Ministry of International Trade
    and Industry (MITI) as being in compliance with the
    disclosure requirements of the Law Concerning
    Development of Middle and Small Scale Retailers, supra
    note 23.   Registration is voluntary, and the
    information contained in the registration statement is

neither approved nor reviewed by either JFA or MITI.

25. In Hamilton v. Casnot Pty. Ltd., (1981) C.L.C. 40-704, the Western Australia Supreme Court held that a cleaning business franchise constituted a prescribed interest under the Companies Act. For a time in Australia, some states (especially Victoria and New South Wales) treated all public offerings of franchises as prescribed interests, while other states declined to do so, proceeding against franchisors only in cases of fraud.

26. NCSC Policy Statement -- Companies Act and Codes: Section 176: Exercise of Exemption Power for Franchising Schemes (Release No. 118, eff. 29th August 1983) See also Zeidman & Blair, Australian Agency Issues Policy Affecting Regulation of Franchise Offerings as Securities, Franchise Legal Digest, January 1984, at 3.

27. See note 19 supra..

28. See e.g., Reg. No. 1983/83, O.J. Eur. Comp. (no. L173) 1 (30th June 1983); Kinkeldey, Pitfalls of Trademark Licensing in the EEC, 72 Trademark Rep. 145 (1982).

29. See generally Brown, Franchising in Latin America (IBA Section on Business Law Committee X program, 6-7th October 1983 incorporated in this work); Kaul & Blair, International Technology Transfer Laws Pose Barriers to U.S. Franchisors, Franchise Legal Digest, October 1982, at 1.

30. See e.g., Japan Fair Trade Commission Antimonopoly Act Guidelines for International Licensing Agreements (24th May 1968).

31. Comments on the Antimonopoly Law in Relation to
     Franchise Systems (Office of the Fair Trade Cimmission,
     20th September 1983) <u>See also</u> Zeidman & Blair, <u>Japanese
     Agency Issues Comments on Application of Antitrust Laws
     of Franchising,</u> Franchise Legal Digest, November 1983
     at 1

32. When the voluntary franchise disclosure law was enacted
     in 1973, <u>see</u> note 23 <u>supra,</u> the Japanese authorities
     were primarily concerned with abuses in connection with
     franchise fees and the vague or indefinite nature of
     many franchise agreements.   More recently, attention
     has shifted to concerns about the competitive effects
     of franchising.   In 1980, the Antimonopoly Study Group
     reported to the JFTC concerning distribution practices
     and vertical restraints generally, with some focus on
     franchising.   In early 1981, the JFTC surveyed Japanese
     franchisors and, in 1982, surveyed a large number of
     franchisees, concerning the value of and need for
     restrictions within franchise systems.   <u>See</u> also note
     20 <u>supra.</u>

33. This appears to have been a quite conscious choice.
     Interview with officials of Japanese Fair Trade
     Commission by Philip F. Zeidman, Tokyo, Japan, 22nd
     November 1983.

34. <u>See generally</u> Saltoun & Soudis, <u>International
     Distribution and Sales Agency agreements: Practical
     Guidelines for U.S.   Exporters,</u> 38 Bus. Law 883
     (1985).

35. <u>See generally</u> Juncadella, <u>Agency, Distribution and
     Representation Contracts in Central America and Panama,</u>
     6 Law. Am (1974.

36. <u>See generally</u> Zeidman & Blair, <u>Foreign Termination and</u>

Nonrenewal Laws, Franchise Legal Digest, June 1982, at 8 (discussing relevant laws in France, Germany, Switzerland, Belgium, Denmark).

37. In order to avoid what they believe would be an unfair result. U.S. courts have occasionally ruled that an obligation greater than "good faith" exits on the part of franchisors. Compare Arnott v. American Oil Co., 609 F.2d 873 (8th Cir. 1979), cert. denied, 446 U.S. 918 (1980), with Jirna Ltd. v. Mister Donut of Canada Ltd., (1975) 1 S.C.R. 2, aff'g (1972(1 Ont. R. 251.

38. The FTC expects to issue its report in the near future, perhaps during 1984.

39. In 1981, the latest year for which statistics are available, 89% of all franchisees eligible for renewal were renewed. Of franchises not renewed, 59% were not renewed because the franchisee did not wish to renew. Similarly, of the 7,181 franchise terminations in 1981, franchisees were responsible for terminating in 3,597 cases. U.S. Dep't of Commerce, Franchising in the Economy: 1981-1983, at 11.

40. This phenomenon is not unlike the course which a typical franchise relationship itself commonly follows. See Zeidman, Antitrust Law: Legal Problems in the Life Cycle of a Franchise, 50 Antitrust L.J. 855 (1982).

INTERNATIONAL FRANCHISING – AN OVERVIEW
M. Mendelsohn (editor)
© Elsevier Science Publishers B.V. (North-Holland), 1984

CHAPTER 5

LEGISLATION AND REGULATIONS AFFECTING FRANCHISING
IN CANADA: AN OVERVIEW
Harvey A. Shapiro *

I   INTRODUCTION

Despite the prominent role that franchising has achieved in retail and service industries, there are few legislative enactments aimed directly at franchising in Canada.   The lack of an effective franchise lobby, fragmented and underfinanced groups of franchisees in a wide variety of industries, the almost total absence of reported and well-publicised abuses, together with governmental budgetary constraints have conspired to make franchising a relatively low priority item on federal and provincial legislative agendas.   Nor is there any evidence of impending change in Canadian legislative attitudes.

In Canada, solicitations and sales of franchises are currently regulated only by the Province of Alberta, which has adopted a registration and disclosure system similar to that in use in a number of jurisdictions in the United States.   Currently, no other province requires the registration of franchisors or of franchise offerings prior to a sale or solicitation, nor the use of any form of disclosure statement.   However, many of the business practices endemic to franchising are subject to regulation

---

* The author gratefully acknowledges the assistance of his associates, Arthur J. Trebilcock and John G. Temesvary and Edward Morgan, a summer student with Goodman and Carr, in preparing and reviewing this paper

by laws of general application, notably the Combines
Investigation Act, the Trade Marks Act and the Foreign
Investment Review Act.

The following summary focusses upon those Canadian federal
and provincial statutes which have a significant impact on
the practices and activities customarily associated with the
franchise method of distribution.

II   REGISTRATION AND DISCLOSURE REGULATION

Currently, there is no federal legislation in effect
governing the sale, solicitation or other trades in
franchises and, of the ten provinces, only Alberta has thus
far enacted legislation regulating trades in franchises.
The Alberta Franchises Act, as amended by the Franchises
Amendment Act, 1983 (assented to June 6, 1983) is patterned
after the original California franchise investment law and
is a disclosure-registration statute.   Little attempt is
made to regulate the substantive aspects of the franchise
relationship.

The Act is administered by the Alberta Securities
Commission, and all communications and applications are
supervised by the Director or Deputy Director of the
Commission.

The Acts forbids any trade in a franchise in Alberta
unless:

(a)   an exemption is obtained and a Statement of Material
      Facts is filed with the Commission; or

(b)   an application for registration of the franchise
      offering together with a prospectus containing full,
      plain and true disclosure of all material facts
      relating to the franchise being offered is filed with

the Commission and a receipt therefor is issued to the franchisor.

"Trade" is defined to include a purchase, sale, disposition or other dealing or solicitation in connection with a franchise, including any advertisement or negotiation in furtherance of any of the foregoing. A trade is deemed to occur in Alberta if the offer or acceptance is made in that province, if the franchisee is domiciled or normally resident there or if the franchise is to be operated in Alberta. As such, the regulatory net cast by the Act is expansive.

Similarly, the term "franchise" is broadly defined as an oral or written agreement between two or more persons by which a franchisee is required to pay, directly or indirectly, a franchise fee in consideration for the right to engage in various types of business arrangements. Such arrangements include:

(a) the sale or distribution of goods or services manufactured, supplied or organised by the franchisor;

(b) the sale or distribution of goods or services according to a marketing plan prescribed by the franchisor;

(c) licensed use of the trade marks of the franchisor; or

(d) the recruitment of additional franchisees.

"Franchise fee" is defined as any consideration paid in exchange for the granting of the franchise, including any payment for goods or services (other than in reasonable amounts at current wholesale market rates), any services that the franchisee is required to perform and any loan, guarantee or other commercial consideration provided by or exigible from the franchisee.

Exemptions from the Act's disclosure requirements are available only on a partial basis. Under Section 2 of the Act, a franchisor with a net worth of at least $5,000,000 (or $1,000,000 if such franchisor is 80% owned by another corporation with a net worth of at least $5,000,000) and which has had 25 franchisees conducting business at all times during the five years preceding the trade (or which is 80% owned by a corporation which has met the five year practice test) can be exempted from the prospectus requirements. For purposes of meeting the exemption thresholds, franchises operated in foreign jurisdictions may be taken into account.

Additionally, Section 3 of the Act (as amended) provides for discretionary exemption: the Director of the Commission may exempt a trade in a particular franchise from any one or more of:

(c) Section 4 (requirement to file with the Commission a Statement of Material Facts and obtain from the Director an acknowledgment of the Section 2 exemption);

(d) Section 5 of any part thereof (specifying the contents of the Statement of Material Facts and requiring delivery of Statement of Material Facts to prospective franchisee);

(e) Section 6 (requirements to file an application and prospectus, and obtain a receipt therefor); and

(f) any regulation, or part thereof, under the Act;

if the proposed trade is not prejudicial to the public interest. An exempting order under Section 3 may be subject to such terms and conditions as the Director considers necessary, and may be made retroactive at the direction of the Director. In reaching his determination the Director will be likely to consider, among other things, the financial responsibility of the franchisor, its business experience, its ability to provide the goods and services it advertises, and its general success in the franchise field. As a matter of practice, the Director exercises broad discretion in determining whether or not to grant a particular exemption. Unfortunately, no regulations or policy statements are available to indicate the specific guidelines used by the Director in applying the foregoing criteria; accordingly, it is difficult for one to determine in advance whether an exemption will be available in any particular case.

In order to obtain an exemption under Section 2, on the other hand, the franchisor is required to file an application in prescribed form setting out information substantially the same as that indicated below with respect to the Statement of Material Facts, together with a copy of the audited comparative balance sheet of the franchisor for the last two complete years of business, statements of income and expenses and of source and application of funds for each of the last three fiscal years preceding the date of the balance sheet, and a Statment of Material Facts.

The application for exemption and accompanying financial statements do not form part of the public record and will be maintained in confidence by the Commission. On the other hand, the Statement of Material Facts is a part of the public record, and requires disclosure of information under 25 enumerated subject headings. The subjects of which disclosure is required include:

(i) the corporate and trade name of the franchisor;

(ii) the franchisor's principal business address and the name and address of his agent for service in

Alberta;

(iii) the franchisor's business form, whether corporate, partnership or otherwise;

(iv) the business experience of the franchisor;

(v) a copy of the typical franchise contract proposed for use or in use in Alberta;

(vi) a statement of the franchise fee charged or proposed to be charged;

(vii) a statement of any payments other than franchise fees that the franchisee is required to pay;

(viii) a statement indicating whether the cash investment required for the franchise covers fixtures and equipment;

(ix) the conditions under which the franchise agreement may be terminated or its renewal refused by the franchisor;

(x) a statement of whether the franchisee is able to sell the franchise and under what conditions;

(xi) a statement regarding the obligation of the franchisee to purchase goods or services from the franchisor;

(xii) a statement of whether the services or other goods relating to the franchise are available from sources other than the franchisor;

(xiii) a statement as to the limitations imposed upon the

franchisee in respect of the goods or services which may be offered by him;

(xiv) a statement of whether the franchisor has agreed with a third party that the products or services of the third party will be available to the franchisee on a discount or bonus basis;

(xv) the terms and conditions of any financing arrangements offered directly or indirectly by the franchisor;

(xvi) a statement concerning the practice of the franchisor regarding the discounting of notes or other obligations of the franchisee;

(xvii) the data upon which a statement of estimated or projected franchisee earnings, if any, has been based;

(xviii) a statement concerning any exclusive territorial or selling rights granted to the franchisee;

(xix) a statement of whether the franchisee is required to participate in a franchisor promotion;

(xx) a statement of whether any patent or liability insurance protection of the franchisor is extended to the franchisee;

(xxi) a statement regarding the availability of arbitration for the resolution of disputes;

(xxii) a statement as to whether continuing assistance is provided by franchisor and the nature, extent and cost of such assistance;

(xxiii) a list of other franchisees operating in Alberta or, if there are no Alberta franchisees, a list of franchisees operating in the next closest jurisdiction;

(xxiv) provisions governing withdrawal from the franchise agreement;

(xxv) provisions relating to the right to rescind the franchise agreement.

An exemption under Section 2 is subject to annual renewal no later than 30 business days prior to the expiry date of the exemption. Renewal is effected by filing with the Director an application in prescribed form, together with an updated copy of the franchisor's Statement of Material Facts.

Additionally, any material adverse change relating to the franchise offering, as reflected in the Statement of Material Facts, must be disclosed to the Director as soon as practicable and, in any event, within 10 days from the date the change occurs.

In the absence of an exemption, subsection 6(1) of the Act forbids any trade in a franchise in Alberta, unless an application for registration of a franchise in prescribed form and a prospectus has been filed, together with certain ancillary documents, and a receipt for the prospectus has been obtained from the Registrar of the Securities Commission. Such an application requires disclosure of substantially the same information as is required for a Statement of Material Facts, together with additional information relating to the franchisor's business and franchising history and details relating to bankruptcy and outstanding litigation affecting the franchisor. The prospectus must provide full, plain and true disclosure of all material facts relating to the proposed franchise, and both the form of application for registration and the prospectus must contain a certificate to this effect. The application must be accompanied by an application form for registration of each salesman of the franchisor who will be selling franchises in Alberta, a personal history form for each director of a corporate franchisor, and in certain circumstances performance bonds for the salesmen. The performance bonds will generally be dispensed with where the salesman is a full-time employee of the franchisor.

The information appearing in the application for registration must be contained in the prospectus, although the ordering of the information may be different. A cross-reference sheet showing the location of such information in the prospectus must be provided to the Commission.

The prospectus must include comparative balance sheets for the last two complete years of the franchisor, together with statements of income and expense and sources and application funds for each of the preceding three fiscal years. If the financial statements are over 120 days old from the date of filing, they must be accompanied by unaudited financial statements not over 90 days old from the date of filing and a comfort letter from the applicant's auditor relative thereto. All of these materials must be accompanied by the consent of the franchisor's auditor, confirming that the information set out in the prospectus which is derived from the financial statements contained therein or which is within his knowledge is in his opinion, presented fairly and is not misleading.

The face page of the prospectus is required to indicate clearly the following:

(a)   a warning concerning speculative risks;

(b)   a statement of the right to receive a prospectus;

(c)   a statement concerning selling and withdrawal rights; and

(d)   the statement "No regulatory body in the Province of Alberta has in any way passed upon the merits of the franchise offered hereunder and any representation to the contrary is an offence."

The Director must provide either a deficiency letter to the franchisor, or issue a receipt for the prospectus, within 30 days of his receipt of the application for registration and the prospectus. If a material change occurs in relation to the franchise offering before a receipt is issued, an amendment to the application must be filed with the Commission as soon as practicable and, in any event, within 10 days from the date that the charge occurs.

Although the Act does not contain any provisions regulating the substantive aspects of the franchisor-franchisee relationship, in the exercise of his broad discretionary authority the Director may require inclusion of reasonable termination and renewal rights in the franchise agreement. The Director may further require that the franchise agreement be governed by Alberta law and that any action upon the contract be brought in Alberta. In addition, the Director currently requires that companies incorporated outside of Alberta be registered as extra-provincial corporations under the Business Corporations Acts (Alberta) before they are eligible for registration under the Franchises Act.

If the franchisor has no assets in Alberta, the Director, as a matter of policy, will require the franchisor to post a bond with the Commission. The amount will vary according to the particular franchisor and may range from $10,000 to $150,000, depending upon the circumstances. Additionally, the Director may order the escrowing of franchise fees or other funds paid by franchisees, if the Director is concerned about the franchisor's ability to fulfill its obligations to provide improvements, equipment, inventory, training or other items including in the offering. Finally, the Act requires a franchisor to maintain a complete set of books and records at its principal place of business in Alberta. Generally, in lieu of this requirement the Director will accept an undertaking from non-Alberta corporations to provide the books and records to the Commission upon request. A statement to this effect must be included in the prospectus or Statement of Material Facts.

The Act establishes numerous rights and remedies of franchisees, the first of which is embodied in the requirement that the franchisor deliver a copy of the prospectus or Statement of Material Facts to the prospective franchisee either before or within four business days of entering into the franchise agreement. Once the franchisee receives the Statement of Material Facts or prospectus, he has a further four day "cooling-off" period in which he may elect to rescind the franchise agreement by notice in writing to the franchisor. The franchisee may also rescind the agreement if the prospectus or Statement of Material Facts contains an untrue statement of a material fact or omits to state a material fact necessary to make any statement therein not misleading. The latter right of rescission is subject to a two-year limitation period, computed from the later of the date on which the prospectus or Statement of Material Facts if received by the franchisee and the date that the franchise agreement is entered into. However, the Act states that no right of rescission exists if either the untruth of the statement or the fact of the omission was unknown to the franchisor, and could not have been known to it through the exercise of reasonable diligence, or if the franchisee was aware of the inaccuracy at the time that he purchased the franchise. It should be noted that the rights of rescission contained in the Act are in addition to and without derogation from any other right that the franchisee may have at law.

The Act establishes numerous rights and remedies of franchisees, the first of which is embodied in the requirement that the franchisor deliver a copy of the prospectus or Statement of Material Facts to the prospective franchisee either before or within four business days of entering into the franchise agreement. Once the franchisee receives the Statement of Material Facts or prospectus, he has a further four day "cooling-off" period in which he may elect to rescind the franchise agreement by notice in writing to the franchisor. The franchisee may also rescind the agreement if the prospectus or Statement of Material Facts contains an untrue statement of a material fact or omits to state a material fact necessary to make any statement therein not misleading. The latter right of rescission is subject to a two-year limitation period, computed from the later of the date on which the prospectus or Statement of Material Facts is received by the franchisee and the date that the franchise agreement is entered into. However, the Act states that no right of rescission exists if either the untruth of the statement or the fact of the omission was unknown to the franchisor, and could not have been known to it through the exercise of reasonable diligence, or if the franchisee was aware of the inaccuracy at the time that he purchased the franchise. It should be noted that the rights of rescission contained in the Act are in addition to and without derogation from any other right that the franchisee may have at law.

The Act was judicially considered by the British Columbia Supreme Court in Nike Infomatic Systems Ltd. v. Avac Systems Ltd et al (1979), 8 B.L.R.196. The Court was asked, on a preliminary motion, to determine the proper choice of law of the contract. While the Court held that the proper law of the contract was that of British Columbia, it went on

to state that even if the laws of Alberta applied to the
contract, the failure to comply with the requirements of the
Act did not have the effect of making the franchise
agreement void or voidable, but only made the franchisor
susceptible to the punitive sanctions of the Act and to the
rights of rescission conferred by the Act on the franchisee.
This decision is seemingly of academic interest only, and
ought not to impact on the rights of disaffected franchisees
in Alberta to rescind their franchise agreement as a result
of a franchisor's failure to provide a Statement of Material
Facts or prospectus. Of course, even if the franchisee can
successfully obtain rescission, it may still be open for a
franchisor to claim compensation on a quantum meruit basis,
if the franchisee has actually utilized the franchisor's
trade mark or other elements of the franchisor's system in
the operation of his business.

Violations of the Acts are punishable on summary conviction
by fine or imprisonment or both. The maximum fine that may
be imposed under the Act is $2,000 for individuals and
$25,000 for corporations. Directors of corporations are
liable on a joint and several basis for breaches of the Act
by the franchisor, if they authorized, permitted or
acquiesced in the offence;the liability of an individual
director will be limited to a fine of not more than $2,000
or to imprisonment for a term of not more than one year, or
both.

Of greater significance is the fact that under Section 39 of
the Act, every purchaser is deemed to have relied on the
statements contained in the prospectus, whether or not the
purchaser actually received the prospectus. If the
prospectus contains a material false statement, every
director of the corporate franchisor issuing the prospectus
is jointly and severally liable with the corporation for any
damage or loss suffered by the franchisee as a result of the
purchase, unless he can establish that the prospectus was

filed without his consent, that he had grounds for believing the statements were true, that reliance was placed upon experts or information contained in public documents, or that he advised the Commission of the withdrawal of his consent upon becoming aware of the false statement.

The Act requires continuing disclosure of all material adverse changes in the information contained in a prospectus or Statement of Material Facts filed with the Commission, and requires that an amended prospectus or Statement of Material Facts be filed with the commission as soon as practible and, in any event, within 10 days from the date that the change occurs.

The registration of a franchise offering expires one year from the date of registration and may be renewed for additional one-year periods by filing a Registration Renewal Statement, in prescribed form, at least 30 days prior to expiration of the registration.

The Act also requires registration of salesmen acting on behalf of a franchisor whose franchise is registered under the Act. As with registration of a franchise offering, the registration of a salesman expires one year from the date of registration and must be renewed at least 30 days prior to expiry.

In December, 1979 the Province of Quebec amended its Securities Act to include franchising within the definition of "security". The amending legislation (Bill 70) stated that it was to remain inoperative pending the promulgation of regulations establishing compliance requirements for franchise offerings in Quebec.

On November 16, 1982, the Province passed Bill 85, replacing Bill 70, which is to come into force upon a date fixed by proclamation. The Bill specifically provides that it replaces Bill 70 in its application to franchising and it further states that regulations of forms of investment covered by the Securities Act will be subject to the provisions of the Bill. To date no regulations concerning franchising have been passed; presumably, if Quebec still intends to regulate franchising, such regulations will be effected under Bill 85 following its proclamation.

III.   COMBINES INVESTIGATION ACT

The Combines Investigation Act is Canada's anti-trust or competition statute, and impacts on an assortment of franchise practices as well as the drafting of franchise agreements. It is administered by the Director of Investigation and Research (the "Director") in conjunction with the Restrictive Trade Practices Commission (the "RTPC"), both of which are under the auspices of the federal Department of Consumer and Corporate Affairs.

The Director is empowered to receive informal complaints and to conduct full investigative inquiries, including the power to search and seize documents, on the basis of there being a "reason to believe" that a violation of the Act has been or is about to be committed. The RTPC, on the other hand, is an administrative agency empowered to review particular business practices and to issue orders concerning such reviewable practices, pursuant to an investigation conducted by the Director.

Part 1V of the Act identifies various "reviewable trade practices" which are subject to investigate inquiry by the RTPC. The RTPC can order a reviewable trade practice to be stopped if it is found to be anti-competitive in nature and effect. These practices do not constitute offences, per se, but rather give rise to administrative review only.   A person suspected of engaging in a reviewable trade practice

has a statutory right to a hearing, which includes the right
to cross-examine witnesses and produce documents on his own
behalf, in order to establish either that his actions do not
constitute a reviewable trade practice, or that such a
practice is necessary in order to compete effectively in the
market and does not, in fact, impede competition or the
entry of new products or services into the relevant market
(Director of Investigation and Research v.Bombardier
Limited (1981), 57 C.P.R.(2d) 216).

Part V of the Act sets out various activities which
constitute criminal offences per se, among which is the
contravention of an RTPC cease-practice order. The Director
is responsible for investigation and prosecution of Part V
offences, which, as in any criminal prosecution, must be
proved beyond a reasonable doubt.

In addition to reviewable trade practices and criminal
offences, the Act establishes civil remedies. A consumer
can bring an action for recovery of damages suffered by
failure of a person to abide by an order of the RTPC, or by
conduct of a person that is contrary to the criminal
provisions of the Act. However, there is no parallel to the
Sherman Act provision for treble damages.

As indicated in the Bombardier case, in order for the RTPC
to issue a cease-practice order the Director must first
prove on the balance of probability that the activity in
question not only meets the statutory definition of the
particular reviewable trade practice alleged, but is as well
anti-competitive in effect. It should be noted that although
there is no provision in the Act for appeal of an RTPC
order, judicial review of any such administrative order by
the federal Court is available pursuant to s.28 of the
Federal Court Act if:

(a) there has been a breach of natural justice;

(b)   the RTPC has erred in law in making its decision;

(c)   a decision has been made on an erroneous finding of fact due to a fact-finding process which can be characterized as perverse or capricious; or

(d)   the RTPC has either refused to exercise or has acted beyond its discretion.

The reviewable trade practices of primary concern to franchisors are those of refusal to deal, tied selling, market restriction and exclusive dealing. Regarding the refusal to deal provisions (s.31.2 of the Act), a supplier is not prohibited under the Act from refusing to sell a product, so long as he is not thereby engaging in a conspiracy or resale price maintenance scheme, and is not a party to an attempt to monopolize the market. However, under s.31.2 the RTPC may order that one or more suppliers of the product in the market accept a complainant customer within a specified time and on usual trade terms. As conditions precedent for the making of such an order, the RTPC must be satisfied that the complainant is unable to obtain the product elsewhere due to a lack of competition among the suppliers, his business is substantially affected due to the impossibility of obtaining adequate supplies of the product anywhere in the market on usual trade terms, he is willing and able to meet the suppliers' usual trade terms, and the product is in reasonably ample supply. However, it should be noted that the fact that a product is distinguished from other products of a similar nature by a trade mark or a proprietary name does not enable the RTPC to make an order regarding the trade-marked product, unless the complainant can establish that his ability to carry on business has been substantially affected by the refusal to deal, and the trade-marked product occupies such a dominant market position that alternative brands are either unacceptable or unavailable. Therefore, where a brand name is so well-known to the public that a similar product under a different name will not suffice to allow a retailer to effectively carry on business, the trade-marked item will probably constitute a separate product to which a cease-practice order can apply (R.v.Grange, (1978) 5 W.W.R. 39)

The practice of tied selling consists of a supplier of a product (the "tying product") requiring a purchaser to purchase another product from the (the "tied product") as a condition of his purchase of the tying product.

However, a franchisor can legitimately engage in tied selling if it is based on a technological relationship between the products in question, or is part of a security agreement resulting from loans made to the franchisee.

The practice of exclusive dealing consists of a supplier requiring his distributors to deal exclusively in the supplier's products or products designated by him. However, such practices have been held to be beyond the scope of RTPC review if there is no evidence that the supplier's action leads to a substantial reduction in competition among all suppliers of the product in the market.

The practice of market restriction consists of a supplier of a product requiring a purchaser, as a pre-condition of any sale, to limit his distribution to a defined market area. As such, although a franchisor may contractually delimit the territory in which a franchisee is guaranteed exclusivity, any clause purporting to restrict a franchisee's market area is subject to administrative review. It should be noted that, under s.31.4(5) of the Act, market restrictions regarding food and beverage products marketed under a franchisor's trade mark are exempt from administrative review. In addition, if exclusive dealing, market restriction or tied selling is engaged in for the purpose of facilitating the entry of a new participant or product into a market,then the practice is immune from administrative review.

The underlying aim of the reviewable trade practice sections of the Act is the elimination of those practices which tend to create added costs and rigidities in the marketplace. Despite this avowed purpose, the threshold requirements of the Act have thus far proved to be an insuperable barrier to the application of the reviewable trade practice provisions in most supply-oriented franchise systems. Indeed, as of this writing there have been only two cases of record in which the exclusive dealing and tied selling provisions have been considered.

In Director of Investigation and Research v. Bombardier Ltd. (1981), 57 C.P.R. (2d) 216, the RTPC, in determining whether the exclusive dealing requirements practised by Bombardier Ltd. had the effect of substantially lessening competition in the market areas in question, relied on two principal factors:

(a) the degree of market share enjoyed by Bombardier Ltd; and

(b) the ease of entry of competitors into the market areas in question.

Although Bombardier's sales accounted for almost 10% of the North American market, the RTPC found that Bombardier's market share had remained constant for a substantial period of time,while the combined market share of Bombardier's competitors had increased over that period. The RTPC found that Bombardier's competitors were able to overcome "whatever barriers to their expansion were created by Bombardier's exclusive-dealing policy". The RTPC also noted that, while it was difficult for competing suppliers to find dealer outlets, the high rate of dealer turnover strongly

suggested that this was a problem which affected the
industry generally, and did not arise by reason of
Bombardier's excluisve-dealing policy. As a result, the RTPC
concluded that Bombardier's exclusive-dealing policy had not
resulted in a substantial lessening or reduction of
competition,nor in a likelihood thereof, in the market areas
in question.

In   Director of Investigation and Research v. BBM Bureau of
Measurement (1982), 60 C.P.R.(2d) 26, the RTPC issued a
cease-practice order prohibiting BBM from continuing to
engage in tied selling to its members of radio data and
television data. The members of BBM included advertisers,
ad agencies and radio and TV stations and networks. BBM
measured Canadian radio and TV audiences and provided
statistical reports of these measurements to its members.
BBM had tied its radio data to its TV data in such a manner
that, if a member wished TV data, it would be forced to
accept radio data as well, since the fee charged for
acquiring radio data or TV data alone exceeded the fee
charged for both types of data purchased as a unit.

The evidence indicated that A.C. Nielsen Company of Canada
Ltd.,the only other competitor of BBM, suffered a severe
disadvantage in selling its television rating data, because
of BBM's tied-selling practice. The commission found that
BBM controlled approximately 88% of the relevant market, and
further concluded that an important factor in Nielsen's
failure to expand in that market was BBM's tied-selling
practice. The RTPC also concluded that it was virtually
impossible for a new entrant in the radio data market to
overcome the advantage attained by BBM through the use of
its tied-selling practice.

The per se criminal offences under the Act carry a penalty
of five years imprisonment or a $1,000,000 fine or both.
Although it has occasionally been suggested that the amount

of the fine should reflect the profits gained by the defendant in violating the Act, the Courts have never adopted such a standard. Indeed, in R. v. Levi Strauss of Canada Inc. (1979, Ont.Co.Ct. unreported) the fact that, subsequent to charges being laid, new management had instituted changes in the operation of the business favourably influenced the Court in passing sentence.

The per se criminal offences under the Act cover the entire spectrum from horizontal restrictive arrangements to vertical arrangements which are considered anti-competitive. The horizontal trade offences (s.32) include entering any agreement to unduly restrain or injure competition, whether by limiting the transportation, production, storage or supply of a product or by unreasonably enhancing the price of a product, or otherwise. Section 32 is worded so that it is an offence to enter such an agreement, even though it was not intended to or would not have the effect of eliminating competition. Indeed, it is an offence for a company carrying on business in Canada to carry out a directive or instruction to further such an agreement entered into outside of Canada, even if the directors or officers of the company in Canada had no knowledge of the conspiracy. However, enforcement of s.32 has been limited by the repeated lack of successful prosecutions, so that the Section is not relied upon to the same extent as are the provisions prohibiting vertical arrangements.

The first significant vertical arrangement forming the subject matter of criminal proscription is the practice of price discrimination (s.34). A franchisor that engages in the practice of knowingly discriminating among franchisees, by granting any discount, rebate, allowance, price concession or other advantage to one franchisee which is not similarly granted to other competing franchisees in respect of the sale of articles of like quality and quantity, commits an offence under the Act. However, a franchisee selling products to consumers at different prices cannot come within the ambit of the price discrimination provision, since one consumer is not in competition with another consumer. Similarly, a franchisor selling both to franchisees and directly to consumers through company-owned outlets ("dual distribution"), may apply different pricing policies to the franchisees and the consumers, since the franchisees and the consumers are not in competition with each other. A franchisor may also practice price discrimination among territorially-separated franchisees, so long as there is no actual competition between such franchisees.

To contravene the price discrimination section of the Act, one must engage in the practice of price discrimination. Accordingly, temporary concessions are permissible. In addition, the practice of granting volume discounts is legitimate, so long as the discounts are offered to all competing franchisees and are structured so that small franchisees can realistically take advantage of the volume discount. Of course, a difference in transportation costs or the sale of different brand names of similar products may provide a justification for price discrimination among franchisees. The franchisor should be aware that the offence of price discrimination can occur with respect to such practices as granting credit terms, cash discounts, allowances for early payment or bonuses in the form of free goods.

A practice of underpricing, which has the effect of substantially lessening competition or eliminating a competitor, or is designed to have such effect, constitutes an offence under the price discrimination Section of the Act. Likewise, predatory pricing aimed at monopolization of a market by a financially-strong competitor, through an uneconomic price reduction campaign, falls under the provisions of Section 34.

Another common arrangement which constitutes an offence under the Act is that of price maintenance (s.38), which is any direct or indirect attempt to achieve a price increase or to set minimum price levels of any product sold or advertised within Canada. S.38(3) of the Act states that any influence exerted by a franchisor in suggesting minimum resale prices of a product supplied by him to his franchisees, other than a mere non-obligatory suggestion accompanied by a suitable disclaimer, constitutes price maintenance, as does any advertising or promotion carried out by the franchisor in which reference is made to the price at which any product may be sold by a franchisee, unless the advertisement or promotion makes it clear that the franchisee is free to sell at a lower price. The Director has indicated that the use of the words "or less" after the price reference will satisfy this requirement. The prohibition in the Act does not extend to setting price ceilings, although the wording of contractual clauses stipulating maximum prices must be carefully drafted to avoid triggering Section 38.

The elements of the offence of price maintenance consist of both an attempt to increase prices and some form of threat, agreement or promise. Thus, a franchisor acting unilaterally (e.g. in an advertisement) in specifying the prices of products sold by the franchise system may escape liability under Section 38. However, any attempt by a franchisor to enforce minimum prices, or by a franchisor or other franchisees to boycott a particular franchisee whose prices undercut other prices in the system constitutes an offence which is strictly enforced. S.38(9)(a) establishes a defence to such a charge where the party with whom the accused has refused to deal is engaging in bait-and-switch techniques, below-cost pricing for certain visible items (loss leadering), or an unacceptable reduction in the level of customer servicing.

The practices of "pyramid selling" and "referral selling" constitute criminal offences under the Act. As a result, systems which utilize such practices are relatively uncommon in Canada. Examples of pyramid selling in the franchise context would be the payment of a participation fee by a franchisee who then receives a fee (a "head-hunting fee") for any franchisees subsequently recruited by him into the scheme, or the purchase of products by independent distributors from a manufacturer, if the distributors were entitled to bonuses upon resale. Similarly, the offence of refferal selling is committed where the buyer of a product is induced to purchase on the promise that he will receive a head-hunting fee or commission upon his subsequent referral to the vendor of other purchasers.

The most actively enforced criminal proscriptions of the Act are those which prohibit practices grouped under the generic heading of "misleading advertising". Of primary importance in this field is the projection, in any form of media advertising, of misleading or unsubstantiated claims. For example, it is a criminal offence under s.36 of the Act to make a false or misleading representation to the public regarding prices, quality of goods, availability of products, profitability of dealerships or franchise outlets, or any other matter that may mislead the public in a material respect. Similarly, misleading or inaccurate warranties or guarantees of a product, or the publication of inaccurate or deceptive test results, constitute offences under s.36.

The test of materiality will take into account both the strictly literal meaning of the words used, and the "general impression" conveyed by, the advertised message to the public at large. As such, special care must be taken in representing to the public the price at which goods are ordinarily sold, and representations of "special one-time sales" and "bargains" must be truthful and accurate in every respect in order to avoid liability under s.36. Thus, for the duration of an advertised sale, it is an offence to charge a higher than advertised price in the market area to which the advertisement relates, unless the advertisement is accompanied by explicit notice that the prices are subject to change.

The common law prohibition of "bait and switch" gimmickry is embodied in the Act, with the result that products advertised at a bargain price must be available for sale in reasonable quantities, which will be determined in accordance with the size of the market, the advertiser and the advertising campaign. The Act specifies that the market to which an advertisement relates is that which the advertisement can reasonably be expected to reach. However, an express geographic limitation contained in the advertisement should serve to narrow the relevent market area.

Under s.36.1 of the Act, it is a criminal offence to publish, as part of an advertising campaign any testimonial which is unauthorized by the endorser. In addition, a breach of s.36.1 is deemed to have occurred if the advertiser, although publicizing a testimonial which has specifically been authorized, has distorted the scope of the testimonial or endorsement.

It should be noted that a respresentation articulated on a product, its wrapper or any other accompanying paraphernalia, a decorative display, door-to-door or telephone communication, or any similar manner of representation is deemed by the Act to be made to the public, thus bringing the representation within the ambit of s.36 of the Act. Thus, the advertising-related offences are not limited to traditional uses of mass media. S.36(2) stipulates, however, that a representation is deemed to be made to the public only by the person who caused the representation, thus allowing a franchisee to escape liability where he simply offers for a sale a product which has been the subject of misleading advertising by the franchisor.

The Act sets out several defences which may be available to an accused facing prosecution under its various criminal provisions. The first of these defences is known popularly as the "publisher's exemption", and is most pertinent to the advertising-related offences. The provisions dealing with misleading advertising do not apply to the printer, publisher or distributor of a representation or advertisement on behalf of another person within Canada, so long as the printer, publisher or distributor receives the representation from the advertiser in good faith and in the ordinary course of business. The publisher's exemption does not,however,extend to the printer, publisher or distributor of misleading advertisements where the representations were received from an advertiser situated outside of Canada.

Of more general applicability to all of the provisions of the Act is the judicial introduction of a defence based on due diligence. Although it has been held that the criminal offences under the Act do not require proof of mens rea, there appears to be a defence of due diligence, as articulated by the Supreme Court of Canada in R.v. City of Sault Ste. Marie (1978), 85 D.L.R. (3d) 161.Once it is shown that the accused did the prohibited act, the burden is on the accused to avoid liability by showing that he operated under a reasonable mistake of fact, or that he otherwise took all reasonable care in attempting to avoid committing the offence. When applied specifically to a misleading advertising offence, however, there is an added consideration: it was held in R.v.Consumers Distributing Company Limited (1981), 54 C.P.R. (2d) 50 that in order to qualify under the due diligence defence,the accused must show not only innocent mistake in the misrepresentation, but that immediate corrective action was taken by notifying the public that a misrepresentation had been made.

IV. TRADE MARKS ACT

Under Canadian common law, trade mark rights can be acquired through usage independently of registration. However, the protection afforded to a trade mark by the common law is predicated upon the doctrine of unfair competition, and is thus limited to the area in which the trade mark has in fact been used. As a result, at common law a trade mark owner would have no right to prevent a third party from using the mark in a different geographical area.

Since the degree of protection afforded to trade marks by the common law is relatively minimal, it is imperative that a franchisor obtain registration of his trade marks under the Federal Trade Marks Act, since the Act provides cross-Canada protection to trade marks, including protection in geographical areas where the trade mark is not used. The Act also provides a statutory cause of action for infringement of the trade mark.

"Trade Mark" is defined in Section 2 of the Act as "a mark that is used by a person for the purpose of distinguishing or so as to distinguish wares or services manufactured , sold, leased, hired or performed by him from those manufactured, sold, leased, hired or performed by others" and includes a certification mark, a distinguishing guise, and a proposed trade mark.

A certification mark is defined in Section 2 as being a mark used to distinguish wares or services that are of a particular character or quality or have been produced within a particular area or by a particular class of persons. Generally speaking, certification marks do not play a major role in business-format franchise systems.

A distinguishing guise is defined in Section 2 of the Act as "the shape of wares or their containers, or a mode of wrapping or packaging wares, the appearance of which is used by a person for the purpose of distinguishing his wares from the wares of others".   As with certification marks, distinguishing guises generally do not play a major role in business-format franchise systems.

It is critically important that a trade mark be distinctive. Although the Registrar of Trade Marks may not refuse to register a trade mark on the ground that it is not distinctive, Section 18 of the Act provides that the registration of such a trade mark will be invalid if the trade mark has not become distinctive at the time proceedings are commenced bringing the validity of the registration into question. Under Section 2 of the Act, a trade mark is distinctive if it "actually distinguishes the wares or services in association with which it is used by its owner from the wares or services of others or is adapted so to distinguish them".

Once a trade mark has been registered, unless the registration is shown to be invalid it gives the owner the exclusive right to use the trade mark throughout Canada, in conjunction with the wares and services listed in the registration. Unlike the common law trade mark, a trade mark registered under the Act does not have to actually be used throughout all of Canada in order to gain protection throughout Canada. This is fundamentally important to a new franchise system, because it enables the franchisor to gain cross-Canada protection of the mark before he has expanded his franchise system into all market areas.

Under Section 16 of the Act, an application for registration of a trade mark may be based on one or more of the following grounds:

(a)   actual use in Canada;

(b)   making known in Canada;

(c)   registration and use abroad;

(d)   proposed use in Canada.

Section 4 of the Act provides that, with respect to wares, use occurs when the wares are sold in association with the trade mark in the ordinary course of trade, and with respect to services, use occurs when the trade mark is displayed in the performance or advertising of the services.   Under Section 29 of the Act, an application based on actual use in Canada is required to set forth a number of specific pieces of information.   These include:

(a)   a description of the specific wares or services in association with which the mark has been used;

(b)   the date of first use of the mark;

(c)   the address of the applicant's principal office or place of business in Canada, or if the applicant has no office or place of business in Canada, the address of his principal office or place of business abroad and the name and address in Canada of some person to whom any notice in respect of the application or registration may be sent;

(d)   a drawing of the mark, unless the application is for the registration of a trade mark which consists only of a word or words not depicated in a special form; and

(e)   a statement that the applicant is satisfied that he is entitled to use the mark in Canada in association with the wares and services described in the application.

An application based on "making known in Canada", must
contain items (a), (c), (d) and (e) above, together with the
name of a country that is a member of the Union for the
Protection of Industrial Property (constituted under the
1883 Convention of the Union of Paris), in which the mark
has been used by the applicant or his predecessors in title,
and the date from and the manner in which the applicant or
his predecessors have made the mark known in Canada in
association with the wares and services described in the
application.   Section 5 of the Act provides that a trade
mark is made known in Canada if it is used in a country of
the Union (other than Canada) and has become well known in
Canada by reason of the distribution of the wares or
services in Canada, or by reason of the advertising of the
wares and services in any printed publication circulated in
Canada, in the ordinary course of commerce, among potential
dealers or users of the wares and services, or by reason of
radio broadcasts ordinarily received in Canada by potential
dealers or users or the wares and services.   The difficulty
with basing an application on "making known in Canada" is
demonstrating achievement of the requisite degree to which
the trade mark must be made known in Canada.   The case law
suggests that a trade mark is not well-known in Canada
unless knowledge of it pervades Canada to a substantial
extent.

An application based on "registration and use abroad", must
contain items (a), (c), (d) and (e) above, together with
particulars of registration in a country of the Union and,
if the trade mark has neither been used in Canada nor made
known in Canada, the name of a country in which the trade
mark has been used by the applicant or his predecessors in
association with the wares and services described in the
application.   "Registration and use abroad" enables an
applicant to obtain priority before any use or making known
in Canada, provided that the Canadian application is filed
within six months of the first application for registration

in a foreign country. If such a filing is made, convention priority may be claimed, and the applicant will be entitled to priority in Canada as of the date of filing in the foreign country.

An application based on "proposed use in Canada" must contain items (a), (c), (d) and (e) above, together with a statement that the applicant intends to use the trade mark in Canada in association with the wares and services described in the application. An application based on proposed use enables the applicant to obtain priority over another person who uses the trade mark before the applicant, but did not use it prior to the applicant's filing date. If an application is based upon proposed use, the application will be allowed without the necessity of commencing use of the mark, but evidence of use must be submitted before registration will be granted.

It is important to be aware of the assortment of statutory grounds permitting the Registrar of Trade Marks to refuse registration. Firstly, section 16 of the Act provides that an application for registration of a trade mark will be refused if the proposed trade mark is confusing with:

(a)   a trade mark that has been previously used in Canada or made known in Canada by any other person;

(b)   a trade mark in respect of which an application for registration has been previously filed in Canada by any other person; or

(c)   a trade name that has been previously used in Canada by any other person.

In addition, section 37 of the Act provides a procedure by which a person may file a statement of opposition to an application to register a trade mark. The filing of a

statement of opposition may delay the registration of the
trade mark for up to three years and may defeat registration
entirely.   The merits of the opposition are assessed in the
first instance, by the Registrar, with a right of appeal to
the Federal Court.

Under Section 12 of the Act, a trade mark is not registrable
if it is a word that is primarily merely the name or the
surname of an individual who is living or who has died
within the preceding 30 years. Customarily, the Trade Marks
Office will check the telephone directories of major
Canadian cities and reject the application if the proposed
trade mark is listed as a surname and does not have a
"secondary" meaning.   However, if a trade mark which is a
surname has acquired a secondary meaning (e.g: "Dr.
Pepper"), registration of the mark usually will not be
refused.

Registration of a trade mark will also be refused if the
mark, whether depicted, written or sounded, is either
clearly descriptive or deceptively misdescriptive of the
character or quality of the wares or services in association
with which it is used. The purpose of denying registration
of a purely descriptive mark is simply to prevent a person
from appropriating to himself the whole right to use a word
that is in common use, thus placing his competition at an
undue disadvantage. The purpose of denying registration to
a deceptively misdescriptive mark is to prevent the public
from being misled with respect to the wares and services.
The descriptive/ deceptively misdescriptive prohibition may
be avoided if the applicant disclaims the exclusive right to
the use of that part of the mark which is objectionable.

A trade mark is not registrable if it causes confusion with
another trade mark or trade name. The use of a trade mark
will cause such confusion if its use in the area in question
would likely lead to the inference that the wares or

services associated with the confusing trade mark and those
associated with the other mark, or the business carried on
under the trade name, are manufactured, sold, leased, hired
or performed by the same person, whether or not such wares
or services are of the same general class. In determining
whether trade marks or trade names are confusing, subsection
6(5) of the Act requires the Court or the Registrar, as the
case may be, to have regard to all the surrounding
circumstances, including:

(a) the inherent distinctiveness of the trade marks or
     trade name and the extent to which they have become
     known;

(b) the length of time the trade marks or trade name have
     been in use;

(c) the nature of the wares, services or business;

(d) the nature of the trade; and

(e) the degree of resemblance between the trade marks or
     trade name in appearance or sound, or in the ideas
     suggested by them.

In addition, section 9 of the Act provides that a trade mark
is unregistrable if it consists of, or confusingly
resembles:

(a) royal, vice-regal or governmental partronage or arms,
     crests, flags, etc.;

(b) national flags and emblems;

(c) scandalous, obscene or immoral words or devices;

(d) any matter that may falsely suggest a connection with

any living individual, including the portrait or signature of an individual who is living or who has died within the preceding 30 years;

(e) any badge, crest or mark adopted by any Canadian public authority, any university or Her Majesty's forces as an official mark; and

(f) the name "Royal Canadian Mounted Police" or the initials "R.C.M.P."

A major area of concern to franchisors involves the appropriate procedure for licensing others to use the trade marks. At common law, the owner of a trade mark could not licence another to use the mark without destroying the goods or services, thus losing any right to protection of the mark.

Section 49 of the Trade Marks Act establishes a statutory procedure for licensing another to use the trade mark. Section 49(3) of the Act states that the use of a trade mark by a "registered user" has the same effect as use by the registered owner. Accordingly, if a registered trade mark is licensed to a registered user, the distinctiveness of the trade mark in identifying the owner as the source of the wares or services is statutorily preserved.

Concurrently with or at any time after filing an application for registration of a trade mark, an application for registration of a person as a registered user of the mark may be made. The regisered user application must include particulars of the relationship, existing or proposed, between the owner of the mark and the proposed registered user, including particulars of the degree of control by the owner over the permitted use of the mark. In addition, the application must contain a statement of the wares and services for which registration as a user is proposed, and must specify particulars of any conditions or restrictions proposed with respect to the characteristics of the wares or services, the mode or place of permitted use, and any other matter. Information as to the duration of the permitted use must be provided, together with such further documents, information and other evidence as may be required by the Registrar, in his discretion.

Although Section 49(7) of the Act requires that the Registrar consider whether or not approval of the registered user application would be in the public interest, as a practical matter the Registrar will normally grant approval.

Registration of a person as a registered user may be cancelled in a number of circumstances. The Registrar may cancel a user registration upon the application of either party, or on his own motion in respect of any wares or services for which a trade mark is no longer registered. Additionally, the Federal Court may order cancellation, on the application of any person, if the trade mark is used otherwise than by way of permitted use, or in such a way as to cause, or be likey to cuase, desception or confusion. Similarly, midrepresentation or failure to disclose material facts, that if accurately represented or disclosed would have justified the Registrar in refusing the application for registration of the registered user, may give rise to cancellation, as may a significant change of circumstances or the vesting of rights in third parties. In this regard, it should be noted that a registered user is not empowered to transfer his right to use the trade mark to a third party.

V. FOREIGN INVESTMENT REVIEW ACT

The Foreign Investment Review Act establishes procedures for screening acquisitions of Canadian businesses by foreigners (called "non-eligible persons" in the Act), as well as the establishment of new businesses in Canada by non-eligible persons. While the Act is not directed specifically to franchising, it does impact directly upon the business planning of a foreign franchisor who wishes to commence operations in Canada.

The Act defines "business" as including any undertaking or enterprise carried on in anticipation of profit, and defines "non-eligible persons" as including:

(a)   an individual who is neither a Canadian citizen nor a permanent resident within the meaning of the Immigration Act, 1976, and

(b)   a corporation (whenever incorporated) that is controlled, in any manner that results in control in fact, either directly or indirectly by a non-eligible person or by a group of persons which includes a non-eligible person.

The Act requires every non-eligible person, and every group of persons which includes a non-eligible person, that proposes to acquire control of a Canadian business or that proposes to establish a new business in Canada to give notice in writing to the Foreign Investment Review Agency ("FIRA") in prescribed form.

Preliminary screening of the applicant giving notice is carried out by FIRA, with the final decision being made at the federal Cabinet level. The test upon which any approval or rejection is based is contained in the broadly-phrased statutory requirement that the proposed acquisition or new business must be "of significant benefit to Canada". The Act lists an assortment of criteria to be considered, in determining "significant benefit", including: the degree of Canadian ownership, the economic benefit to Canada through employment, purchase of Canadian goods, services and materials; Canadian participation in management; product innovation; and the general effect of the new business on the competitive market.

A foreign franchisor wishing to establish company-owned outlets in Canada must first submit to the review process, since the operation of a company-owned outlet in Canada will constitute the establishment of a new business in Canada by a non-eligible person. Even if there are no company-owned outlets, in Canada, a franchisor may still be caught by the Act if it maintains administrative offices in Canada, or if the franchise agreement with the Canadian franchisee contains controls going beyond that degree reasonably necessary to protect the trade marks and the elements of the system, since FIRA could then argue that the franchisor is the true operator of the franchised business. Even if the franchisor in no way acquires or controls a Canadian business, a franchise agreement which permits the franchisor to acquire of the franchisee's business upon some contingent event will trigger FIRA review. Careful drafting, however, can defer the review process to a time when the event is no longer a contingent one.

Non-resident franchisors should be aware that the Act requires FIRA review when a foreign franchisor with operations in Canada is itself taken over by a non-eligible person, regardless of the level of significance played by the Canadian operations of the franchisor in the context of its total business operations.

The review process is generally lengthy and complex, requiring the applicant to file with FIRA detailed corporate information. The franchisor's proposed Canadian operations must be suspended for the 30 to 60 days required to prepare the documentation for filing and for the up to six month period which FIRA generally takes to consider the

application.   Recently, however, the process has been
somewhat simplified in order to abridge the time consumed.

The application must identify the applicant, its affiliates
and the persons ultimately in control.   It must also
describe the proposed business, including the form of
business organisation; location of the business; type,
source and cost of plant equipment; types of goods and
services to be produced; markets to be served; sources of
materials and supplies; and the overall operation and
control of the business.   Abbreviated procedures are
available under the Act if the business in question
generates less than $5,000,000 in gross assets and has less
than 500 employees.   However, even if such initial
requirements are met, the Act gives FIRA administrative
discretion to require the long-form review process in all
circumstances.

As part of the review process, the applicant will usually
negotiate undertakings to FIRA, directed toward meeting the
"significant benefit" test contained in the Act.   FIRA
usually will require undertakings directed toward increasing
the degree of Canadianisation of the enterprise, which may
include local staffing requirements, a higher degree of
local participation in ownership or management, or the
incorporation of a Canadian subsidiary to own company-
operated outlets.

An acquisition of a Canadian business with gross assets of
under $250,000 and gross revenues for the most recent one
year period of under $3,000,000 is not reviewable under the
Act, if such business is related to a business already
carried on in Canada by the foreign acquiror.   However, the
gross assets and gross revenues of other enterprises
associated with the target business by the interrelationship of management, ownership or financing are added
to those of the target business for the purposes of the

exemption test, unless the associated enterprises constitute distinct entities for reasons of business efficacy and not for the purpose of circumventing the Act.

If a foreign franchisor does not operate company-owned outlets in Canada and does not maintain a permanent establishment or office in Canada to which its employees ordinarily report, the Act is normally inapplicable. As already indicated, however, excessive controls in the franchise contract may trigger FIRA review despite the franchisor's complete lack of physical presence in Canada.

Although provisions in a franchise agreement calling for acquisition of the outlet by the franchisor on default by the franchisee do give rise to FIRA review, these can be dealt wth in a number of ways. For example, where such provisions are expressly made subject to obtaining approval under the Act, FIRA review is deferred from the date of signing of the contract to the date of actual acquisition by the franchisor. Even then, prior to acquisition of the franchised outlet the franchisor must either undergo FIRA review, or find a suitable Canadian assignee, thus providing for the continuance of the business by an eligible person. FIRA has indicated that it may be willing to give informal approval (contained in a "no action" letter) for a foreign franchisor to operate a franchised outlet following termination, for a limited period of time, upon the foreigner undertaking to transfer the business to a Canadian as soon as possible. If a no-action letter is not forthcoming, a franchisor willing to undergo the risk may simply acquire the business of the terminated franchisee and subsequently apply to FIRA for retroactive approval. If such approval is not obtained, the franchisor will be required to divest itself of the business.

VI.   TAX CONSIDERATIONS

The first significant point to note in an evaluation of the Canadian tax system is that jurisdiction to levy income taxes in Canada is divided between the provincial and federal governments. Of equal significance is the fact that the tax base is not founded upon citizenship of the taxpayer, but upon his residency in Canada or his employment or carrying on of business in Canada.

For personal income tax, the federal government and the provinces (with the exception of the Province of Quebec) collaborate in a joint computation and collection mechanism. the provincial tax is "piggy-backed" as a percentage of the federal tax payable, all of which is collected in one tax return by the federal government and subsequently distributed to the provinces. The Province of Quebec alone computes tax without reference to the federal legislation, and such tax is collected by the Quebec government directly from the taxpayer.

For all Canadian taxpayers, personal income tax is computed on a graduated rate strcture, depending on the level of income.   Corporate income taxes, on the other hand, are computed at a fixed rate and are collected separately by the federal and provinicial governments. The combined federal-provincial corporate income tax burden varies from province to province, although on the average it is a 50% rate, subject to reduction if the corporation qualifies for the "small business" deduction (resulting in a tax rate of approximately 25%) or is entitled to an "incentive reduction" in respect of manufacturing and processing operations.

A non-resident franchisor based in a country with which Canada has a tax treaty and operating without a permanent establishment in Canada is usually exempt from most Canadian income taxes (those contained in Part 1 of the federal Income Tax Act) by virtue of the provisions of the tax treaty. A resident of a non-treaty country, on the other hand, is subject to full Canadian taxation so long as he "carries on business" in Canada (which term is defined in an extremely broad manner, and includes even the soliciting of orders in Canada).

A non-resident parent of a Canadian subsidiary must be aware of the "thin capitalisation" rules, which stipulate that a Canadian subsidiary is limited in deducting interest payments on inter-company loans from a foreign source, to the extent that the loan exceeds by a factor of 3 the foreign company's equity investment in the Canadian subsidiary. Thus, if the non-resident franchisor finances the Canadian subsidiary through inter-company loans, if the interest charged is to be withdrawn from Canada a debt-equity ration of 3:1 in the subsidiary should not be exceeded.

Under Part XIII of the Income Tax Act, non-residents are subject to a withholding tax of 25% on income produced in Canada, including payments received for the right to use trade marks, patents, properties, and industrial and commercial know-how. The 25% rate has been reduced to 15% under most current tax treaties.

Ongoing payments such as royalties or rents are also subject to 25% withholding tax under Part XIII, which is reduced to 15% by most current tax treaties. To the extent that profits are not classified as royalties or rents, under most treaties withholding tax is not exigible. Accordingly, it may be possible to argue that the initial lump sum franchise fee payable in most systems is exempt from taxation under the applicable treaty. In addition, most treaties, including the U.S.-Canada tax convention, exempt from income and withholding taxes industrial and commercial profits of the non-resident enterprise, to the extent that such profits are not allocable to a permanent establishment in Canada. Royalties and rents are excluded from this exemption and remain taxable at the treaty rate. Other service charges incidental to the franchise relationship are subject to a 15% withholding tax under Part XIII of the Income Tax, although this does not include fair market value purchases of goods and services from the non-resident.

Of equal concern to a foreign franchisor is the fact that the Customs Act imposes liability for customs duties on an importer of any goods into Canada, the classification of which is based on the value of such goods in the country of origin. Similarly, the Excise Tax Act imposes a sales tax on the resale price of all goods imported into Canada. The sales tax is 10% for wholesalers or manufacturers and applies to all imported products, including brochures, operation manuals, other marketing materials and finished products.

A Canadian-resident franchisor need not consider any special tax provisions in regard to his status or the nature of his business, but should be aware of the income tax rules of general applicability to resident commercial enterprises. By way of illustration, the initial capital outlays by a franchisor, whether depreciable or currently deductible, are treated similarly to those incurred by any other business. As with any commercial endeavour, expenditures incurred for the purpose of producing income from a business are deductible as current expenses, whereas those expenditures properly characterized as outlays for depreciable capital property are subject to an annual capital cost allowance in accordance with the class of the capital property to which the subject matter of the expenditure belongs. Detailed lists of class of depreciable property are annexed to the Income Tax Act.

Numerous statutory deductions of general applicability to business may be relevant to a franchisor. Theses can include such items as: manufacturing and processing expenses, inventory allowances, employment tax credits, small business deductions, investment tax credits, interest payments, research costs, landscaping costs, site location analysis costs, costs of representations to government bodies (e.g. for licences, permits or zoning by-laws), costs of warranties on products, soft costs of real estate, and general fees for legal and accounting services necessary for the taxpayer's ongoing business. Additionally, statutory deductions of specific relevance to a franchisor's business include: advertising and market research expenses, costs of preparation of an operation manual for the franchise system, costs of representations to the Alberta Securities Commission and costs of the prospectus required under The Franchises Act. The underlying test for timing of the deduction is centred upon the taxpayer's ability to match expenses with revenues in computing annual income from business.

Legal expenses incurred in terminating a franchisee and reacquiring property and other rights are generally treated as non-deductible costs of preserving assets. However, a specific statutory deduction is allowed for payments made by a lessor to reacquire the remaining term of a lease from a lessee, although the deduction must be spread proportionately on an annual basis over the remaining term of the lease. Similarly, losses arising from the non-repayment of loans advance to the franchisee are deductible as long as such loans are either provided in order to protect the franchisor's goodwill or represent an established business practice of the franchisor. Compensatory payments made by the franchisor to the franchisee in terminating the franchise have been held to be deductible if, in the ordinary course of business, the franchisor brings all receipts of franchise fees into income.

On the income side of the taxation equation, the fee
received from a franchisee in consideration for the granting
of a franchise is generally treated as income to the
franchisor, and not a payment on capital account, since the
franchisor is usually in the business of granting
franchises.

Royalty payments received by the franchisor in consideration
for the franchisee's use of the trade marks and other
property rights will be taxed as income from business, since
the franchisor is usually in the business of granting such
property rights. Likewise, royalties and other fees
received by the franchisor in consideration for managerial
and supervision services and ongoing assistance to the
franchisee are taxed as income from the franchisor's
business. Needless to say, profits resulting from the
arm's-length sale of goods by the franchisor's to the
franchisee represent business income. Non-arm's length
sales are similarly treated, with the sale price being
deemed to be the fair market value of the goods sold.

Although the specific income tax provisions pertinent to a
franchisee's business are too numerous to catalogue in the
present context, there are several basic Canadian taxation
concepts of which anyone going into business as a franchise
should be aware. Firstly, a franchise fee paid upon
entrance into the franchise system for a fixed term
constitutes an expenditure for depreciable capital property,
if paid in a lump sum, and qualifies for annual capital cost
allowance treatment. On the other hand, a franchise fee
paid upon entrance into the franchise system for an
indefinite period, or for a fixed period infinitely
renewable at the option of the franchisee, while
constituting a capital expenditure, does not qualify for
capital cost allowance treatment. It will, however,

consitute an "eligible capital expenditure", if purchased for business purposes, one-half of which forms part of the "cumulative eligible capital" of the franchisee's business. Up to 10% of cumulative eligible capital may be deducted annually from business income.

Royalty payments to the franchisor based on the franchisee's sales constitute a deductible business expense. Similarly, ongoing managerial fees charged by the franchisor also represent a deductible expense for the franchisee, provided that the managerial services are actually supplied and the fee is not really just an additional element in an original non-deductible franchise fee.

VII. QUEBEC CHARTER OF THE FRENCH LANGUAGE

On August 26, 1977 the Assemblee Nationale du Quebec assented to Bill No. 101, thereupon passing into law the Charter of the French Language. The avowed purpose of the Charter is to assure to Quebecers the quality and influence of the French language in all aspects of government, law, everyday work, instruction, communication, commerce and business.

Unfortunately, from the lawyer's point of view, the Charter is in many instances drafted with less than the degree of precision found in most statutes. The result is that some sections of the Charter appear to be in conflict with other sections and with regulations passed under the Charter; indeed, several provisions of the Charter may well be unconstitutional. For example, the Charter requires various business firms and semi-public agencies to obtain francization certificates (see below), failing which their activities may be curtailed; to the extent that the activities of such agencies or firms are regulated by the federal government, these provisions of the Charter may be unconstitutional.

The Charter proclaims French as the offical language of Quebec. In addition, the Charter provides certain fundamental rights to the people of Quebec, including the following of particular interest to franchisors:

(a) the right of every person to have all business firms doing business in Quebec communicate with him in French;

(b) the right of workers to carry on their activities in French; and

(c) the right of consumers of goods and services to be informed and served in French.

Notwithstanding the foregoing fundamental rights, wherever the Charter does not explicitly require the exclusive use of the French language, French plus another language may be used. However, the French version of the text must have at least equal prominence with the foreign-language version (ss.89, 91).

While the Charter contemplates, in certain cases, the lawful coexistence of the French language with a foreign language, the Office de la langue francaise (the "Office") may, as a condition to granting a francization certification or a provisional certificate, require that only the French language be used. As will be seen, the Office has complete discretion with respect to the granting of francization certificates.

The Charter regulates the use of the French language in various aspects of society, including use of the French language in commerce and business. The Charter and regulations thereunder provided certain exceptions to the "French only" theme; however, as a matter of practice, a franchisor or franchisee carrying on business in Quebec will usually conduct his business using the French language.

Inscriptions on products, product containers or wrappings, leaflets, brochures or cards supplied with products, including directions for use and warranty certificates, must be in French; menus and wine lists must also be in French (s.51). Because French is not required to be used exclusively, the provisions of s.89 apply. The Office is permitted to grant exceptions to the rule in s.51, by regulation. An extensive list of exceptions is contained in the Regulation Respecting the Language of Commerce and Business, promulgated by the Office and herein called the "Business Regulations". With the exception of ss.5(c) of the Business Regulations (exempting products in limited use, with no equivalent replacement in French available in the Quebec market) and s.11 thereof (granting in exemption so long as force majeure obliges a firm to obtain a non-complying product), the Business Regulations do not provide any meaningful exemptions to the s.51 requirements as far as franchisors are concerned.

Catalogues, brochures, folders and similar publications must be in French (s.53). Because French is not required to be used exclusively, the provisions of s.89 apply. Contracts predetermined by one party (contracts of adhesion) or containing printed standard clauses, and all related documents must be in French unless, at the express wish of all of the parties, the contract and documents are drawn up in another language. It would seem that so long as the parties to the contract are on an equal basis regarding bargaining power, a contract drafted entirely in English would be one "drawn up in another language at the express wish of the parties". Nevertheless, the accepted practice has been to indicate the express wish of the parties to the contract by inserting standards clauses, in both English and French, to this effect. Application forms for employment, order forms, invoices, receipts and "quittances" must be in

French.   Because French is not required to be used
exclusively, the provisions of s.89 apply.

On the other hand, signs, posters and commercial advertising
must be in French exclusively, except as otherwise provided
in the Charter or in the Business Regulations (s.58). S.58
is one of several sections in the Charter requiring the
exclusive use of French, and as such, precluding the
operation of s.89.   Sections 59 to 62 provide certain
exceptions to the rule of s.58; these sections deal with
advertising in news media that publish in another language,
signs and posters of firms employing not over four persons,
including the employer, signs and posters respecting the
cultural activities of a particular ethnic group and signs
and posters of commercial establishments specializing in
foreign national specialties or particular ethnic
specialties.   The Business Regulations define "signs and
poster" as "any message of public interest intended for the
public and displayed in public view or in a public place".
However, section 17 of the Business Regulations permits the
distribution in a public place of catalogues, brochures,
folders and similar advertising in a language other than
French, if they are available as well in French under no
less favorable conditions of accessibility and quality.
However, the French text must constitute a separate
publication.   In addition, catalogues, brochures, folders
and similar advertising in a language other than French may
be distributed privately to a natural person pursuant to his
written request for such literature.   The remaining
exemptions from s.58 contained in the Business Regulations
deal mainly with cultural or educational products and are
therefore of little use to franchisors.

Names of business firms must be in French (s.63) and,
subject to s.68 of the Charter, only the French version of a
firm name may be used in Quebec (s.69).   The restriction in
s.69 precludes the operation of s.89.   Section 68 permits a

firm name to be accompanied by a version in another language for use outside Quebec, but most incorporation statutes preclude the use of two versions of a corporate name. Among the exceptions to this general rule are the Canada Business Corporations Act and the Ontario Business Corporations Act. "Business firm" is defined by regulation as "a natural person, a cooperative, a partnership of natural persons, or an artificial person engaged in farming, industrial, commercial, financial or professional activities in Quebec"; and "firm name" is defined by the Business Regulations as "any designation of a firm". Section 67 of the Charter permits family names, place names, coined names and expressions taken from other languages to appear in firm names in accordance with the Business Regulations. The Business Regulations permit an expression taken from another language to be used as a distinguishing part of a firm name, if that distinguishing part is used with a French generic element (e.g., Limitee, Incorporee, Inc. or Ltee.) For example, "Golden Harvest Investments Ltd." could be changed for use in Quebec to "Placements Golden Harvest Inc."

It should be noted that Section 17 of the Business Regulations permits a firm name to appear in a foreign language in any document drawn up in that foreign language. In addition, in any document drawn in both French and in a foreign language, the firm name may appear both in French and in the foreign language.

Finally, s.16 of the Business Regulations permits the following to appear exclusively in a foreign language on signs, posters, in commercial advertising, in product inscriptions and in any other document;

    (i) the firm name of a firm established exclusively outside Quebec;

    (ii) a trade mark which was registered or in respect of

which an application was pending before the
Legislative Assembly assented to the Charter
(August 26, 1977);

(iii) a name of origin, a denomination of a typical
product or specialty with a foreign name (e.g.
sauerkraut), a heraldic or any other non-
commerical motto;

(iv) a place name, a family name, the name of a
personality or character, the distinctive name of
a cultural product (e.g., "mozzarella", "pierogy")
or the distinctive name of any other product if
the name was used before July 25, 1979.

In addition to the Charter provisions specifically
applicable to language use in various commercial contexts,
the Charter represents an attempt to regulate the
development of the French language generally. The Office de
la langue francaise was established to define and implement
policy on terminology and on francization. Francization is
a procedure intended to ensure that the French language
becomes, as much as possible, the language of
communications, work, commerce and business.

The duties of the Office are to standardize terminology,
establish research programs with respect to terminology and
francization, draft regulations under the Charter, and
define francization procedures and oversee such procedures.
The use of standardized terminology approved by the Office
is obligatory in the civil adminstration and in signs and
posters. As a branch of the Office, the Commission de
toponymie has been formed to establish criteria for the
selection of place names and the rules of spelling place
names. The use of standardized place names is obligatory in
civil administration, traffic signs and public signs and
posters.

Francization programs have as their object the generalized use of French at all levels of a business firm. Firms of 50 or more persons must obtain a francization certificate from the Office by dates specified in accordance with the regulations under the Charter. The Office is empowered to define various classes of businesses and to schedule the dates by which such business must obtain francization certificates, based on the nature of the activity and the number of employees in the firm. A francization certification attests that the business firm in question is applying or has completed a francization program approved by the Office (s.138). As a matter of practical necessity, provisional certificates may be granted by the Office to those firms which have made "appropriate arrangements" to adopt a francization program (s.139).

The Charter requires the Office to grant a francization certificate or a provisional certificate "if the Office is of the opinion that a firm has complied with the requirements of Sections 138 or 139". Therefore, the grant of francization certificates appears to be in the complete discretion of the Office. If a business firm fails to comply with the francization program it has undertaken to follow, or is in breach of any provision of the Charter or the regulations passed thereunder, the office may suspend or cancel its francization certificate or provisional certificate (s.154).

For the purposes of ongoing regulatory control, the Charter establishes the Commission de surveillance de la langue francaise to enforce the provisions of the Charter and the regulations passed thereunder. The Commission is composed of a chairman, investigation commissioners, inspectors and other staff. The function of investigation commissioners is to inquire into non-compliance with the Charter. Any person or group can petition an inquiry by an investigation commissioner; an investigation commissioner can himself institute such an inquiry and the Office can request that an inquiry be made into any business firm.

The function of the Commission's inspectors is to assist the investigation commissioners in their investigation, to verify and establish the facts of non-compliance, and to submit reports and recommendations to the investigation commissioners. Following investigation, an investigation commissioner may put an offender in default under the Charter and require the offender to conform to the Charter within a stipulated time (s.182). If the offender does not so conform, the investigation commissioner may forward the record to the provincial Attorney-General for his consideration.

Every person who contravenes the Charter or any regulation made under the Charter (including regulations made by the Office) is guilty of an offence and is liable, in addition to costs:

(a)   for a first offence, to a fine of $25 to $500, in the case of an individual, and $50 to $1,000 in the case of an artificial person; and

(b)   for any subsequent offence within two years of a first offence, to a fine of $50 to $1,000, in the case of an individual, and of $500 to $5,000, in the case of an artificial person.

A business firm which fails to obtain a francization certificate in accordance with s.136 of the Charter is liable, in addition to costs, to a fine of $100 to $2,000 for each day during which it carries on business without such a certificate (s.206). The Attorney-General or his agent may institute, by way of summary proceedings, prosecutions of persons or firms alleged to have committed an offence under the Charter. In addition, Section 208 of the Charter permits a court of civil jurisdiction, on motion by the Attorney-General, to grant a mandatory injunction requiring the removal or destruction (at the defendant's expense) of any poster, sign, advertisement or billboard not conforming with the requirements of the Charter. Indeed, in view of the fact that much of the Charter appears to deal with matters of public order, it may be open to the Court, in addition to imposing the penalities provided in the Charter, to hold that a document not in conformity with the requiremetns of the Charter is a nullity.

The Charter also establishes the Conseil de la langue francaise to advise the Minister responsible for the Charter on policy regarding the French language in Quebec and on questions regarding the interpretation and application of the Charter. The Conseil also advises the Minister with respect to regulations proposed by the Office. The Conseil consists of 12 persons, being a chairman, secretary and two persons representing each of five different sectors of society.

VIII. RECENT JUDICIAL DEVELOPMENTS IN FRANCHISING

Despite the impressive growth of franchising in Canada, franchise-related litigation has remained at a relatively modest level. This is a result of a number of factors.

First, the absence of franchise regulation gives franchisors broad discretion in developing franchise agreements which frequently impose onerous restrictions on franchisees regarding rights of termination, purchase of product and rights of assignment. The enforceability of such clauses will usually be governed by general contract law principles. Accordingly, unless there is evidence of a material breach by the franchisor, or of a manifest disparity in bargaining position, the agreement will generally be enforced.

Secondly, unlike U.S. anit-trust law, the private
enforcement rights contained in the Combines Investigation
Act offer little assistance to most franchisees. The
marketing practices which are the greatest source of abuse
in most franchise systems are those of exclusive dealing and
tied selling. As previously indicated, these restrictions
are classified as reviewable practices under the Act, and
thus will not give rise to a right of action unless a cease-
practice order is issued by the Restictive Trade Practices
Commission and such order is subsequently violated by the
franchisor. Canadian experience has clearly demonstrated
that no relief under the Act will lie, except where the
franchisor occupies a substantial share of the market area
in question.

Thirdly, the lack of effective class action procedures make
it difficult and expensive for individual franchisees to
pursue claims against franchisors. This fact, coupled with
the prohibition in effect in most Canadian jurisdictions
regarding the use of contingency fee arrangements,
effectively prevents franchisees with limited resources from
pursuing their legal remedies, regardless of the merits of
their claim.

Despite the dearth of legal decisions, there have been
several cases which have played a significant role in
shaping the franchise relationship in Canada.

In <u>Jirna Ltd. V. Mister Donut of Canada Ltd.</u> (1975), S.C.R.
2, the court laid to rest the notion that the franchisor-
franchisee relationship is fiduciary in nature. In that
case, the franchisor had earned secret profits as a result
of the purchase by the franchisee of materials from
suppliers designated by the franchisor. These purchases
were made pursuant to a stipulation the franchise agreement
that the franchisee purchase its requirements of product
from the franchisor or suppliers approved by it. The

Supreme Court of Ontario held that a quasi-fiduciary duty arose as a result of the dependence of the franchisee on the franchisor, and the franchisor was therefore obliged to account for secret profits arising out of the franchise,s purchase of product from such suppliers.

The Court of Appeal disagreed. Relying on a finding that the franchisee was a sophisticated businessman, experienced in commercial matters, and had taken independent legal advice prior to entering into the franchise agreement, the Court rejected the principle that the franchise relationship was fiduciary in nature. The Court relied on and gave effect to a clause in the franchise agreement which characterized the relationship between the parties as one of independent contractors, and held that the franchisor was under no obligation to account (or indeed to disclose) to the franchisee the existence of secret arrangements regarding the purchase of products. In spite of this, Canadian franchisors have typically made disclosure of such secret arrangements in their franchise agreements, in order to avoid allegations of mispresentation by the franchisee.

The general reluctance of Canadian courts to interfere in commercial transactions made between businessmen, simply because one party was subjected to an onerous bargain, was again demonstrated in the decision of the Supreme Court of Canada in <u>Ronald Elwin Lister Ltd. v. Dunlop Canada Limited</u> (1982, 42 N.R. 181. In that case, Mr. and Mrs. Lister, after extensive negotiations with Dunlop, entered into a pre-printed form of franchise agreement through a corporation incorporated specifically to operate the franchise. The franchisee also executed a demand debenture, which was personally guaranteed by the Listers. The evidence indicated that representations concerning the purchase of product and the profitability of the franchise had been made by representatives of Dunlop, but these representations were not incorporated into the agreement.

The franchise operation eventually encountered financial difficulty, and Dunlop purported to terminate the franchise agreement and to enforce its rights under the debenture and under the personal guarantees. Following further negotiations, a settlement agreement was entered into providing for payment of the amounts owing to Dunlop, and confirming the guarantees which had been given by the Listers. The evidence indicated that throughout the negotiations the Listers had enjoyed the benefit of independent legal advice. In 1973, the Listers and the corporate franchisee brought action against Dunlop on a number of grounds, including misrepresentation and breach of an oral collateral contract. As well, the Listers asked for relief from the settlement agreement, based on unconscionability.

Citing the fact that the Listers had received independent legal advice and were experienced in commercial matters, the Supreme Court of Canada concluded, somewhat reluctantly, that the Listers were bound by the settlement agreement. The fact that their bargaining power had been grievously impaired and that there was available to them no real alternative to signing the settlement agreement was not sufficient, in the Court's opinion, to alter this result.

Regarding the issues of negligent misrepresentation and collateral contract, the Court relied on the disclaimer clause contained in the franchise agreement, which negated the effect of any representations not expressly stated in the conclusion; however, it is worth noting that Madam Justice Wilson, dissenting, would have found that the personal guarantees executed by the Listers were not enforceable, since they contained no similar exclusionary clause and had been induced by the same representations which had been made in connection with the franchise agreement. The Supreme Court of Canada found it unnecessary to consider this argument, however, since the settlement agreement contained an express acknowledgment of the guarantee made by the Listers in favour of Dunlop.

The decision of the Supreme Court of Nova Scotia in A & K Lick- A-Chick Enterprises Ltd. v. Cordiv Enterprises Ltd. (1981), 119 D.L.E. (3d) 440 stands in stark contrast to the foregoing decisions. In that case an existing franchisee was induced, through high pressure tactics of the franchisor, to execute a revised franchise agreement for an existing location. The evidence indicated that the franchisee was subjected to a continuing stream of threats of termination from the franchisor, and had been discouraged from seeking independent legal advice. The revised franchise agreement contained onerous termination provisions, including a buy-back clause in favour of the franchisor at a substantial discount. The franchisee argued that the contract was unconscionable and thus unenforceable. The Court agreed, citing the inexperience of the franchisee and the undue influence exerted by the franchisor's representatives. This case indicates the great importance which Canadian courts will place on independent legal advice in the negotiation and execution of franchise agreements.

The trilogy of cases discussed above clearly demonstrates the conservative attitude of Canadian courts in interpreting franchise agreements. The dilemma raised by this attitude is eloquently stated by M.H. Ogilvy in his analysis of the Lister decision:

"The adjudication of the fact situation in the Lister case is a tragedy of lost opportunity. Rarely do cases with such a rich mix of important policy issues go to the Supreme Court. Too few will venture there in the immediate future. The obstinate refusal of the court to cast aside outdated contractual principles and to explore instead new concepts and policy directions

deprives the highest court of the respect and
integrity which it ought rightfully to have in the
determination of the future development of the law
of contract. Avoidance of the real issues and the
incantation of narrowly conceived and applied
principles of yesteryear suggests a lack of self-
confidence and jurisprudential maturity in the top
court which is beginning to produce stagnation and
chaos in Canadian curial contractual analysis.
This need not be so; even in Lister the Supreme
Court acknowledged the existence of inequality of
bargaining power and of economic duress, if in the
wrong contexts, and in the past the court has
developed new themes in contract law.
Unfortunately, however, the decision of the
Supreme Court of Canada in Ronald Elwyn Lister
Ltd. v. Dunlop Canada Ltd. looks backward rather
than forward and reminds one of the dictum
ascribed to Talleyrand in describing the Bourbons:
"They have learned nothing, and forgotten
nothing"

It is fair to conclude that, for the time being at least,
the drafting and interpretation of franchise agreements will
of necessity continue to be founded upon technical
principels of contract law rather than upon specialised
doctrines uniquely applicable to the franchise
relationship.

CHAPTER 6

FRANCHISING IN LATIN AMERICA
H. Stephen Brown

I.   INTRODUCTION

Unlike that found in the United States and other countries, there is no legislation in Latin American countries that deals exclusively or explicitly with franchising. However, there are rules and regulations that have been adopted by certain Latin American countries that concern and affect franchising. The degree of regulation imposed by the countries ranges from the highly regulated scheme of the countries that make up the Andean Common Market to the moderate, but stringent regulations found in Brazil and Mexico and finally the regulations of Chile.

Despite over-regulation in some areas, Latin American countries provide an excellent opportunity for substantial economic gain to both foreign franchisors and franchisees.

Industries that should find franchising especially attractive in Latin America include tourism, i.e. hotel and transportation, fast foods, service and manufacturing.

II.   Franchise Legislation Found in Latin America

A.   Andean Pact Franchise Legislation

The principal legislation of the Andean Common Market dealing with franchising is the "Common Code for the Treatment of Foreign Capital and Trademarks, Patents,

Licenses and Royalties," better known as Decision 24.(1) Decision 24 was intended to protect the potentially lucrative Andean Market from foreign domination and to diminish the possibility of competition between member countries. Decision 24 was not intended to deter foreign investment, but because of its requirements, Decision 24 has lessened the attractiveness of the Andean Market to foreign investors. Decision 24 has been amended since its passing in 1970, but these amendments do not directly affect franchising.(2) Decision 24, along with Decisions 84 and 85, forms the basis of franchising legislation in the Andean Pact.(3) However, the Andean Part Decisions are not all encompassing in the field of foreign investment. Each member country has the right to enact additional requirements, but to this point, only Venezuela and Columbia have passed additional legislation.(4)

B. Brazilian Franchise Legislation

The Government Agency in Brazil that foreign investors must deal with is the National Industrial Property Institute ("INPI"). The Brazilian regulation of foreign investment began initially through the income tax. The 1958 Income Tax Law imposed a ceiling on the amount Brazilian licensees could deduct for royalties and technical assistance fees. This limit on the amount of available deductions also had the practical effect of limiting the amount of royalties and assistance fees that foreign investors could charge.

The Remittance Law of 1962 put a ceiling on monies that could be remitted abroad. This law also prohibits the payment of any royalties by a licensee which is controlled directly or indirectly by a foreign licensor.

The Industrial Property Code of 1971 placed restrictions on transfers of foreign technology to Brazil. Normative Acts 15, 30 and 32 issued by the INPI have further expanded regulations in the area of foreign investment.(5)

C. Chilean Franchise Legislation

Chile was a charter member of the Andean Common Market but withdrew in 1976. A desire for more liberalized trading relationships with countries outside the Pact was most assuredly one reason for Chile's withdrawal.

After Chile's withdrawal from the Pact, a new Decree-Law No. 600 was enacted by the legislature. Previously, an old Decree-Law No. 600 had been enacted but the new Decree-Law No. 600 made important modifications in the old law with respect to foreign investment. And even though Decision 24 was negated upon Chile's withdrawal, the Central Bank still prohibits certain restrictive business practices contained in Article 20 of Decision 24.(6)

Patents and trademarks are both protected by Article 10 of the Constitution and by Decree-Law No. 958.(7)

D. Mexican Franchise Legislation

Mexico for a long time has regulated and limited the role of foreigners in its economy and culture, but not until recently has the legislation been codified.

The Transfer of Technology Law of 1972 (Technology Law) created the National Registry (Registry) of the Transfer of Technology.(8) The Technology Law requires the registration of all technology agreements with the Registry. In 1973, the Law to Promote Mexican

Investment and Regulate Foreign Investment (Foreign Investment Law) was enacted to govern foreign equity participation. All foreign investments must be approved by the Foreign Investment Commission (FIC).

The law of Inventions and Trademarks (Trade Mark Law) requires all licenses, trade names, patents, and agreements on know-how, trade secrets and others to be approved by the Registry.

III.   Required Clauses and Practices

A. Andean Pact

(Author's Note: The following discussion of Andean Pact required clauses and practices includes general guidelines for all foreign franchisors in Latin American countries.   When reading the discussions dealing with Brazil, Chile and Mexico, this section should be referred to.)

1. Governmental Approval

Each member country has an agency that must review and approve all franchise agreements. The agency typically rules on major terms of the agreement including the royalty payments and the length of the agreement. The agency will also compare the terms of the agreement with the guidelines set forth in Decision 24 and member country's separate regulations, alsong with the subjective policies of the agency.(9) Important factors that member governments take into account include the priority given to foreign investment by that particular government, initial local equity, employment practices, introduction of new technology and know-how, use of local materials, import requirements and the number of existing similar firms.(10)

2. Terms of Franchise

Decision 24 requires that all franchise contracts must include a clause on the terms of the franchise.(11) However, these types of requirements are general and each member country is given wide latitude in enforcing these requirements. Each government can make its own determinations on what is required in a franchise agreement.

3. Contractual Value

The franchise agreement must include a clause stating the contractual value of each of the elements concerned in the transfer of technology.(12) The phrase "the elements concerned in the transfer of technology" is ambiguous and could mean know-how, patent, trademark and/or trade secrets among other elements. It has been stated that in most member countries, the review is limited to a cursory, legalistic review of the franchising contract to eliminate prohibited provisions as well as to try to bargain for lower royalty payments or other favorable modifications.(13)

4. Time Period

The franchise agreement must include a clause on the "determination of the time period involved."(14) The individual member governmental authority will typically attempt to bargain for a shorter contract term. In one case in Venezuela, a franchise term was limited to five years.(15)

5. Royalty

The major consideration for the foreign franchisor
when deciding whether to franchise anywhere is the
receipt of a royalty. The form, amount, and the
term of the royalty must be determined before the
economic feasibility of the international business
relationship can be evaluated. Royalties should
reasonably reflect the value of input by the
franchisor. In many cases, franchisors do not
know how much they should reasonably claim as a
royalty from a foreign franchisee. The amount of
royalty will primarily depend on the value of the
industrial property being licensed and on sales
possibilities. As a rule of thumb, the average
royalty is five (5%) per cent of gross sales.(16)

When the method of determining the royalty is
decided upon, the foreign franchisor should then
provide the franchisee with detailed definitions
of all important terms included in the
calculation. The franchisor should also attempt
to keep the calculations simple. By keeping them
simple, the franchisor can eliminate potential
future disagreements over the amount of the
royalty. The franchisor should attempt to make
the royalty as fair as possible. The franchisor
should keep in mind that problems tend to arise
when the franchisee fails to make money.

The following considerations on the terms of the
royalty should be taken into account when
negotiating and preparing an international
agreement. The bankruptcy or insolvency of either
party should be grounds for immediate termination
by the solvent party. A franchisor will normally
attempt to obtain a broad power to terminate

whenever in his judgment the franchisee's management, financial standing, quality control, or general operations adversely affect the interests of the franchisor. On the other hand, a franchisee should make every attempt to define very closely the circumstances in which a franchisor could exercise this option. In any event, the agreement should provide that upon termination, the franchisee cease immediately to use the franchisor's patents, trademarks, know-how blueprints, designs and other proprietary information. Some provision should also be made for disposing of the licensed products at termination.

In the Andean Common Market, the royalty fee must be submitted for examination and approval to a specific national body in the country under negotiation. When negotiating the royalty with an Andean Pact franchisee, the foreign franchisor should be aware that there are problems with its receiving the amount specified. Some of these problems are:

(a) Repatriation of royalty payment;

(b) The appropriate foreign national body reviewing and approving the royalty term and amount;

(c) The tax consequences of the payment in both the franchisor's and franchisee's country;

(d) Currency, rate of exchange, and fluctuation of currencies;

(e) The current political climate in both

countries. (17)

The foreign franchisor can mitigate its risks by considering the following:

(a) A clause in the franchise agreement requiring the franchisee to deposit the royalty in a separate account for the exclusive use of the franchisor. This will keep the royalty safe in case of an order from the government prohibiting its remittance.

(b) Provisions in the franchise agreement on currencies, rate of exchange and fluctuation of currencies. A typical international franchise agreement will include a provision requiring payment of the royalty in United States currency at the official rate of exchange recognised by the International Monetary Fund.

(c) The appropriate tax entity, state and country of incorporation to obtain favorable tax benefits. Important factors include double taxation treaties, foreign tax credit, capital gains versus ordinary income, etc.

(d) A joint venture arrangement providing the foreign franchisor with security collateral by allowing the Andean Pact franchisee to invest in the foreign franchisor's assets in its resident country.

(e) A careful screening of the foreign franchisee for compatibility, technical know-how, financial status and integrity.(18)

B. Brazil

1. Governmental Approval

Every agreement relating to the transfer of technology must be registered with the INPI. Parties must submit their agreements and comply with the provisions of Normative Act No.15 and the INPI requirements. The types of agreements that are required to be registered can be classified as:

(a) License agreements for the exploitation of a patent;

(b) License agreements fr the use of a trademark;

(c) Contracts for the supply ofindustrial technology;

(d) Contracts for technical - industrial co-operation; and,

(e) Contracts for specialised technical services. (19)

It is important to note that the INPI requires separate instruments to be drawn covering different and specific transactions. If one agreement contains more than one of the type of categories listed above, then there must be separate contracts for each one. Therefore, it is virtually impossible to have a legally enforceable franchise agreement in a single contract. Also, if payments are due to a foreign party the agreements must be registered with the Central Bank of Brazil.(20)

2. Terms of Franchise

INPI has the authority to approve the foreign franchise agreement. The terms set forth in the franchise agreement are subject to the scrutiny of the INPI.

3. Time Periods

Normative Act No. 15 governs the time periods allowable for franchise agreements. The Act sets limits for the maximum length of the agreement (these periods commence on the filing of an application):

(a) Patent of invention - 15 years
Patent of utility model - 10 years
Patent of industrial model or design - 10 years

(b) Trademark Licenses The contract resulting from the granting of the license may not exceed the period of validity of the protection of the industrial property rights relating to the registration of the trademark.

(c) Supply of Industrial Technology The contract must establish the term considered to be necessary to enable the receipient to master the technology, through adequate use.

(d) Technical Industrial Co-operation The contract must establish the term necessary for the recipient to master the technology.

(e) Specialised Technical Service The period necessary for the rendering of services by the technicians.(21)

4. Royalty

The first limitation on the amount of royalties came through the Income Tax Law of 1958. The Income Tax Law of 1958 authorised the Minister of Finance to prescribe a scale of royalties, not exceeding five (5%) per cent, which a franchisee may deduct for income tax purposes. If only trademarks are licensed, the maximum royalty is one (1%) per cent.

The Central Bank has interpreted the Profit Remittance Law of 1962 as directing that the maximum amount that can be deducted by the franchisee is also the maximum amount that can be remitted to the franchisor.(22) This limit was extended to royalties including trademarks and payments for technical and administrative assistance.

Normative Act No.15 puts the ceiling as a percentage of net sales instead of gross sales. However, since legislative provisions are superior to the Normative Acts, Normative Act No. 15 has no effect in this instance.(23)

The payment period can be more important than the actual amount of the license. Under a patent license, payment can begin only after the patent has been issued. The patent must be issued in Brazil for the franchisor to be entitled to royalties and for the royalties to be remitted abroad. There is usually a substantial delay between the filing of a patent application and the date of issue, and, consequently, a long delay

before payments can be remitted.(24) When the
Brazilian patent expires, there will be no
entitlement to royalties.   There also must be
proof that the patent has not expired in the
country of origin.

Brazil is a party to the Paris Convention and the
Buenos Aires Pan-American Convention of 1910.
Owners of patents and trademarks in other member
countries have a right of priority in Brazil, but
they must claim it within one (1) year from the
date of application in other member countries.
The applicant must then file a copy of the
original application within one hundred and eighty
(180) days. If a foreign franchisor obtains a
Brazilian patent or trademark other than through
this procedure, the license will be ineffective
regarding royalties.(25)

When dealing with industrial technology or know-
how agreements, subjective factors become
important in determining the length of royalty
payments.   Normative Act No. 15 lists criteria
that the INPI will consult when determining the
length of time needed for a successful transfer of
technology. The INPI presumes that five (5) years
is an adequate length of time for royalty
payments, but this term may vary according to "the
period required to transfer all the content of the
technology and for full and complete assimilation
thereof by the recipient."(26)

Trademark royalties can be paid after the
trademark is registered in Brazil, but they can
only be paid during the ten (10) year term of
registration.(27)

C. Chile

1. Governmental Approval

Article 16 of the Decree-Law No. 600 requires certain investments to be approved by the Foreign Investment Committee. The investments that need Foreign Investment Committee approval are:

(a) those exceeding the value of 5 million U.S. dollars;

(b) those relating to activities customarily reserved for the state;

(c) those including the communications media; and

(d) those made by a foreign state or institution. (28)

Those investments not covered by these categories can be authorised by the Executive Secretary of the Committee, provided the President of the Committee has given his approval. All foreign investments must be approved in some fashion by the Foreign Investment Committee.(29)

In reaching its decision on whether to accept the foreign investment, the Committee will consider the profitability of the franchise, the possibility of local employment, the effect on national development plans and the effect of the imported technology on Chile's existing technology.(30)

2. Other Considerations of Franchising in Chile

Chile's withdrawal from the Andean Pact can be interpreted as a move on its part to liberalise trading relationships with foreign countries. Even though Chile has updated and revised Decree-Law No. 600, the laws governing foreign investment in Chile are still very general.

The Committee exercises unrestricted discretion in reviewing potential foreign investment in Chile.(31) Apparently there are no explicit requirements for the foreign franchisor in Chile today. There are, however, certain things that the foreign franchisor should be aware of when considering contacting possible Chilean franchisees.

Patents are protected by Decree-Law No. 58. The patent application must be submitted through a procurador de patentes to the Conservador de Patentes, Ministerio de Economia, Departmento de Propiedad Industrial, along with necessary plans and descriptive notes. For approval, the originality of the patent must be proved. With respect to foreign patents, the length of the patent license in Chile cannot exceed the balance remaining on the patent in the originating country.(32)

Trademark registration is similar to the procedure required for patent registration. The trademark application must include:

(a) two copies of the label;

(b) evidence that the name belongs to the applicant of consent of the owner; and

(c) a notarised power of attorney if the applicant resides in a foreign country.(33)

A summary of this application must be published in a Santiago newspaper and the Diario Official. Trademarks can be registered for ten (10) years with renewal available for another ten (10) years.

Patents and trademarks are transferable by proper assignment.

D. Mexico

1. Governmental Approval

The Transfer of Technology Law requires that agreements that call for licensing of industrial property, or for the transfer of know-how, technical assistance or service be registered with the Technology Transfer Registry. The Registry is responsible for approving and registering foreign agreements through the application of the Transfer of Technology Law. Registration includes the answering of an extensive questionnaire pertaining to:

(a) capital structure of the licensee;

(b) principal products;

(c) income and profits;

(d) relationship of licensor with licensee;

(e) description of license;

(f) projected production and sales; and

(g) royalties.(34)

In order for the Registry to accept and register an agreement, the agreement must be written in Spanish.

2. Length of Contract Term

The maximum permitted length of a contract term is ten (10) years. However, the Registry may limit the contract to a shorter period if it believes ten (10) years are not needed to assimilate the technology.(35)

3. Royalty

There are no formal limitations on royalties. However, the franchise agreement may be rejected on the basis of excessive royalty rates and fees. The excessiveness of rates and fees is determined on a case-by-case basis. it has been reported that royalties in excess of three (3%) per cent of gross income will be considered excessive.(36)

III.   Prohibited Clauses and Practices

A. Andean Pact

The Foreign Investment Code of the Andean Pact countries prohibits certain types of franchising clauses and practices. These prohibitions are often subject to broad, liberal constructions.

1. Tying Practices

Franchise contracts should not require the purchase of materials from specific suppliers; nor can the contract require the permanent employment of specific personnel.(37)

2. Price Fixing

Andean Pact countries are prohibited from authorising clauses in the franchise agreement which allow the franchisor the right to fix sale or resale prices.(38)

3. Restrictions on Volume and Production

Article 20(c) prohibits any restrictions regarding the volume and structure of production. "In practice, the amount of output may be effectively controlled through the way in which performance standards or quality controls are applied."(39)

4. Competitive Technologies

Franchise agreements are not allowed to prohibit the use of other sources of know-how. By the use of an approved supplier program, however, the franchisor may effectively minimise the competitive technology prohibition.

5. Option to Purchase and Grant-Backs

Franchising agreements cannot grant purchase options to the franchisor,(40) nor can franchise agreements require the transfer of improvements of know-how or technology from the franchisee back to the franchisor.(41) "Usually, it is permissible to provide that the user shall inform the supplier of any improvement and give the latter the option

of licensing under terms to be negotiated between
the parties."(42)

6. Patents or Trademarks Not Utilised

If the franchisor is the owner of patents or
trademarks that are not utilised by the Andean
franchisee, then the franchisor is prohibited from
charging a royalty for the unutilised patent or
trademark.(43)

7. Export Restrictions

Generally, Article 25(a) of Decision 24 prohibits
clauses that would limit or deny the franchisee
the right to export or sell. Exceptions have been
allowed, but not on exports to other member
countries.(44)

B. Brazil

1. Tying Practices

Normative Act No. 15 prohibits agreements that
stipulate that materials required for
manufacturing or other materials, machines, or
equipment must be purchased from the franchisor or
any source that the franchisor may determine.(45)

2. Pricing Fixing, Volume and Production

Law 4.137 of September 10 1962 may be violated by
controlling prices, volume or production.(46)
(See 5 below.)

3. Grant-Backs

Unpatented improvements made by the franchisor during the term of the contract must be transferred to the Brazilian party without additional compensation. These improvements will containue to be owned by the franchisee after the contract expires. Improvements made by the Brizilian party also must be transferred to the franchisor.(47)

4. Control by Franchisor

The franchisor is required to exert control over the quality of the products so that such quality will be comparable with the franchisor's standards.(48)

5. Restrictions of Franchisee's Business

No clause can be included which restricts the activities of the franchisee by regulating, determining, altering, or limiting the production, sale, price or publicity of the product.(49)

6. Competition

Provisions requiring the franchisee not to compete either during or after the expiration of a franchise agreement will be objected to under Normative Act No. 15.(50)

7. Territorial Restrictions

The exclusion of certain foreign markets may be accepted by INPI only in the following cases:

(a) when permitted by legislation;

(b) by special legislation in the franchisor's resident country; and

(c) by international act or convention to which Brazil is a member.(51)

8. Local Participation

There is no required local participation. However, an unwritten policy requiring sixty (60%) per cent or more Brazilian voting capital is enforced when:

(a) the Brazilian company seeks subsidised financing from government owned banks; or

(b) the Brazilian company applies for benefits, reductions, or exemptions under Industrial Development Programs administered by special agencies of the Brazilian government.

Management of the Brazilian franchise may be assigned to individuals or companies residing in Brazil or abroad. If the manager is abroad, he must delegate day-to-day administrative powers to a resident of Brazil. The resident manager does not have to be a citizen of Brazil.(52)

C. Chile

Although Chile has withdrawn from the Andean Pact, prohibitions against certain restrictive business practices contained in Article 20 of Decision 24 enacted by the Andean Pact are still imposed by Chile. "For example, some tie-in clauses have been permitted on the theory that Chile must meet international marketing standards to increase her exports."(53)

The Foreign Investment Committee has not issued any guidelines concerning the criteria which will be applied in a franchise arrangement. The Committee is allowed to exercise virtually unrestricted discretion in reviewing all transfer projects. Therefore, even though the Central Bank may impose some of the restrictions of Article 20 of Decision 24, it is not bound by it. Each new proposed franchise agreement will be judged on its own merits.

Chile's decision to encourage foreign investment (which led to its withdrawal from the Andean Pact), is evidenced by the ease of entry into the Chilean market. All that is required is the filing of an application which the Foreign Investment Committee and to qualify as a "fit and reliable" applicant. Approval, in all likelihood, will be granted shortly thereafter.(54)

D. Mexico

The franchise agreement must be approved by the Transfer of Technology Register.

1. Tying Practices

The agreement will not be approved by the Registry when the Franchisee agrees to acquire equipment, supplies or raw materials exclusively from the franchisor or a designee of the franchisor since the Transfer of Technology Law prohibits clauses requiring the franchisee to deal only in products or services supplied or designated by the franchisor.(55)

2. Price Fixing and Restricting of Production

Article 28 of the Mexican Constitution and the Law

of Monopolies both prohibit any agreement permitting one or more persons to impose prices for goods or services. The Transfer of Technology Law prohibits clauses which impose prices at which the franchisee must sell its products.(56) The Law of Monopolies can also be interpreted as prohibiting any clause that gives the franchisor the right to limit production.

3. Grant-Backs

Clauses are prohibited that oblige the franchisee to grant to the franchisor patents, trademarks, innovations or improvements obtained by the franchisee during the course of the agreement. This type of clause is prohibited even if the franchisor would be required to pay valuable consideration for the grant-back.(57)

An agreement will not be registered if upon the expiration of the franchise arrangement, the franchisee is not permitted to use the technology transferred to it; the lone exception being patents in effect.(58)

4. Export Restrictions

The Transfer of Technology Law forbids clauses which prohibit or limit exports by the franchisee or which require the franchisor's consent before exporting; however, these clauses may be allowed if the franchisor has already granted exclusive rights to the third parties in the importing countries.(59)

5. Competition

An agreement may be rejected if it requires the franchisee to restrict itself to the exclusive operation of the franchised business.(60)

6. Local Participation

The general rule is that a new company may not be organised with more than forty-nine (49%) percent foreign capital. Some industries allow even less foreign investment, and in a few industries foreign investment is totally prohibited.

Foreigners are only allowed to acquire twenty-five (25%) percent of the capital or forty-nine (49%) percent of the fixed assets of already organised companies. As far as management is concerned, the Foreign Investment Law provides that the degree of foreign participation in management may not exceed its participation in the capital.(61)

IV. CONCLUSION

The franchisor who wishes to franchise in the Andean Pact, Brazil, Chile and/or Mexico is confronted with various legislative schemes that can at best be described as confusing. The Andean Pact legislation has discouraged many potential investors; whereas Chile's new Foreign Investment Legislation invites foreign investors. Brazilian and Mexican legislation appears to be a compromise between Andean Pact Legislation and Chilean legislation although when compared to Chile's requirements, Mexican and Brazilian requirements are lengthy and cumbersome.

Although the risks of operating in Latin American countries are many, including the political climate, cultural differences, and taxes to name a few, the Foreign franchisor still stands to make a substantial profit with proper

preparation, persistence, ingenuity, and continual
reassessment of precautions.(62)

FOOTNOTES

1. The Andean Foreign Investment Code was approved by the Andean Common Market Commission on December 31, 1970, and went into effect on June 30, 1971. Foreign investors or franchisors who are not nationals or residents of a member country are subject to the provisions of the Code.

2. Decision 37 amended Articles 3(c), 17, 28, 30, and 35 of Decision 24. Decision 37(a) amended Article 1 of Decision 24

    Decision 84, On the Basis for a Subregional Technological Policy (1974), provides in part:

    Notwithstanding the common criteria which may be established in accordance with that provided in Article 2 of Decision 24, the national entities of the member countries shall evaluate the applications for technology importation on the basis of the following effects, among others:

    (a) Effects on technological development in regard to matters such as the creation of a demand for scientific and technological activities in the subregion, use of local engineering and consulting services and the possible effects derived from the technology incorporated in the project;

    (b) Effects of the technology on employment;

    (c) Contribution to specific development plans of interest to the country or subregion;

    (d) Effects on the balance of payments and income generation; and

(e) Effects on the environment.

Article 8. In the application for approval of technology importation contracts related to investment projects which the entities consider of national interest the applicant shall present to the national entity the information available to said applicant on alternative technical solutions, sources from these could be obtained and the conditions for their negotiation, as well as the reasons justifying the selection made.

Article 9. The national entity may require, in addition to the data indicated in Articles 2 and 19 of Decision 24, that applications for the importation of technology be accompanied by information permitting the identification, in a disaggregated form, of the modular and peripheral technologies encompassed in the importation. Such disaggregation of the technological components will permit, among others, a distinguishing of those elements which must necessarily be obtained abroad and those which can be supplied locally.

Article 10. The national entities responsible for granting the respective authorizations shall orient users on the disaggregations of the technology indicated in the previous Article, when this is necessary. For this purpose, they shall jointly collaborate with the other national entities which are able to co-operate in this effect, and they shall promote the participation of the national research entities.

Article 11. The member countries shall incorporate into the norms, guidelines, criteria for preparation, evaluation, financing, bidding and the execution of studies and projects, clauses which assure the application of the principles relating to the importation of technology established by Decision 24 and this Decision.

Annex

Norms for the Transmittal of Information from the Member Countries to the Junta of Technology Importation.

The contracts for the importation of technology shall be distinguised by the following data:

User (name and activity)

Supplier (Name and nationality)

Relation of affiliation between the user and the supplier, if any

Definition of the technology being transferred and its application

Specification of methods which are the object of the contract: process technology, product technology, trademarks(s), patent(s), technical assistance, operational know-how, training

Form of payment of the royalties (fixed and variable payments, and the base for the variable payments), amount of the fixed sums or periodic payments, and percentage in the case of variable payments.

(transl. in 13 Int'l Leg. Mat's 1478 (1974))

Decision 85 on Industrial Property (1974) provides as follows:

Article 5. Patents shall not be granted for:

c) Pharmaceutical products, medicines, active therapeutic substances, beverages and foods for human, animal or vegetable use,

d) Foreign inventions the patent for which is applied for one year after the date of presentation of the patent application in the first country where applied for. Once the period has lapsed no right deriving from such applications shall be recognised, and

e) Inventions which affect the development of the respective member country of the processes, products or patentability by the governments.

Article 10. The first application for a patent of invention originally presented in any member country shall give the owner the prior right for one year from the date of said application to apply for a patent for the same invention in any other member country.

Article 20. If the definitive examination (of the patent application) was favourable, the patent shall be granted.

If it was unfavourable, it shall be denied, based on an explanatory ruling.

Article 24. When the inventions are of national security interest, or are related to processes, products or groups of products reserved by the government, or when provisions of law so determine, the granting of the patent may be subject to conditions of exploitation. In such case, the administrative act which authorises said patent shall so specify.

Article 29. A patent shall be granted for a maximum term of ten years from the date of administrative issuance. It shall be initially granted for five years and may be renewed provided the owner demonstrates to the competent national office that the patent is being adequately exploited.

Article 30. The owner of a patent shall be required to:

a) Communicate the initiation of exploitation of the patent to the competent national entities within three years from the date of issuance. Failure to provide this communication shall be cause for presuming that exploitation has not been initiated for purposes of granting the obligatory licenses provided in Article 34.

b) register with the competent national office all contracts for the cession, license or other forms of utilisation of the patent by third parties, in any way.

Article 31. Exploitation shall be understood to mean the permanent and stable utilisation of the patented procedures or the production of the product covered by the patent to supply the market with the resulting final product under reasonable conditions of commercialisation, provided that such events occur within the territory of the member country which granted the patent, except for the provisions contained in the sectoral industrial development programs referred to in Articles 33 and 34 of the Cartagena Agreement.

Article 34. After three years from the date of issuance of the patent any person may apply to the competent national office for the granting of an obligatory license to exploit the patent if at the time of application, and lacking a legitimate excuse recognised by said office, one of the following events has occurred:

a) The patented invention has not been exploited in the country;

b) The exploitation of said invention has been suspended for more than one year;

c) The exploitation does not satisfy, under reasonable conditions of quantity, quality or prices, the national market demand; or

d) The owner of the patent has not granted contractual licenses under reasonable conditions such that the licensees may satisfy the national demand under reasonable conditions of quantity, quality and price.

After five years from the date of issuance of the patent the obligatory license may be granted by the competent national office without the necessity of proving the occurrence of one of the events indicated in letters b), c) or d) of this Article.

The obligatory licensee shall pay to the owner of

the patent an adequate compensation.

Article 35. The competent national office may at any time grant a license if applied for by the owner of a patent the exploitation of which necessarily requires the use of another, which must be duly proven before the respective office.

Article 36. The amount of compensation shall be determined by the competent national office after a hearing with the parties. Once the administrative process has been completed the matter may be appealed to the competent jurisdictional entity within thirty working days following notification.

The appeal shall not impede the exploitation nor affect the time periods then running. The presentation of an appeal shall not impede the owner of the patent from receiving, in the meantime, the royalties determined by the office for those elements not subject to the appeal.

Article 39. When patents are of a public health nature or are of interest to national development needs the government of the respective member country may submit the patent to obligatory license at any time, in which case the competent national office shall grant the license so requested.

Article 69. The registration of a trade-mark shall be valid for five years from the date granted may be renewed indefinitely for periods of five years.

Article 70. In order to have the right of renewal

the interested party must demonstrate, before the respective national competent office, that the trademark is being utilized in any member country.

Article 73. The acceptance of the application for the registration of a trademark in a member country shall give a prior right for six months to the applicant to apply for registration in the other member countries.

Article 75. The owner of a trademark may not oppose the importation or presence of goods or products originating in another member country which bear the same trademark. The competent national authorities shall require that the imported products be clearly and sufficiently distinguished by reference to the member country where they were produced.

Article 82. All license contracts must contain provisions which assure the quality of the products or services provided by the licensor.

Article 83. The member countries shall abstain from unilaterally entering into agreements on industrial property with third countries or with international organizations which contravene the provisions of these regulations.

4.   For Venezuelan laws see Decree 746 (11 Derecho de la Integracion, March and July 1975, p. 318.) and Decree 2442 (Gac.of 2,100 Ex.November 15, 1977). See also, John R.Pate, The Andean Common Market, ABA Technology Transfer: Laws and Practice in Latin America (Rev. Ed.) 59, 62 (1980).

5.   Frank E.Nettier, Brazil ABA Technology Transfer: Laws and Practice in Latin America (rev. Ed.) 145, 148 (1980).

     Ato Normativo No.15 of 11 September 1975, Rev. Da Propriedade Industrial No.256 of 16 September 1975.

     Ato Normativo No.30 of January 1978, Rev. Da Propriedade Industrial No.19 of January 1978.

     Ato Normativo No.32 of 5 May 1978, Rev.Da Propriedade Industrial No.394 of 9 May 1978.

6.   Roger C.Wesley Chile, ABA Technology Transfer: Laws and Practice in Latin America (Rev.Ed.) 135, 137 (1980).

7.   Article 10 states: "The Constitution ensures to all the inhabitants of the republic....(ii) Exclusive property in every discovery of production, for such time as the law may concede.   If the law required its expropriation, the author or investor shall be given suitable indemnification." See id at 140. See also. Constitution of the Republic of Chile (1925), as amended, in III. A. Blaustean and G. Flanz, Constitutions of the Countries of the World (Oceana, 1977).   Decree Law 58 specifies what is patentable.

8.   Alan L. Hyde and Guston Ramirez De La Corte, Mexico, ABA Technology Transfer: Laws and Practice in Latin America (Rev. Ed.) 1, 5 (1980).

9.   H.Stephen Brown Franchising in the Andean Common Market, ABA Forum Committee on Franchising, Third Annual Forum,2,3 (1980).

10. U.S.Department of Commerce, Overseas Business Reports, "Current Development and Trends in the Andean

Common Market", 12 (February,1978).

11. Article 19(a) of Decision 24.

12. Article 19(a) of Decision 24.

13. Supra note 4, Pate, at 65.

14. Article 19(c) of Decision 24.

15. Supra note 9, at 4.

16. Id. at 5.

17. H.Stephen Brown, Negotiating and Protecting the
     International Royalty, 1 ABA Newsletter on
     Franchising, 5, 8 (Winter 1980).

18. Supra note 9, at 7,8.

19. Irece De Azevedo Marques Trench and Juliano Laura Bruna
     Viegas, Foreign Laws Affecting Franchise Operations
     Brazil, ABA Survey of Foreign Laws and Regulations
     Affecting International Franchising, 6 (1982).

20. Id. at 30.

21. Id. at 20-22.

22. Supra note 5 at 162.

23. Id. at 163.

24. Id.

25. Id. at 164,165.

26. Normative Act No.15, <u>supra</u> note 5, at 1-4.2(h).

27. <u>Id.</u> at I-3.1.1. See also, Profit Remittance Law, No.4,131 of 3 September 1962, amended by Law No. 4390 of 29 August 1964, at Art.II.

28. <u>Supra</u> note 6 at 136 .

29. Decree-Law No.600 of March 18, 1977, art.17.

30. <u>Supra</u> note 6 at 138.

31. <u>Id.</u>

32. <u>Id.</u> at 141.

33. <u>Id.</u> at 142.

34. Alexander C. Hoagland, Jr., <u>Foreign Laws Affecting Franchise Operations-Mexico,</u> ABA Survey of Foreign Laws and Regulations Affecting International Franchising,7,(1982).

35. <u>Id.</u> at 8.

36. <u>Id.</u>

37. Article 20(a) of Decision 24.

38. Article 20(b) of Decision 24.

39. <u>Supra</u> note 4, Pate, at 93

40. Article 20(e) of Decision 24.

41. Article 20(f) of Decision 24.

42. Supra note 4, Pate, at 94.

43. Article 20(g) of Decision 24.

44. Supra note 4, Pate, at 95.

45. Supra note 5, Normative Act No. 15,I-2.5.2.(b)(ii).

46. Law 4.137 is also known as Brazil's Anti-Trust Law.
     This law regulates the abuse of economic power. Forms
     of abuse of economic power are defined by the law:

     1.   Actions that dominate domestic markets or
          obliterate competition........;

     2.   the increasing of prices without cause.......,with
          the purpose of increasing profits without
          increasing production;

     3.   to provoke monopolistic conditions.......;

     4.   to form economic groups, by aggregations of
          companies, which may be detrimental to buyers or
          sellers, by means of certain specific actions;

     5.   to make unfair competition......;
          See supra note 19 at 36-37.

47. Supra note 19 at 33.

48. Id. at 32.

49. Id. at 33.

50. Id. at 39.

51. Id. at 35-36.

52. Id. at 14.

53. Supra note 6 at 137.

54. Peter C.O.Schliesser, Outline of Laws Affecting New Foreign Investment Under Decision 24 in Colombia, Peru and Venezuela, and the Chilean Foreign Investment Statute, ABA Current Legal Aspects of Doing Business in Latin America, 10 (1981).

55. Supra note 34 at 9,11.

56. Id. at 10-11.

57. Id. at 9.

58. Id.

59. Id. at 11.

60. Id. at 9.

61. Id. at 5.

62. Supra note 17.

INTERNATIONAL FRANCHISING — AN OVERVIEW
M. Mendelsohn (editor)
© Elsevier Science Publishers B.V. (North-Holland), 1984

CHAPTER 7

FOCUS ON FRANCHISING IN THE ASIA/PACIFIC REGION
JOINT VENTURES, REGULATION OF INVESTMENT, TAX
David R. Shannon *

INTRODUCTION

There are over thirty different countries in the
Asia/Pacific region. This paper refers only to the 12 that
are most important in economic terms. It takes the
perspective of an international franchisor looking at the
broad structuring of franchising operations in the region,
with particular attention to joint ventures, foreign
investment regulation and tax.

1. Economic Priorities in Asia/Pacific Countries

The opportunities for franchising in the Asia/Pacific
region vary greatly from one country to another. The
degree of economic diversity can be seen from the
following table:-

---

* Material for this paper was compiled in collaboration with
various Baker & McKenzie lawyers from the Asia/Pacific
region - in particular Michael Ahrens (Australia), Charles
Conroy (China), James Rider and Mark Goetze (Singapore,
Indonesia and Malaysia), Tim Woodhouse (New Zealand),
Shinichi Saito and Kiyoshi Odaka (Japan), Leo Dominguez
(Philippines), Jennifer Lin (Taiwan) and Suchint
Chaimungkalanont (Thailand).

Country	Population (millions)	GNP (US$ billions)	Per capita income US$
Australia	15	153	8658
China	1008	260	229
Hong Kong	6	24	4600
Indonesia	151	84	520
Japan	119	860	8999
South Korea	41	63	1636
Malaysia	15	26	1797
New Zealand	3	17	5540
Philippines	53	11	815
Singapore	2	12	4071
Taiwan	18	46	2360
Thailand	50	39	816

Source: Far Eastern Economic Review
Asia 1983 Yearbook

All countries in the region seek to encourage the importation of technology and expertise on favourable terms. Some countries -generally those that are less developed -draw the distinction between "real" technology and the marketing expertise that is a major part of many franchise systems. This policy differentiation is most neatly illustrated in the Philippines, where the Technology Transfer Board (TTB) imposes different royalty rate ceilings depending on the kind of technology involved and the use to which it will be put. Technology licenses which are considered "highly meritorious" (particularly those which license sophisticated technology not locally available to produce essential commodities and capital goods or which promote exports or provide significant employment) may be allowed a royalty rate of up to 5% of net sales. Licenses for other approved industrial projects are generally allowed a royalty rate of up to

3%. However, for franchise and trade mark agreements, the royalty rate is limited to 1% of net sales.

Similar discrimination against franchising is found in different forms throughout the Asia/Pacific region. It is most acute in developing countries, where the main concern in this respect is to ensure that scarce foreign exchange is spent on the areas of greatest economic need. Mere trade mark rights are not given high economic priority. Where the choice is between spending a dollar on acquiring advanced industrial technology on the one hand, or acquiring the right to put a famous trade mark on a bottle of perfume, the trade mark right is unlikely to be preferred.

In several countries, full service franchise agreements are treated as though they were mere trade mark licenses. This is particularly the case where the technology involved does not appear likely to make a significant economic contribution to the country. New ways of frying chicken or selling donuts are not considered to be of high economic priority by comparison with the expertise for improving farm output, steel-making and the production of computers.

Such ranking is superficially sensible. The development of high technology industries does seem more important than the service and marketing concepts of franchising. Most government economic planners and academic economists throughout the world seem to be in agreement on this point. Yet despite such overwhelming consensus, it must be said that it is only half of the truth. It is true that technology is important. It is also true that trademarks and marketing concepts have a very important role to play in promoting economic growth. There is little point in debating whether technology should be ranked higher than marketing. It is clearly necessary to have both.

In 1979 the Secretariat of the United Nations
Conference on Trade and Development (UNCTAD) published
a paper titled "The Role of Trade Marks in Developing
Countries". This paper views trade marks as
instruments of exploitation. It asserts that trade
marks contribute little in the way of net benefits to
society. It claims trade marks cause prices to
increase without a corresponding increase in quality.
It states that persuasive advertising leads to a
misallocation of resources. it is particularly
critical of foreign-owned trade marks, because of the
role they play in building a larger share of the local
market for the foreigner, ultimately leading to an
adverse effect on balance of payments and the
distortion of consumption patterns away from "basic
needs" to the sophisticated preference of affluent
foreigners.

In free enterprise societies, the persuasive power of
advertising and other marketing techniques is the
engine of economic growth. This engine would not be
effective without trademarks. Yet nowhere in the
UNCITAD paper is there any recognition of the crucial
role of trademarks in promoting economic growth.

Whether they express their economic priorities in terms
of specific industrial sectors and numerical targets,
or in more general terms, there is one thing that all
the countries of the Asia/Pacific region have in
common. They have a single-minded dedication to
economic growth. Leaving aside Australia and New
Sealand, the major economies in the region have
achieved outstanding growth rates in recent years, and
are determined to keep on growing.

Franchising is essentially a rapid-growth technique. It has the added attraction of disseminating business expertise more widely than would a wholly-owned operation, and it maximises the opportunities for local equity participation. All of these characteristics are entirely compatible with the economic aspirations of the region.

Economic planners in the Asia/Pacific region are for the most part pragmatic. Rarely does political or economic ideology stand in the way of a practical idea for growth and expansion. So far the region has prospered by concentrating on the supply side -the line of thought being that if only we produce rice and steel and watches and computer parts of better quality and at a lower price, somebody will want to buy them. Hopefully it will be somebody in another country, providing foreign exchange through export earnings. Little thought has been given to the fact that one man's export is another man's import, and that in a game where everybody wants to export more than they import there must be as many losers as there are winners. And very little emphasis has been given to the marketing concept and the developent of strong brand franchises. The idea of promoting growth by stimulating domestic demand is still in the early stages of being adopted in most Asian countries. The large advertisers in the region are mainly American, Japanese and European-based multi-national corporations.

Too often the domestic market is viewed as a cake of constant size, with any shares obtained by a foreign franchise system resulting in less for local people. This view is seldom valid. New methods of advertising, marketing and distribution have gone hand in hand with new production techniques to create national wealth in every advanced industrial country. Franchising not only gains market share, but also promotes economic growth.

However clear this may be to a true believer, the task of demonstrating it conclusively to a government economist is never easy. Technology will always seem more important than trademarks. Yet advances in the efficiency and quality of production are worthless unless accompanied by corresponding growth in demand and distribution capacity. To be finally accepted in the region, franchising must demonstrate the contribution it is able to make across the full spectrum in production, distribution and demand stimulation. Such demonstration must occur in the context of economic growth within domestic markets, because an incoming franchise will rarely produce exports.

2. Laws Regulating Foreign Investment

With the exception of Hong Kong, all major countries in the region regulate foreign investment. The mechanism for regulation is typically a requirement that foreign investment proposals be submitted to a central government agency for approval. Most countries also have an exchange control system, requiring approval for the importation and repatriation of capital, and for the payment of dividends and royalties.

A foreign franchisor has a choice of three basic structures in a foreign country. It can set up an arms-length franchise arrangement with an unrelated domestic entity; it can set up a joint venture with a local partner, or it can franchise through a wholly-owned subsidiary within the country. Which of these basic structures is most desirable in commercial terms varies with the particular facts of each situation. However, as a matter of general impression it seems that most full-service franchisors prefer a joint venture or a subsidiary operation to an arms length agreement. This preference runs contrary to the direction favoured by foreign investment policy. In most countries it is easier to obtain approval for an arms-length franchise than for a joint-venture participation, and easier to obtain approval for a joint venture controlled by residents of the country concerned than for a wholly-owned subsidiary operation.

Arms-length franchising is in fact an ideal way to comply with foreign investment guidelines in most countries, becuase it leaves ownership and control of the business solely in the hands of local residents. The only area of concern to Asia/Pacific governments in respect of this structure is the royalty rate.

The regulation of foreign investment and exchange control in each of the major countries may be briefly summarised as follows:

Australia - Exchange Control approval is required for all contracts and transactions between a resident and a non-resident (other than for the sale of goods). Exchange control approval can be expected as a matter of simple formality. Most new franchising proposals will not require approval from the Foreign Investment Review Board. It is open to a foreign franchisor to operate through a wholly-owned subsidiary in Australia, and most foreign franchisors in fact operate in this way. The preference for a subsidiary rather than a branch is usually based on factors of administrative convenience. One advantage of using a subsidiary for Australian sub-franchising is that Exchange Control screening does not extend beyond the initial head license from the parent to the subsidiary.

China - carefully regulates foreign investment. China has recently developed detailed laws and regulations regarding the establishment of joint ventures, controls of foreign exchange and the taxation of joint ventures and royalties. The preferred ways of operating in China are through joint ventures, both of the equity and contractual type, and through an arms length franchise agreement. The use of a wholly owned subsidiary is effectively precluded. As with other areas, the trademark system in Chila has developed significantly in the past few years and the Chinese recognise the need to offer protection to foreign owners of the trademarks. It is necessary to obtain prior approval from the foreign exchange control authorities for the remittance of royalties, dividends and capital. This is generally not a problem for an approved joint venture or franchise.

Indonesia - does not impose exchange controls, but it does have tough foreign investment laws. It is not possible for a foreign franchisor to operate through a wholly-owned subsidiary. Joint venture operations are only permitted in relation to business sectors on the government's priority list. This does not include the majority of franchisable businesses, and in practice the only option open is an arms-length franchise to an Indonesia resident.

Japan - has both exchange control and foreign investment regulation. Prior notification to relevant ministries through the Bank of Japan is required to set up a branch, subsidiary or joint venture operation. Franchises which fall under the category of "technical introduction contracts" and which are not specifically exempted are also subject to the prior notification requirement. Most franchise proposals are likely to pass the prescribed waiting period without any directive of amendment from the government. There is no legal reason to prefer a joint venture over alternative structures, but most successful foreign franchise operations in Japan are structured either as arms-length franchises or as joint ventures. There is no difficulty in remitting dividends, royalties or capital. Exchange control approval is not normally required.

South Korea - has both exchange control and foreign investment regulation. Foreign franchising is not encouraged. Operation in Korea through a branch or subsidiary is most unlikely to be approved. Operation through a joint venture in which Korean interests hold at least 50% is in theory possible, although restrictions placed on the terms of the franchise to the joint venture entity are likely to make it unattractive. A franchisor seeking to deal at arms length with a South Korean franchisee would face a series of difficulties, both in obtaining acceptable terms and in effective protection of franchised rights during the course of the relationship.

Malaysia - has both exchange control and foreign investment regulation. Operation through a branch or wholly owned subsidiary is effectively precluded, but operation through a joint venture or on an arms-length franchise basis is permitted. In practice dividends, royalties and capital may be freely remitted abroad. In the manufacturing sector, licence agreements must be approved by a government department. The government normally seeks to limit royalties to 2-3% of sales. Such limitation is not yet applied to franchise agreements, but it may be so applied in future as part

of a more generalised system of regulating licence
agreements.

New Zealand - has both exchange control and foreign
investment regulation. Although there is no legal
requirement to conduct franchise operations in the form
of a joint venture rather than as a branch or
subsidiary, the joint venture approach is encouraged by
the Overseas Investment Commission. The required
O.I.C. approval is more easily obtained in the industry
sectors where franchising is likely to occur if the
proposal is structured to give New Zealand ownership
and control. Once initial exchange control approval is
obtained there is no difficulty in repatriating
dividends, royalties and capital. The New Zealand
Reserve Bank is generally more critical as to the
percentage royalty it will allow than is its
counterpart in Australia. However, royalty payments up
to 10% of gross sales have been allowed in appropriate
circumstances.

The Philippines - has both exchange control and foreign
investment regulation. There are three levels of local
participation requirements. Most franchising activity
occurs at the highest level, made up of those
industries where foreign investment is permissable but
not encouraged. In this group, the local participation
requirement is 70%. Effectively, a foreign franchisor
may operate with a 30% joint venture interest, or
through an arms-length franchise. The maximum royalty
rate generally allowed on franchise and trade mark
agreements is 1% of net sales. However, in cases where
the franchisee is allowed to export the licenced
products, a bonus royalty of 2% of net foreign exchange
earnings is allowed. Repatriation of dividends and
royalties pursuant to approved contracts is freely
permitted. Capital repatriation may only be made in

installments. Technology licenses are required to be governed by Philippine law. They must not provide for a fixed term in excess of 5 years. Renewal beyond 5 years requires TTB approval, and generally the TTB endeavours to reduce the royalty rate on renewal.

Singapore - has no exchange control, and in most industry sectors there is no legal requirement to obtain government approval for foreign investment. Retailing is one of the few sectors where approval is required, and many franchise operations are required to obtain approval because they involve retailing. This requirement applies only where the foreign franchisor is investing in Singapore. No approval is required for mere licensing. The relevant authority is the Ministry of Trade and Industry (Domestic Trade Section). The Singapore government expects foreign companies to pass on relevant skills to Singapore residents, and expatriate work permits are often restricted to ensure that this occurs.

Taiwan - has strict exchange control and foreign investment regulation. For a branch or subsidiary to secure the right to repatriate profits and capital, it is necessary to obtain Foreign Investment Approval ("FIA") status. This is unlikely to be granted for most franchising activities, with the result that in practice a foreign franchisor must operate through a minority joint venture interest or through an arms-length franchise. In order to obtain exchange control approval for repatriation of royalties, the franchise agreement must be approved under the Statute for Technical Co-operation. This approval is unlikely to be granted for a franchise agreement if the royalty fee is greater than 5% of net sales. A franchise agreement is unlikely to be approved for a term in excess of five years.

Thailand - has both exchange control and foreign
investment regulation.   Business activities are
classified into three categories.   Most franchising
activity falls into categories A or B, and as such is
unlikely to be approved for majority foreign ownership.
Effectively a non-U.S. foreign franchisor must operate
either through a Thai controlled joint venture or on
the basis of an arms-length franchise.   United States
franchisors are exempt from Alien Business Control Law
restrictions by virtue of the Thai-U.S.   Friendship
Treaty.   The process of remitting royalties to a
foreign franchisor is generally straightforward,
although sometimes difficulties may be encountered in
obtaining approval for royalty payments in respect of
activities which are considered not beneficial to the
Thai economy.   Fast food is one such activity.   There
is no official limitation on the royalty rate, and 6-8%
is considered reasonable.

In jurisdictions which impose limits on foreign equity
participation and franchise fees, it may be possible to
obtain a relaxation of the constraints by justifying
the franchise in terms of the economic objectives of
the country concerned.   Although the objectives vary in
detail from country to country, they usually include
the introduction of new technology and skills, the
promotion of exports, the promotion of tourism, the
development of remote or decentralised regions, and the
utilisation of local resources or components.
Sometimes it is feasible to structure a franchise
operation so that it makes a significant contribution
to one or more of these objectives.   For example, a
fast food franchise might entail the development of a
particular grade of meat or vegetable, and the
franchisor might undertake to contribute the necessary
technology.   This might facilitate not only local
purchasing by the franchise system, but export as well.

Some franchise systems may be justified in terms of increasing foreign currency earnings from tourism. Precisely how the submissions are framed will depend on the facts and circumstances of each case, but with a little flexibility and imagination it is sometimes surprising how strong a case can be made for relaxing the constraints.

3.   Joint Ventures

The imperatives for operating as a joint venture fall into two broad categories.

Firstly, a strong joing venture partner can be invaluable in negotiating political and bureaucratic obstacles, particularly in jurisdictions where the language, culture and legal system are very different to anything with which the franchisor is familiar. This imperative applies throughout the region. Even in Hong Kong, with no restrictions on foreign investment and a familar British legal system, a strong local partner understanding the local market and its largely Chinese population can mean the difference beteen success or failure.

The second imperative for operating as a joint venture is that a branch or wholly-owned subsidiary operation is not permitted, and a local equity interest may be required as a precondition of obtaining government approval.   The jurisdictions where such requirements apply are mentioned in section 2 above.   As well as direct legal requirements for local equity, several jurisdictions in the region have a policy of restricting expatriate visas, leaving the franchisor with a choice of either managing indiginous staff at a distance of thousands of miles, or relying on a joint venture partner.

Joint ventures at best have the advantage of spreading the risk, importing local-market expertise and ensuring that local management has a real interest in efficient, profitable and high quality performance. At worst, they become a burden of deadlocked decision-making and mutual discontent. This difference between success or failure is usually a matter of picking the right partner.

The most important contribution a lawyer is able to make to the success of a joint venture is to ensure that the potential areas of future discord are discussed fully before the agreement is signed, and if possible incorporated expressly in the document. The key elements of any joint venure agreement are capitalisation, voting, future funding, appointment and control of staff, selection and appointment of franchisees, access to records, quality control, term, termination and rights on termination. The right to retain all rights in the franchised trademark upon termination of the venture is of critical importance.

Where the joint venture vehicle is a corporation, there will usually be three inter-related documents to prepare - the joint venture agreement, a franchise agreement and the constitution of the company. It is sometimes possible to negotiate additional minority protection provisions in the constitutional document - for example, the franchisor may be given special voting rights in relation to defined issues concerning quality control and protection of the trademark.

Where rights are equal between the parties, joint ventures are in theory highly unstable. Where the franchisor has a minority position, it is usually impossible to incorporate into the document the degree of protection enjoyed by the majority interest. Yet even in the absence of ideal contractual protection, many joint ventures in the region appear to work very well indeed. A note of caution should be added to this; it is only the successful ventures that survive to be visible, and any lawyer experienced in this area of practice will have stories of acrimonious failures as well as success.

4. Tax Planning

From the perspective of the franchisor, the key questions in relation to franchising in a foreign jurisdiction may be formulated as follows:-

(a) If the operation is conducted through a branch, subsidiary, or joint venture company what income or profits tax will be applicable?

(b) What tax is applicable to dividends paid by a subsidiary or joint venture company?

(c) Where capital is contributed by way of a loan to a branch, subsidiary or joint venture, what tax is applicable to interest payments?

(d) What tax is applicable to royalty payments made to the foreign franchisor?

(e) Are royalty payments deductible by the franchisee?

(f) Are there opportunities to take out training or management fees on a tax-free basis?

(g) Are there opportunities for taking receipts in a lowtax jurisdiction such as Hong Kong?

(h) To what extent can foreign taxes be taken as credits against tax in the home jurisdiction?

(i) Where the franchise system involves the sale of goods, to what extent are there opportunities for reducing overall tax exposure through adjustments to transfer prices?

(j) What tax will be imposed on expatriate executives in the foreign jurisdiction?

The answers to these questions will vary depending on the countries concerned, whether or not tax treaties are applicable, the overall position of the franchisor in relation to foreign tax credits, and the particular operation of the franchise system. Although a full multi-jurisdictional tax treatise is far beyong the scope of this paper, the following table proves a broad idea of the tax position in the region.

Jurisdiction	Tax on Subsidiary or joint venture company (%)	Tax on branch (%)	Withholding tax on dividend paid to USA franchisor (%)	Withholding tax on royalty paid to USA franchisor (%)
Australia	46	51	15	*
China	33	44	10	10
Hong Kong	16.5	16.5	0	1.65
Indonesia	20-45**	10-45**	20	20
Japan	55	55	10	10
S. Korea	40	40	10.75	10.75
Malaysia	50	50	0	15
N. Zealand	45	50	30	15
Philippines	35	35	20	25
Singapore	40	40	0	40***

Taiwan	35	35	35	20
Thailand	40	40	20	25

* In Australia royalties paid to the USA are taxed as Australian source income at the rate of 51% calculated on the net royalty after deducting attributable expenses. The new USA-Australia tax treaty is expected to be ratified in October. It will impose a withholding tax ceiling of 10% of gross royalties.

** Indonesia imposes tax on a graduated rate scale. For an audited company with profits of less than Rp100m p.a., (approx. US$100,000) the rate is 20%. Between Rp100m and 250m the rate is 30%. Above Rp250m the rate is 45%.

*** The 40% Singapore withholding tax on royalties is not a final tax, and a reduction in the effective rate is possible if the franchisor is willing to submit accounts and provide evidence of deductions allowable against the royalty income.

This table provides a rough guide only - the rates of tax applicable may vary in certain circumstances. For example, several jurisdictions impose lower withholding taxes where the foreign investment is in an economic sector promoted by the government. Some jurisdictions vary the withholding tax depending on the degree of equity participation by the franchisor in the franchisee.

The region provides two ideal jurisdictions in which to locate a franchisor. A franchisor based in Hong Kong may be structured so that no Hong Kong tax is payable in respect of franchise fees received from other countries. A franchisor set up as a non-resident Singapore company will not be subject to Singapore tax on foreign source franchise fees provided the fees are not remitted to Singapore. A corporate franchisor caught in a sophisticated and far-reaching tax net such as that cast by the IRS in the United States may not be able to take full advantage of thes jurisdictions. Others may be more fortunately situated.

The U.S. Federal income tax consequences of a U.S. company establishing a foreign (non-U.S.) subsidiary to licence property in the Asia/Pacific region may be briefly stated as follows:

As an intial matter, the U.S. parent company will have to determine whether it will be required to pay tax on the transfer of licensing rights to any foreign subsidiary that it might use for this purpose.

Once such a transfer has been made (with or without payment of tax), the "subpart F" rules will undoubtedly become an important tax consideration. These rules attempt to restrict the use of a foreign company to shelter foreign sources income from U.S. taxation.

A foreign company will generally not be subject to U.S. Federal income tax on its foreign licensing income. Therefore, a foreign subsidiary, by arranging its affairs properly, can escape all U.S. taxes. However, the U.S. parent, by virtue of its stock ownership of the subsidiary, will be subject to U.S. income tax if the latter company has "subpart F income" (sometimes known as "tainted income").

Generally, a "United States shareholder" will be

subject to tax on its pro rata share of the tainted income of a "CFC". (a "controlled foreign corporation.") For this purpose, a "United States shareholder" includes a corporation formed under U.S. law that owns (or is considered to own by attribution rules) 10 percent or more of the total combined voting power of all voting stock of the foreign company at issue. A CFC is defined as any foreign company in which U.S. shareholders own (or are considered to own) more than 50 percent of the total combined voting power of such company's stock. In this situation, the foreign subsidiary would be a CFC by virtue of its parent's ownership of all (or most) of its stock.

Tainted income includes royalties. Royalties, however, are not considered tainted if they are derived from the active conduct of a trade or business from a non-affiliated person. This exception, however, is narrow. Therefore, it may be of limited usefulness to many companies. Of greater practical application is the "10/70" rule, which allows the parent to escape tax under the subpart F provisions on relatively small amounts of tainted income of its subsidiary. Therefore, in many situations a subsidiary with large amounts of non-tainted income can be used for licensing purposes without adverse U.S. tax consequences.

An analysis of the subpart F rules shows that the U.S. parent could defer U.S. tax on the earnings and profits of the subsidiary indefinitely as long as the latter company has little or no tainted income. When the accumulated earnings and profits of the subsidiary are repatriated (made available to the parent by way of dividend, for example), the parent will be subject to tax on such repatriated funds. In short, the benefit of avoiding tainted income is the ability to defer U.S. Federal income tax liability. Of course, the deferral of tax is itself a great benefit. Furthermore, deferral allows flexibility in the timing of repatriation, which permits the minimisation (or, in some cases, the elimination) of tax liability. For example, funds can be repatriated so as to take the best advantage of the parent's deductions, losses, and credits.

The U.S. tax laws also contain the "foreign personal holding company" rules, which like the subpart F provisions, prevent U.S. taxpayers from using foreign companies to shelter foreign royalty income from U.S. tax. For purposes of this brief summary it is sufficient to note that the U.S. tax rules, such as the subpart F and foreign personal holding company provisions, should be an important consideration for any U.S. company contemplating the use of a foreign subsidiary for licensing purpose.

It is also important to consider any withholding taxes on royalty payments that may apply. The use of a foreign subsidiary entitled to tax treaty benefits could result in substantial savings.

5. Rights and Remedies

Some jurisdictions in the Asia/Pacific region provide rights and remedies equal to any in the world. Australia, Hong Kong and New Zealand are outstanding in this regard -industrial property rights may be registered, protected and enforced by a foreign franchisor or potential franchisor in these jurisdictions without any difficulty whatsoever.

Not all jurisdictions are equally accommodating. The protection of trademarks, patents and copyrights as intellectual property is essentially a western concept which was introduced to the region in the early part of the 20th century. In many jurisdictions this concept has not been a major concern of legal thought and philosophy. Instead, the virtues of learning by imitation have been advocated. The process is one of learning to make a "perfect" imitation of the work of a master before setting out to create something new. Moreover, imitations of foreign goods and services are not seen as being wrong. Do they not bring profits to local businesses, and are they not cheaper and more readily available than genuine foreign products?

Each of the 12 countries referred to in this paper have laws providing for industrial property rights. For the most part these laws are adequate in their terms, and local attorneys are willing and ready to perform registration services for foreign companies. However, it is one thing to be registered in respect of various rights, and quite another to be able to effectively enforce those rights.

Several important issues may arise in relation to enforcement. Are foreign companies not having a place of business in the jurisdiction able to initiate proceedings in the local courts? Can enforcement proceedings be taken by private action, or only through the good offices of the local police? Are there adequate facilities for obtaining "search and sieze" orders, discovery and interrogatories? Do the courts impose serious penalties on those who violate trademarks and similar rights? Can injunctions be obtained to effectively protect confidential information, or to restrain future violation of registered rights. Where effective action depends on the local police force, what can be done to stimulate them into action.

A franchisor seeking to establish and protect rights in an Asian jurisdiction must obtain detailed answers to all of these questions. Elaboration on that detail is beyond the scope of this paper, but a rough guide can be given by looking at the jurisdictions where imitations are on flagrant display. Look-alike imitations of foreign products and trademarks are rarely found in Australia or New Zealand. They are more common in Hong Kong, not so much by virtue of any deficiency in the legal system as through lack of vigilence on the part of foreign trademark owners. Japan was once the world's greatest imitator but now provides effective rights and remedies. Singapore and Malaysia have legal systems based on the British system, but imitations are frequently found, particularly in relation to copyright. Taiwan, Thailand, South Korea and the Philippines still have many imitations, although Taiwan in particular has in the past year taken serious steps to provide more effective remedies. In several instances of counterfeiting reported in Korea in 1982, it was the Korean licensee of the foreign company that was the infringing party.

The Asia/Pacific region projects strong economic growth prospects in the immediate and intermediate future. Opportunities for foreign franchisors in the region are abundant but not easy. McDonalds, 7-Eleven, Pizza Hut, Coca Cola, Pepsi, Denny's, Mr. Donut and many others have already succeeded in difficult jurisdictions.

INTERNATIONAL FRANCHISING – AN OVERVIEW
M. Mendelsohn (editor)
© Elsevier Science Publishers B.V. (North-Holland), 1984

CHAPTER 8

FRANCHISING IN EUROPE - UNITED KINGDOM
Martin Mendelsohn *

1. **TRADITIONAL METHODS**

The traditional methods which have developed in International Franchising are:-

(i) Master Licence : the granting of a licence to a company or person in the target territory granting rights for the whole territory. The licensee will either, operate all outlets under his ownership and control or will sub-franchise within the territory or have a combination of both.

(ii) Direct Licence : the grant by the overseas franchisor of a licence direct to the operational franchisee with the franchisor providing direct back up and support possibly by some sort of presence in the target territory.

(iii) Branch or Subsidiary Operations : the establishment by the franchisor of a direct presence or by setting up a subsidiary to exploit the territory by granting franchises and servicing the Franchisee

---

* The author acknowledges the assistance of his partners Manzoor G.K. Ishani and G. Roland Hayes in the preparation of this paper.

(iv) <u>Joint Venture</u> : the establishment of a joint company or partnership with a company or person in the target territory to which a licence is granted for exploitation of the territory by operating their own outlets or by sub-franchising or a combination of both.

Which method is chosen is a commercial and not a legal decision. However it is significant that in the author's experience it is not the legal aspects which give rise to most difficulties. Most of the difficulties which arise seem to flow from two basic problem areas.

A.   The franchisor is not prepared or able to devote the financial and manpower resources to the venture to a degree which is necessary to ensure success.

B.   The difficulty in finding and selecting the right person which whom to work in the target territory whichever method of doing business is chosen.

2.   **LEGAL BACKGROUND**

(i)   **No Franchise Laws except those affecting Pyramid Sales**

By way of contrast with the USA there are no specific franchise laws in the U.K. The relationship between franchisor and franchisee is regulated by the general law which affects all commercial transactions and the contract is the governing factor. The only legislation which may be said to have any connection with franchising is that which tackles the subject of pyramid selling. The provisions are contained in Part XI of the Fair Trading Act 1973 and apply to what are described as Trading Schemes.

"118. <u>Trading Schemes to which Part XI applies</u>

(1) This Part of this Act applies to any trading scheme which includes the following elements, that is to say:-

(a) goods or services, or both, are to be provided by the person promoting the scheme (in this Part of this Act referred to as "the promotor") or, in the case of a scheme promoted by two or more persons acting in concert (in this Part of this Act referred to as "the promoters"), are to be provided by one or more of those persons;

(b) the goods or services so provided are to be supplied to or for other persons under transactions effected by persons (other than the promoter or any of the promoters) who participate in the scheme (each of whom is in this Part of this Act referred to as a "participant");

(c) those transactions, or most of them, are to be effected elsewhere than at premises at which the promoter or any of the promoters or the participant effecting the transaction carries on business; and

(d) the prospect is held out to participants of receiving payments or other benefits in respect of any one or more of the matters specified in the next following subsections

(2) The matters referred to in paragraph (d) of subsection (1) of this section are:

(a) the introduction of other persons who become participants;

(b) the promotion, transfer or other change of status of participants within the trading scheme;

(c) the supply of goods to other participants:

(d) the supply of training facilities or other services for other participants;

(e) transactions effected by other participants under which goods are to be supplied to, or services are to be supplied for, other persons

(3) For the purposes of this Part of this Act a trading scheme shall be taken to include the element referred to in paragraph (b) of subsection (1) of this section whether the transactions referred to in that paragraph are to be effected by participants in the capacity of servants or agents of the promoter or of one of the promoters or in any other capacity

(4) In determining, for the purposes of paragraph (c) of subsection (1) of this

section, whether any premises are premises at which a participant in a trading scheme carries on business, no account shall be taken of transactions effected or to be effected by him under that trading scheme

(5) For the purpose of this Part of this Act such a prospect as is mentioned in paragraph (d) of subsection (1) of this section shall be taken to be held out to a participant-

(a) whether it is held out so to confer on him a legally enforceable right or not, and

(b) In so far as it relates to the introduction of new participants by him or extends to the introduction of new participants by other persons

(6) In this Part of this Act "trading scheme" includes any arrangements made in connection with the carrying on of a business, whether those arrangements are made or recorded wholly or partly in writing or not

(7) In this section any reference to the provision of goods or services by a person shall be construed as including a reference to the provision of goods or services under arrangements to which that persons is a party".

This section is neither easy to follow or to understand; let us consider its basic features.

1. This part of the Act applies to "any trading scheme".
    Subsection 6 provides a non-exclusive definition of the
    expression "trading scheme" to include "arrangements"
    made in connection with the carrying on of a business
    (1). There are two factors to consider at this stage:

    (a) The expression "scheme" suggests that there is a
         systematic promotion of activities by the
         "promoter" and not isolated transactions which
         have no linking features or pre-planning.
         Something spontaneous and unexpected (e.g.
         gratuitously making a payment to a franchisee for
         introducing a new franchisee) would not be within
         a "scheme"

    (b) The expression "arrangements" is not defined, but
         is clearly intended to be wider than just a
         binding contract particularly in view of Section
         118(5) (a) and by way of contrast the reference in
         S.119 (3)(a) to "an agreement in writing" which
         must in context mean a binding contract. It would
         seem therefore that a "gentlemen's agreement"
         could be an arrangement and that any informal non-
         binding obligations would be included in this
         expression. "Arrangements" must mean that there
         has been some degree of consensus or a common
         purpose or at the very least some advance
         understanding of what each party expects of the
         other

2. Assuming that there is a trading scheme it must include
    all four elements referred to in Section 118(1). It is
    safe to assume that all basic franchise schemes as
    commonly understood would be schemes. The question
    arises whether any particular one would be a trading

scheme to which part XI of the Act applies, i.e. does it include all elements. That apart, as will be seen below, not all trading schemes which are within the definition in S.118 of the Act are necessarily affected by its provisions.

3.   The first element to be satisfied requires that goods (2) or services are to be provided by the promoter (i.e. the person promoting the scheme). Under subsection 7 this includes a reference to the provision of goods or services under arrangements to which that person is a party. This latter provision is obviously an anti-avoidance provision to prevent an informal off-the-record diversion of the goods or services through an apparently arms-length third party. All business format franchise schemes would be within this element with the expression "promoter" meaning the "franchisor".

4.   The second element to be satisfied requires that the goods or services provided by the promoter are to be supplied to or for other persons (3) under transactions effected by participants (i.e. persons other than the promoters who participate in the scheme). This is intended to catch and include recruitment by participants of third parties. The promoter is not a party to these transactions and the other person to whom the supply is made is neither promoter nor participant until the transaction is concluded. The recruiting participant is therefore in reality acting as a conduit pipe through which the goods or services are supplied. Despite the intention to deal with recruitment this element is drafted sufficiently widely to embrace consumer sales by a participant.

5.   The third element relates to the transactions to be effected by the participant who is ascertained in the

second element.   It is aimed at situations in which
such transactions or most of them are intented to be
carried elsewhere than on the promoter's or the
participant's business premises.   When read together
the second and third elements clearly relate to the
aspect of the scheme which is concerned with the
recruitment of participants.   Subsection (4) of the
section provides that transactions effected by a
participant (eg recruitment of other participants or
product sales) are to be ignored in determining whether
or not any premises are premises at which the
participant carries on business.   Indeed sub-section
(4) means that if the only business carried on by a
participant on any premises is transacted under the
trading Scheme they are not premises at which the
participant carries on business.   He must therefore be
carrying on some other business from the premises if
the premises are to be considered as premises at which
he carries on business.

6.   The fourth element deals with the motiviation of the
        participants; the holding out to any participant the
        prospect of receiving financial or other benefits.
        Section 118(5) makes it clear that the expression
        "holding out" includes a non legally enforceable right
        to benefit by payment or otherwise for the introduction
        of "sub-participants" at a lower level in the
        structure.

The matters in respect whereof the prospect of payment or
other benefits must arise are set out in Section 118(2) They
include benefits from introductions of participants, change
of status within the scheme, supply of goods or training
facilities and commission on the sale of products or supply
of services to other persons.

It should be noted that for this element to have effect it

must be a feature of the scheme (although not necessarily a legally enforceable obligation) that the prospect is held out to participants. It would be unusual to find such features in a bona fide franchise scheme. A participant (franchisee) who uninvited introduces a "friend" as a propective franchisee and who is gratuitously paid a "commission" for having done so would not be within this provision (see page 6)

It should also be noted that the provision does not concern itself with the question of who is the payer of the money or promoter or provider of the benefit. it is enough that a payment or benefit is held out as a prospect in respect of one of the matters referred to.

Section 119 of the Act permits the Secretary of State to make regulations by Statutory Instrument with respect to the issue, circulation or distribution of documents in a wide range of guises, namely:- advertisements, prosectuses, circulars or notices. The regulations may prohibit certain practices and the Secretary of State is permitted to impose such requirements as he considers necessary or expedient for the purpose of preventing participants in trading schemes from being unfairly treated. Regulations, which came into force on 15th November 1973, have been made under the section (4)

Before considering the Regulations it should be appreciated that a trading scheme as defined by Section 118 is not objectionable under the statute provided the Regulations (if they apply) are observed. The fact of the matter is that any bona fide business format franchise which is a trading scheme under the Act would not be able to promote sales of Franchises or to exist economically if it had to observe the Regulations.

The Regulations which have been made under the Act apply to

trading schemes as defined in the Act other than a scheme under which the prospect of payments or benefits are held out to only one participant in the United Kingdom or, alternatively, under which the only prospect of benefit is the receipt of a sum not exceeding £10 in respect of the introduction of other participants

The exclusion of one participant is intended to permit licensing of the UK by an overseas Franchisor to a Master Licensee.

The regulations contain a number of restrictions dealing with such matters as

(a) a limit of £25 on the value of goods to be supplied to a participant in a trading scheme

(b) the prohibition of non-returnable deposits

(c) the prohibition of charging for the provision of training or other services to a participant

(d) contents of advertisements and of the issue, circulation or distribution of documents promoting the trading scheme.

The infringement of the Act and/or the Regulations is a criminal offence. The civil consequences are that sums paid and accepted in contravention of the Regulations are recoverable.   No undertaking or liability to pay sums in contravention of the Regulations is enforceable.

The real danger to be avoided is splitting the UK into two or more areas each to be franchised with a view to sub-franchising subsequently being conducted.

(ii) Antitrust Considerations

(A) Restrictive Trade Practices Act 1976

The provisions of the Act apply both to the supply of goods and the provision of services.

We shall deal with each in turn. First, the provision relating to goods is contained in Section 6 of the Act

> "6. Restrictive agreements as to goods
>
> (1) This Act applies to agreements (whenever made) between two or more persons carrying on business within the United Kingdom in the production or supply of goods, or in the application to goods of any process of manufacture, whether with or without other parties, being arrangements under which restrictions are accepted by two or more parties in respect of any of the following matters -
>
> (a) the prices to be charged, quoted or paid for goods supplied, offer or acquired, or for the application of any process of manufacture to goods;
>
> (b) the prices to be recommended or suggested as the prices to be charged or quoted in respect of the resale of goods supplied;
>
> (c) the terms or conditions on or subject to which goods are to be supplied or acquired or any such process is to be applied to goods;

(d) the quantities or descriptions of
goods to be produced, supplied or
acquired;

(e) the processes of manufacture to be
applied to any goods, or the quantities
or descriptions of goods to which any
such process is to be applied; or

(f) the persons or classes of persons
to, for or from whom, or the areas or
places in or from which, goods are to be
supplied or acquired, or any such
process applied."

It is immaterial -

(a) whether any restrictions accepted by
parties to an agreement relate to the
same or different matters specified in
that subsection , or have the same or
different effect in relation to any
matter so specified, and

(b) whether the parties accepting any
restrictions carry on the same class or
different classes of business."

Second, the provision relating to services is contained in
Section 11 which was brought into effect by virtue of
Section 44 and Schedule 4 paragraph 1(1) of the Act which
provide that Restrictive Trade Practices (Services) Order
1976 applies as if made under Section 11.

(1) The Secretary of State may by statutory
instrument make an order in respect of a class
of services described in the order (in this Act

referred to, in relation to an order under this section, as "services brought under control by the order") and direct by the order that this Act shall apply to agreements (whenever made) which :

(a)	are agreements between two or more persons carrying on business within the United Kingdom in the supply of services brought under control by the order, or between two or more such persons together with one or more other parties; and

(b)	are agreements under which restrictions in respect of matters specified in the order for the purposes of this paragraph, are accepted by two or more parties

(2) The matters which may be specified in such an order for the purposes of subsection (1) (b) above are any of the following:

(a)	the charges to be made, quoted or paid for designated services supplied, offered or obtained;

(b)	the terms or conditions on or subject to which designated services are to be supplied or obtained;

(c)	the extent (if any) to which, or the scale (if any) on which, designated services are to be made available, supplied or obtained;

(d)   the form or manner in which designated
       services are to be made available,
       supplied or obtained;

(e)   the persons or classes of persons for
       whom or from whom, or the areas or
       places in or from which, designated
       services are to be made available or
       supplied or are to be obtained

There are a number of requirements to be satisfied in both
cases before the sections take effect

1.   There must be an agreement and it should be noted that
the Court has the power to declare whether an agreement is
one to which the Act applies (5). Agreement is defined (6)
and includes arrangements which need not be enforceable

2.   It (the Agreement) must be made between two or more
persons carrying on business within the United Kingdom in
the production or supply of goods or the application to
goods of any process of manufacture or as the case may be
the supply of services

Two or more individuals carrying on business in partnership
with each other are treated as a single person (7). Whether
or not a person carries on business in the United Kingdom is
a question of fact but representation by an agent in the UK
does not by itself mean that a person is carrying on
business within the UK (8)

3.   Restrictions have to be accepted by two or more parties
in respect of the matters listed. Restriction includes a
negative obligation whether express or implied and whether
absolute or not (9).

In franchising there is no doubt that the franchisee accepts many restrictions in respect of the matters listed. The franchisor usually accepts none. However, there are two ways in which a franchisor commonly invites application of the Act to his agreement:

(i) Where he grants exclusive territorial rights he will be accepting a restriction under Section 6(1)(f), or as the case may be Section 11(2)(e) (10)

In view of the restrictions which the franchisee inevitably will be accepting this will require the agreement to be registered. In practice very few franchisors grant exclusive territorial rights so as to avoid the need for registration. In commercial terms there is no benefit to a franchisor in encroaching by himself or by appointing another franchisee too close to the operations of the franchisee unless the franchisee fails properly to exploit the business opportunity. It is usually only in the very early stages of the development of the franchise network that this is an issue. In practice many franchise companies who have been unhappy with this consequence of the legal formalities surrounding the formation of the contract and the applicability of the Act have been pleasantly surprised to see how few problems arise in this respect. Additionally, and again in commercial terms supported by experience, it is frequently very difficult to establish in the early stages of the development of the chain what would be an equitable area to grant. Furthermore, if an exclusive area is to be allocated there must be some guarantee to the franchisor that the area will be exploited properly. This would involve establishing minimum sales or performance targets which are as difficult equitably to fix as are territories coupled of course with the difficulty of structuring an escalation of expectation in real market terms allowing for inflation

A further method of approaching this problem, which is used by some, is to grant exclusive rights to the use of the franchisor's name within a defined area. It is argued that this does not come within the list of registrable restrictions. The counter argument is that this is merely another method of imposing the restrictions contained in Sections 6(1)(f) or 11(2)(e) in that the franchisor will not, using that name, either by himself or by appointing a franchisee into that territory be selling goods or supplying services under the established name. If the franchisor were to suppose that since he was free to trade within the territory using any other name and was thus restriction free he would in effect be competing with his own franchise chain. One would question the ethics of such behaviour although for the purposes of the Act it would only be necessary to know that there was no restriction and not actually to set up in business to demonstrate the practical capability

A Foreign franchisor who does not carry on business within the U.K. who enters into a contract with not more than one person who does carry on business in the U.K. will not be affected by this provision.

(ii) Where the principal shareholder and/or director of the franchisee (being a company) is required to enter into the agreement not only to guarantee the franchisee's performance of the contract but also to preserve the trade secrets etc of the franchisor

What one has is a three party contract; Franchisor (1), Franchisee (2) and Guarantor (3) (Director/Shareholder

Assuming the franchisor and the franchisee both carry on business within the UK as provided in the appropriate section the first trigger has been squeezed. The next point to consider is whether two or more parties have accepted relevant restrictions. Again assume the franchisor has not accepted any restrictions, if the franchisee has accepted the usual spread of restrictions one has to consider whether the covenant by the Guarantor amounts to the acceptance of a restriction within the framework of the relevant section.

If the covenant is so framed that the Guarantor is prevented from making use of the know-how trade secrets and confidential information acquired by him as director and/or shareholder in the franchise company there is no restriction accepted by him.

The basic reason is that the Guarantor is not granted any rights under the franchise agreement entitling him to operate the franchise system or use any of the property rights associated therewith including know-how and trade secrets etc. On the other hand by virtue of his position he has acquired knowledge of the franchisor's system, methods, know-how and trade secrets. He is not accepting any restrictions under the relevant provisions in the Act by covenanting not to use or disclose such information since it was never his of which to make use and nor has he ever been licensed to use it for his personal benefit.(10a)

There could be a tripartite agreement with two parties accepting restrictions which does not come under the Act. If the franchisor is a foreign company which does not carry on business within the the UK - a franchisee who does - and the Principal who is an employee or officer of the franchisee but who does not carry on business within the UK. In such a case the franchisee and Principal could accept otherwise registerable

restrictions without the Act applying. The danger in
such an arrangement is that if either the franchisor or
the Principal subsequently carry on business in the UK
in the production or supply of goods or the provision
of services, the Act could then apply

There are also some excepted agreements (11). These
are set out in Schedule 3 to the Act (as amended by the
Competition Act 1980) (12). They cover such matters
as:

- Exclusive Dealing
- Trade Marks
- Patents and registered Designs
- Exclusive Supply of Services
- Know-how about services
- Copyright

Agreements which deal with such matters are excepted
from registration in the limited circumstances
specified in the Act which are unlikely to be of any
value in formulating a franchise agreement

Having made the decision whether or not to become
involved in a registrable agreement the consequences of
registration must be considered. Basically, as has
been explained, the restrictions must be modified or
abandoned or be so insignificant that the Director
advises the Secretary of State that they should not be
put before the Court. If one does not agree to modify
or abandon the restrictions and they are not considered
insignificant then a reference is made to the Court
which has to be satisfied that the case comes within
one of the tests laid down in Section 10 (in respect of
goods) or section 19 (in respect of services)

It is convenient to set out section 19 (as amended by

Competition Act 1980)(13) as services predominate in franchising:

"19. Presumption under Part III as to the public interest

(1) For the purpose of any proceedings before the Court under Part I of this Act, a restriction accepted or informed information provision made in pursuance of an agreement to which this Act applies by virtue of this Part shall be deemed to be contrary to the public interest unless the Court is satisfied of any one or more of the following circumstances -

(a) that the restriction or information provision is reasonably necessary having regard to the character of the services to which it applies, to protect the public against injury (whether to persons or to premises) in connection with the use of those services or in connection with the consumption, installation or use of goods in relation to which those services are supplied;

(b) that the removal of the restriction or information provision would deny to the public as users of any services, or as vendors purchasers, consumers or users of any goods or other property in relation to which any services are supplied, other specific and substantial benefits or advantages enjoyed or likely to be enjoyed by them as such, whether by virtue of the restriction or information provision itself or of any arrangements or operations resulting therefrom;

(c) that the restriction or information provision is reasonably necessary to counteract measures taken by any one person not party to the agreement with a view to preventing or restricting competition in or in relation to the trade or business in which the persons party thereto are engaged;

(d) that the restriction or information provision is reasonably necessary to enable the persons party to the agreement to negotiate fair terms for the supply of services to, or for obtaining services from, any one person not party thereto who controls a preponderant part of the trade or business of supplying such services, or for the supply of services to any person not party to the agreement and not carrying on such a trade or business who, either alone or in combination with any other such person, controls a preponderant part of the market for such services;

(e) that, having regard to the conditions actually obtaining or reasonably foreseen at the time of the application, the removal of the restriction or information provision would be likely to have a serious and

persistent adverse effect in the general
level of unemployment in an area, or in
areas taken together, in which a
substantial proportion of the trade or
industry to which the agreement relates
is situated;

(f) that, having regard to the
conditions actually obtaining or
reasonably foreseen at the time of the
application, the removal of the
restriction or information provision
would be likely to cause a reduction in
the volume or earnings of the export
business which is substantial either in
relation to the whole export business of
the United Kingdom or in relation to the
whole business (including export
business) of the said trade or
industry;

(g) that the restriction or information
provision is reasonably required for
purposes connected with the maintenance
of any other restriction accepted or
information provision made by the
parties, whether under the same
agreement or under any other agreement
between them, being a restriction or
information provision which is found by
the Court not to be contrary to the
public interest upon grounds other than
those specified in this paragraph, or
has been so found in previous
proceedings before the Court; or

(h) that the restriction or information

provision does not directly or indirectly restrict or discourage competition to any material degree in any relevant trade or industry and is not likely to do so;

and is further satisfied (in any such case) that the restriction or information provision is not unreasonable having regard to the balance between those circumstances and any detriment to the public or to persons not parties to the agreement (being users of services supplied by such parties, or persons engaged or seeking to become engaged in any business of supplying such services or of making available or supplying similar services, or being vendors purchasers, consumers or users of goods or other property in relation to which any such services or similar services are supplied) resulting or likely to result from the operation of the restriction or information provision

(2)   In this section -

(a) "vendors", "purchasers", "customers" and "users" include persons selling purchasing, consuming or using for the purpose or in the course of trade or business or for public purposes; and

(b) references to any one person include references to any two or more persons being interconnected bodies corporate or

individuals carrying on business in
partnership with each other"

The provisions of Section 10 are similar save for its
applicability to goods rather than services

It will be seen from the wide ranging nature of this
section that if and when a franchise agreement is
referred to the Court the whole business practice of
franchising is likely to be on trial, not merely the
particular restrictions contained in the referred
agreement. It is also significant for both franchisor
and franchisee that the tests to be satisfied pay no
heed to what is in their respective interests. Indeed
restrictions could be removed from an agreement which
destroy the whole fabric of the franchise scheme and
leave the franchisor without control over substantial
areas of the system

The risk of being involved in the heavy expenditure
which would be incurred in a reference to the Court
with the uncertainty of its outcome does not, in the
authors' view, justify the use of a registrable
agreement. In addition there are of course the
unfortunate consequences which could follow an
accidental omission to register any particular
agreement. With a fast growing franchise chain it
would of course be quite easy for this to happen by
simple clerical error or ommission.

It should also be borne in mind that even if the
agreement is registered and the restrictions considered
to be insignificant at the time of registration, that
does not end the matter. The Secretary of State may,
if requested by the Director, withdraw his direction
under Section 21(2) if there has been a material change
of circumstances (14)

(B) <u>The Competition Act 1980</u>   which came into operation
on 12th August 1980 has the potential to affect
franchise companies. It is concerned with what are
described as anti-competitive practices in the
following terms:-

> "A person engages in an anti-competitive
> practice if, in the course of business,
> that person pursues a course of conduct
> which, of itself or when taken together
> with a course of conduct pursued by
> persons associated with him, has or is
> intended to have or is likely to have
> the effect of restricting, distorting or
> preventing competition in connection
> with the production, supply or
> acquisition of goods in the United
> Kingdom or any part of it or the supply
> or securing of services in the United
> Kingdom or any part of it." (15) (the
> word "person" includes a company or
> firm.)

If it appears to the Director that any person has been
or is pursuing an anti-competitive practice he may
investigate the position (16) and publish a report (17)
The Director has the power to seek information and
obtain documents relevant to his investigations (18).
Time is given to allow for negotiations of undertakings
as to future conduct (19) but if no negotations take
place or are not concluded a competition reference may
be made to the Monopolies and Mergers Commission (20).
The Commission investigate and report on whether the
person was engaged in an anti-competitive practice and
if such practice operated or might be expected to
operate against the public interest (21). The public
interest test is the same as that prescribed for

Monopoly references (22) and is expressed in the following way:-

"In determining for any purposes to which this Section applies whether any particular matter operates, or may be expected to operate, against the public interest, the Commission shall take into account all matters which appear to them in the particular circumstances to be relevant and, among other things, shall have regard to the desirability:-

(a) of maintaining and promoting effective competition between persons supplying goods and services in the United Kingdom;

(b) of promoting the interests of consumers, purchasers and other users of goods and services in the United Kingdom in respect of the prices charged for them and in respect of their quality and the variety of goods and services supplied;

(c) of promoting, through competition, the reduction of costs and the development and use of new techniques and new products, and of facilitating the entry of new competitors into existing markets;

(d) of maintaining and promotion the balanced distribution of industry and employment in the United Kingdom; and

(e) of maintaining and promoting
competitive activity in markets outside
the United Kingdom on the part of
producers of goods, and of suppliers of
goods and services, in the United
Kingdom." (23)

Following the Commission's report there is a procedure
whereby undertakings as to future conduct are sought
(24) but if no agreement can be reached the Secretary
of State may make an order prohibiting the continuation
of the course of conduct which has been held to be
anti-competitive (25).

No exhaustive list of the practices which the Act is
intended to control has been given. However, in a
debate on the Bill in the House of Lords the Government
spokesman indicated the following as being the type of
practices which after considering the degree of market
power a person enjoys could be anti-competitive,
namely:-

supply only to certain classes of trader
tie-in sales
rental only contracts
loyalty rebates
discriminatory pricing
discriminatory discounts
delivered price systems
full-line forcing

Some of these practices will readily be recognised as
familiar features of franchise arrangements so the
scope for investigation of franchise practices is
clear. Five factors are, however, relevant:-

1.   Regulations (26) have been made under the Act

which inter alia exempt companies

(a) with less than £5 million annual turnover in the United Kingdom

(b) who enjoy less than one quarter of a relevant market and

(c) who are not members of a group of interconnected companies which has an aggregate annual turnover in the United Kingdom of £5 million or more or enjoys one quarter or more of a relevant market

This exemption would rule out a large majority of franchise companies

2.   An investigation under the Act is concerned with a practice engaged in by an individual person and not with all those who may be engaged in it or in a similar practice.   There may be differences in the structure of the transaction and the economics of the particular market, which means that what is anti-competitive in one case may not be in another.   Whatever these differences it would seem likely that there will emerge clear indications of the thinking of the Office of Fair Trading, the Secretary of State and the Commission as cases are dealt with.   None of the cases which have so far been dealt with involve franchising or franchise companies or appear to have any specific consquences for franchising.

3.   The present attitude of the Office of Fair Trading appears to be that the members of a franchise chain are not in a competitive or adversary situation inter se. Rather they are analogous to a multiple chain of stores or outlets and competing with others in the market. This should mean that the above practices utilised for

the benefit and strength of the franchise chain and
which strengthen its competitiveness in the market
should be free from complaint under the Act

4.   It seems likely that a person is unlikely to be
able to act anti-competitively unless he enjoys market
power.   This does not mean that he need dominate the
market but that his presence in the market is such that
his behaviour can have the effect stipulated in Section
2.   It is recognised that in some circumstances
practices which would be anti-competitive may be pro-
competitive, for example when employed by a small firm
fighting for entry to a market

5.   The views already expressed by the Monopolies and
Merges Commission in its report on Full Line Forcing
and Tied Sales (27) that in relation to franchising it
did not consider that the public interest would be an
issue.

(C)   The Resale Prices Act 1976 prohibits the enforcement by
suppliers of goods to dealers of any condition
establishing or providing for the establishment of
minimum resale prices to be charged on the resale of
the goods in the United Kingdom

The Act deals with collective action by suppliers or
dealers (28) and individual contractual arrangements
(29)

Sections 1 and 2 set out the prohibitions affecting
collective action by suppliers or dealers

  "1.   Collective agreement by suppliers

  (1) It is unlawful for any two or more
  persons carrying on business in the

United Kingdom as suppliers of any goods to make or carry out any agreement or arrangement by which they undertake -

(a) to withhold supplies of goods for delivery in the United Kingdom from dealers (whether party to the agreement or arrangement or not) who resell or have resold goods in breach of any condition as to the price at which those goods may be resold;

(b) to refuse to supply goods for delivery in the United Kingdom to such dealers except on terms and conditions which are less favourable than those applicable in the case of other dealers carrying on business in similar circumstances; or

(c) to supply goods only to persons who undertake or have undertaking-

(i) to withhold supplies of goods as described in paragraph (a) above; or

(ii) to refuse to supply goods as described in paragraph (b) above

(2) It is unlawful for any two or more such persons to make or carry out any agreement or arrangement authorising -

(a) the recovery of penalties (however described) by or on behalf of the parties to the agreement or arrangement from dealers who resell or have resold goods in breach of any such condition as is described in paragraph (a) of subsection (1) above; or

(b) the conduct of any domestic proceedings in connection therewith."

"2. Collective agreement by dealers

(1) It is unlawful for any two or more persons carrying on business in the United Kingdom as dealers in any goods to make or carry out any agreement or arrangement by which they undertake -

(a) to withhold orders for supplies of goods for delivery in the United Kingdom from suppliers (whether party to the agreement or arrangement or not) -

(i) who supply or have supplied goods otherwise than subject ot such a condition as is described in paragraph (a) of Section 1 above; or

(ii) who refrain or have refrained from taking steps to ensure compliance with such conditions in respect of goods supplied by them; or

(b) to discriminate in their handling of goods against goods supplied by such suppliers

(2) It is unlawful for any two or more such persons to make or carry out any agreement or arrangement authorising -

(a) the recovery of penalties (however described) by or on behalf of the parties to the agreement or arrangement from such suppliers; or

(b) the conduct of any domestic proceedings in connection therewith."

The principal prohibition affecting individual resale price maintenance agreements is contained in Section 9

"9. Minimum resale prices maintained by contract or agreement

(1) Any term or condition -

(a) of a contract for the sale of goods by a supplier to a dealer, or

(b) of any agreement between a supplier and a dealer relating to such a sale

is void in so far as it purports to establish or provide for the establishment of minimum prices to be charged on the resale of the goods in the United Kingdom

(2) It is unlawful for a supplier of goods (or for an association or person acting on behalf of such suppliers) -

(a) to include in a contract for sale or agreement relating to the sale of goods a term or condition which is void by virtue of this section;

(b) to require, as a condition of supplying goods to a dealer, the inclusion in a contract or agreement of any such term or condition, or the giving of any undertaking to the like effect;

(c) to notify to dealers, to otherwise publish on or in relation to any goods, a price stated or calculated to be understood as the minimum price which may be charged on the resale of the goods in the United Kingdom

Paragraph (a) does not affect the enforceability of a control of sale or other agreement, except in respect of the term or condition which is void by virtue of this section

Paragraph (c) is not to be construed as precluding a supplier (or an association or person acting on behalf of a supplier) from notifying to dealers or otherwise publishing prices recommended as appropriate for the resale of goods supplied or to be supplied by the supplier."

Two factors are immediately obvious

1.   The Act is concerned with the prohibitions of MINIMUM resale price conditions. It does not affect MAXIMUM resale price conditions unless there is collusive action by suppliers or dealers

2.   The Act only applies to goods and thus does not

apply to services. A question may arise if the provision of a service includes of necessity the inseverable sale of goods

This point does not appear to have been decided in relation to this Act but the answer may be that it depends on the element of the price which is attributable to the provision of goods compared with that attributable to the provision of the services. (30) If the goods are basically what are being provided with a related service: eg selling a car battery and installing it - then the prohibition would apply. If on the other hand the service is what is being given and the goods incidental: eg cleaning carpets and upholstery in the home and providing the shampoos and cleaning materials - then the prohibition would not apply. These are obviously two extreme examples to illustrate the point and there will be many less clear cases in practice

In many cases a franchisor will not be a supplier of goods. He may nominate suppliers so as to ensure that the quality standards are maintained, but he may have no agreement or arrangement with the supplier as to resale prices or indeed any conditions subject to which the goods are sold. He may have negotiated for all franchisees the benefit of a discount which takes into account the whole of the business of the franchise chain. In such a case Section 1 would not apply. Indeed it would be rare to find any franchisor (being a supplier) who would enter into a contract with a supplier which contained provisions which are unlawful under Section 1

It is also unlikely that the franchisor (with company owned stores) would combine with franchisees to enter into such an agreement or arrangement as is envisaged by Section 2 of the Act. Normally one would expect the franchisor to make whatever arrangements are appropriate for the obtaining of supplies and to ensure that franchisees are able to take advantage of the opportunity thus presented. There is no good reason for franchising to be involved in such practices as are envisaged by this section

So far as Section 9 is concerned one must first consider the definitions. A dealer means a person carrying on a business of selling goods by wholesale or by retail (31). Supplier means a person carrying on a business of selling goods other than a business in which goods are sold only by retail (31).

If a franchisor is a supplier of goods to his franchisees clearly the section would render void any provision in the franchise or sale contract which establishes or seeks to establish a minumum resale price

However, it would appear that the section does not apply if the franchisor does not supply goods. It may be convenient to take an example

A franchisor has evolved a scheme which includes as an element the sale of goods. The franchisor does not sell goods to the franchisee but nominates the suppliers from whom goods of the requisite type and quality must be obtained. The franchisor has agreed with the suppliers a special price list which contains the prices at which goods will be sold to franchisees by the suppliers and which reflects the discount given in anticipation of the volume of business expected to be obtained from the franchise chain. The franchisor imposes in the franchise agreement a price at which such goods must be sold by all franchisees. The reason for the imposition of this provision is to ensure uniformity of price throughout the country for consumers dealing with the franchise chain and to enable the franchisor to advertise goods and prices. There is no agreement or arrangement between the franchisor and any supplier about the price restriction imposed upon the franchisees. The franchisor does have a number of company owned operations through which it trades, obtaining supplies from the same sources as franchisees and at the same prices

In any such arrangement the franchisor and his franchisees would be dealers within the meaning of the definition in the Act. The franchisor would not be a supplier nor acting on behalf of a supplier

In the circumstances described in this section would not apply and the franchisor would be free to incorporate such a provision in the contract. It should be remembered that if there is an agreement which is registrable under the Restrictive Trade Practices Act 1976 such a provision would be a restriction under Section 6(1)(b) or 11(2)(b) as the case may be. Furthermore the arrangements between the supplier and franchisor would have to be carefully organised so that the Restrictive Trade Practices Act did not apply to that arrangement in view of Sections 6(1)(a) and 11(2)(a) and the fact that the franchisor had his own stores which would be accepting the same price list

There is provision in the Act for exemption of goods and these are contained in Section 14. There are not many cases in which exemption has been given and it is unlikely that any business in respect whereof exemption would not otherwise be given would qualify for exemption merely because the marketing system involved is franchising

(iii) <u>Restrant of Trade - Common Law Rules</u>

The basic common law rule is that a covenant in restraint of
trade is void and unenforceable except to the extent that
the person seeking to enforce it can demonstrate that it is
reasonable both as to time as well as area of operation in
order to protect his legitimate interests.

There are two normal provisions in franchise agreements
which may be said prima facie to have the capacity to be in
restraint of trade. In a franchise involving the tied sale
of products there may be an additional such provision.

The first provision is designed to ensure that the
franchisee who is trained to the task and properly motivated
will devote the whole of his time and attention to the
franchised business and to no other. The purpose of this
restraint is intended to be for the benefit of the
franchisee since his business should prosper the better for
his personal attention. The franchisor is of course
concerned also that the know-how acquired for the purpose of
the operation of the franchised business is not being used
to set up a competing business contemporaneously with the
running of the franchised business.

Obviously there are some businesses in which the more able
franchisee will be able to cope with more than one outlet or
to combine the franchise with another type of business. It
is usual to provide for the franchisor's consent to be
obtained if the franchisee wishes to spread his wings is to
enable the franchisor to ensure that the less able but
ambitious do not over reach themselves to the detriment of
their own business and of their own business and of the
whole franchise network.

The second provision covers restraint on the conduct of a similar business both while the contract is running and after termination. The franchisor has, developed a sophisticated bundle of rights and know-how; he will have his own operations; he will have franchisees and he will wish to grant more franchises particularly in an area where a franchisee has failed, has had to be terminated or has withdrawn. His rights and know-how require protection from being gatuitously used by a former franchisee and he has the legitimate right to look for such protection. The question is to what extent does the law permit this.

As already mentioned a covenant in restraint of trade is void at law unless the person seeking to enforce it can show that it is reasonable both as to time as well as area of operation. The courts have not yet determined the approach to adopt to franchising. The normal restraint provision is found either in vendor and purchaser and master and servant cases. In the former case the standard of reasonableness is easier to satisfy than in the latter. Two judges in the Court of Appeal have said different things one said (32) that franchising is neither but is perhaps "betwixt and between". The other said (33) that the franchisee was a cross breed but that for the purposes of that case he was prepared to assume he was an employee and apply the employee tests. In that case which was concerned with an interlocutory application for an interim injunction which was granted to enforce a time and radius clause the full case for franchising was not argued. If it is fully argued one would hope that the courts will conclude that the same standard of reasonableness should be required as that which is required in vendor and purchaser cases.

The additional provision to which reference was made is where there is a tied sale of products from franchisor to franchisee. These types of arrangement are analogous to those which came before the courts involving the petrol

companies' solus agreements.   The courts appear in such
cases to have reached the conclusion that a tied product
sale for a period in excess of five years was unreasonable.
In franchising it is safe therefore to take the same view of
the length of term of the agreement as have been approved by
the courts in the petrol company cases.

However, the courts have indicated that the acceptable
length of the tie will depend on the circumstances in the
particular trade and thus the whole franchise scheme should
be looked in the context of its place in the market.
Franchising is different from the petrol company type of
arrangement. The petrol company arrangement was dealt with
on the basis that the garage proprietor owned his business
before he struck the deal with the petrol company, in
franchising the franchisee does not. He receives a licence
permitting him to trade using the franchisor's name,
goodwill, systme, methods and know how.   If the products
which are an integral part of that scheme are trade marked
or otherwise identified with the franchisor's trade name it
must be legitimate to require that such goods are tied as
part of the overall package, otherwise the franchisor's
trade mark, trade name and goodwill will be adversely
affected and ultimately lead to the devaluation of the
franchise scheme to the detriment of all franchisees as well
as the franchisor.

Even if the goods are not trade marked by the franchisor the
get-up of the business and the franchise chain branding and
goodwill will ultimately be affected and the integrity and
value of the franchise system devalued if each store trades
with a different range of stock. Invariably it is the case
that such arrangements provide for franchisees to effect
purchases at advantageous prices.

Furthermore the franchisee surrenders no freedom which he
previously held.   Prior to the grant of the franchise the

franchisee had no right to exploit the name and goodwill of
the franchisor nor to make use of his system, methods and
know-how. Since the grant of the right to do these things
will be limited by the conditions laid down relating to the
purchase of products it is arguable that there is indeed no
restraint at all, merely a limited right to conduct business
under a licence. On the other hand, if there is held to be
a restraint then perhaps the value of membership of the
franchise chain could be regarded as sufficient
justification for its imposition.

(iv) Liability of Franchisors

(a) Tort

As already pointed out there are no franchise laws in
the U.K. One is left with the application of general
principles to the transaction. While in the U.S.A. the
case law is abundant there is none in England directly
related to business format franchising. There are some
cases which offer guidance since they relate to
analagous transactions and the most fertile source of
such authority are those cases involving the petrol
companies, their leasing and licensing activities and
their tied sales arrangements. The three areas in the
field of tortious liability which are likely to cause
most activity are Negligence, Misrepresentation and
Vicarious liability .

Negligence   in   advising   the   franchisee;
Misrepresentation in selling the franchise; and claims
against franchisors by customers of franchisees

So far as negligent advice is concerned whether it be
given in writing or orally the general body of law
would apply without any special consideration for the
fact that the transaction is a franchise. Further

consideration will be given to this head potential liability below.

So far as Misrepresentation is concerned the scope is considerable.

Negotiations which lead to the sale of a Franchise can take a long time. Franchisors are selective and take time to conclude that a franchise prospect is suitable; franchisees take time to conclude that the franchise is viable and acceptable to them. Franchisees are usually able to see the franchise operation at work having previously been supplied with a description of what is on offer. With negotiations spread over a lengthy period, the business capable of being looked at and with so many areas of business activity where the franchisee relies upon the franchisor for guidance the scope and incentive for representations to be made is considerable. The areas offering such scope include, profit projections site approval, setting up advice, advice on procedures and so on.

In order than one can misrepresent the statement made must express an existing fact. A statement of opinion by someone with particular knowledge (e.g. a franchisor) is factual in the sense that it imports that the person holds the opinion and has grounds for it. A franchisor is likely to be held by the courts to be a person professing particular skills owing to special duty of care and to be warranting that the advice given is sound.(34)

This latter statement is drawn from a judgment of the Court of Appeal in a case involving a lease by a petrol company of a filing station. The petrol company assessed the likely throughput of gallonage and failed to take into account adverse factors known to them, which arose after the initial assessment was made. There are so many parallels to be drawn between the issues in that case and franchising that it must be considered an important case for franchising. This case preceded the Misrepresentation Act 1967 which broadly speaking gave the same remedies for innocent misrepresentation as were available for fraudulent misrepresentation. A franchisor would be liable for an innocent misrepresentation unless he had reasonable grounds to believe and did believe when the contract was made that the facts representated were true (35)

Turning to the issue of vicarious liability

The franchisor is imposing his system and method upon the franchisee. The operation of the system may be:

(i) correct yet result in damage being suffered by a customer of the franchisee.

(ii) incorrect and result in similar damage.

The question then arises as to whether the customer of the franchisee can make a claim against the franchisor. In the first case mentioned above the question to be resolved would appear to be whether the loss by the customer was foreseeable and it is likely that the franchisor could directly be sued by the customer, although of course if the franchisee were sued he would undoubtedly add the franchisor as a third party and the result would be the same.

In the second case the question is wider since it is inherent in the franchise relationship that the franchisor will monitor and regulate standards in order that the name and goodwill should not be devalued. Would a Court investigate the conduct of the franchisor in its monitoring and regulatory functions to see whether it had failed and would it hold that the franchisor owed a duty to consumers who deal with the franchisee because he operated under the banner of the franchisor, which could result in a liability upon the franchisor even where the franchisee had failed or neglected correctly to operate the system. The Court would also in such a case have to investigate the resistance from a franchisee to the franchisors pressure for performance and perhaps even decide whether the franchisor had acted reasonably in the enforcement or non enforcement of his contract and permitting the franchisee to continue under his banner despite his breaches.

(b) Contract

By virtue of the Supply of Goods and Services Act 1982 there is implied in a contract for the supply of a service where the supplier is acting in the course of a business an implied term that the Supplier will carry out the Service with reasonable care and skill (36)

Apart from this statutory provision and the implied warranty referred to above under the heading of Tort the liability of a franchisor under contract will depend upon the nature and extent of his contractual obligations and his performance under the contract.

The question however arises of the extent to which a franchisor may be able in the franchise contract to limit the scope of any clause which may be made against him by the franchisee

Any contact term which attempts to exclude liability for Misrepresentation will be subject to the provisions of S.11(1) of the Unfair Contract Terms Act 1977 which requires "that the term shall have been a fair and reasonable one to be included having regard to the circumstances which were, or ought reasonably to have been, known to or in the contemplation of the parties when the contract was made."

This same test is applied in the case of liability for loss or damage by negligence (37) but does not apply to

> " any contract so far as it relates to the creation or transfer of a right or interest in any patent, trade mark, copyright registered design technical or commercial information or other intellectual property or relates to the termination of any such right or interest"(38)

It is difficult in the absence of guidance from the court to know how far this exemption goes. The termnology for dealing with these proprietory interests does not appear to be compatiable with either the way in which some of them are created or the manner in which they are dealt with. In particular there must be some doubt as to whether the grant of a licence (so common in dealing with these interests) is intended to be and is covered by the wording of this exemption.

(v) **Tax Considerations for the Franchisor and Franchisee**

A. General

1. The Commissioners of Inland Revenue (The Inland Revenue) are charged with administering all direct taxes in the U.K. Someone becomes liable to taxes on income when they are resident in and or have a source

of income in the U.K.   The Capital Gains Tax however
applies only to persons resident or ordinarily resident
(something more than simply resident), (39) and for
present purposes, regardless of where their capital
assets are located.

2.   The Commissioners of Customs & Excise (The Customs &
      Excise) are charged with administering customs and
      other duties and the UK's system of sales tax, the
      Valued Added Tax.   Duties and indirect taxes levied by
      the Customs and Excise now account for approximately
      50% of all central government revenue.

3.   Local property taxes referred to coloquially as the
      "Rates" are imposed by Local Authorities throughout the
      U.K.

4.   Though the same rules apply to both individuals and
      companies in calculating income or capital gains
      individuals are charged to Income Tax at rates between
      30% and 60% (plus an additional rate of 15% on
      investment income) and Capital Gains Tax at 30% whereas
      companies are charged Corporation Tax at 52% (40% for
      some sizes of small companies) in respect of income
      profits and (effectively) 30% in respect of capital
      profits.

5.   It is not relevant to deal with Capital Transfer Tax
      which is a gift and estate tax.   The Capital Transfer
      Tax, although applying to individuals can also apply to
      transactions of certain closely held companies (e.g.
      companies with 5 or fewer shareholders).

B.   The Foreign Franchisor

1.   A non-resident will only be taxed in the UK if he has a
      source of income here.   For businesses the likely

source of income will be trading income. A non resdient only has a source of trading income if he is trading within but not if he is simply trading with The UK (e.g. selling goods from his own country to a UK buyer without himself having any sort of presence in the UK): these two phrases being the classical way of expressing the distinction between taxable and non-taxable foreign trading transactions relating to the UK (40) . Trading within the UK has a very wide definition which would encompass the presence in the UK of a branch or agent. The place where contracts are made is a very important but not conclusive factor (41)

All the basic tests of trading within the UK are limited by the network of double tax treaties into which the UK has entered. A foreign "enterprise" resident in a treaty country will usually only be subject to UK tax if it has a "permanent establishment" in the UK ; this often excludes for example a base used simply and only for warehousing or the use of an independant as opposed to a dependant agent in the UK. An individual offering personal services would take himself outside treaty protection if he had a "fixed base" in the UK.

2. Clearly a Franchisor operating from a branch, subsidiary or fixed base within the UK will be subject to UK taxes. (42) There are no thin capitalisation rules as such but in the absence of treaty protection (which there often is) any interest paid to a non-resident parent with a 75% holding in a UK subsidiary is treated as a dividend.(43) The Inland Revenue can also substitute arms length prices for the ones actually used between non-resident controlling companies and their UK subsidiaries (44) and this basic rule is also usually retained by any double tax

treaty.

3. Other common categories of income received by non-
    residents from sources within the UK will be royalties,
    interest and passive income, and rent for real
    property.   In the absence of treaty protection the
    rates of tax applying to non resident individuals are
    exactly the same as those applying to residents.

    Non resident companies receiving such income which is
    not associated with a branch or agency (45) in the UK
    only suffer tax tax at 30%

    As a mechanism of collection all three of these sources
    are subject to a witholding tax of 30% (46).   Capital
    sums received for a disposal of patent rights or know
    how will also for tax purposes be treated as income and
    might be subject to withholding (47). Under most double
    tax treaties the rate of witholding tax on interest and
    royalties (including know-how royalties) is reduced by
    varying amounts, in the case of the USA/UK treaty no
    witholding tax at all is necessary.   Double tax
    treaties do not usually apply to relieve income from
    immovable property nor certain categories of passive
    income not strictly within the definition of interest
    or royalties.   Transactions can usually be structured
    however so that payments received by a franchisor will
    not be taxed specifically as royalties or passive
    income.   Income from land is not susceptible to such a
    transformation.

4. The Taxes Acts impose customs duties on the importation
    of goods according to category, type and quantity at
    varying rates.

5. Value Added Tax (VAT) is a tax charged at each stage of
    production of particular items and the provision of

services but not as its name suggests on the value
added but on the whole price charged on the transfer of
goods or the supply of services. (48) The supply of
some goods and services is exempt from VAT but most
supplies are either zero rated (potentially chargeable
at some future date) or chargeable to tax at 15% of
their value. Imported goods are subject to VAT in
addition to any customs duties. A business which gains
the status of a registered business,"taxable person",
for VAT purposes acts as a collector for Customs and
Excise of the 15% tax they must charge on supplies. A
taxable person, however, unlike the final consumer has
the advantage of setting off any VAT it has had to pay
on supplies to it or "inputs" against the VAT it has
collected on its supplies to others or "outputs";
needing only to pay the balance of the tax to the
Customs and Excise or as the case may be reclaiming any
deficit on its quarterly VAT accounts from the Customs
and Excise. This can obviously affect cash-flow. With
regard to imports received by a taxable person however
no VAT becomes payable immediately because rules
provide simply for for output VAT only to be charged on
any onward sale of the imported goods. Within this
general context it is clear however that a UK resident
who is not a taxable person could become chargeable to
VAT on the value of imported goods or services supplied
by a non-resident franchisor. A foreign franchisor
operating through a resident subsidiary of a branch
trading within the UK would have to charge VAT on the
value of initial and continuing franchise fees and on
goods supplied to franchisees. Most franchisees
however should qualify for registration (i.e. make
taxable supplies in excess of £18,000 in a 12 month
period) and be in a position to operate the system as
described earlier.

C.   The UK Resident Franchisor

1.   Capital and Revenue Expenses

(a) The initial Capital outlays by a franchisor are
     treated similarly to any other business and on
     first principles no deduction is allowed for them
     against trading income. Further, franchisors,
     particularly those used to USA taxation
     principles, should note that there is no deduction
     allowed generally against UK taxes on income on
     account of depreciation. Specifically, no
     allowance is allowed for depreciation of real
     property. A system of Capital Allowances does
     however exist which gives an immediate tax write
     off of 100% (subject to clawback on a subsequent
     disposal) on the capital acquisition cost of items
     of "plant and machinery"(49). Over the years this
     has come to have a wide definition. One test
     being that plant and machinery has to be an item
     used in the business rather than being part of the
     setting within which the business is carried on.
     There is however no comprehensive, or any, list of
     plant and machinery contained in the Taxes Acts.

(b) Hundreds of cases have been heard on the
     distinction between captial expenditures (not
     deductible) and revenue or Income expenditures
     which are deductible. The use made of the item
     and not the item itself is all important. As a
     rough guide expenditure incurred on assets which
     will be used for the enduring and long term
     benefit of a business will be a capital expense
     whereas frequently recurring expenses, classically
     the acquisition of stock/inventory, will be
     revenue expenses. The incidental costs of
     acquiring assets will similarly be classified as

capital or reveneue expenses depending on the use
an item has. For instance legal expenses incurred
on acquiring real property will be classified as
capital or revenue according to whether the real
property is the base from which a business is
conducted - a captial item or part of the trading
stock of a business dealing in land - a revenue
item.

(c) Overriding everything else, even revenue expenses
will only be deductible as such if they have been
incurred wholly and exclusively for the benefit of
the trade carried on by a business. No
comprehensive list of items allowed as revenue
expenses exist in the Taxes Acts though section
130 Income and Corporation Taxes Act 1970 contains
a list of items which are not allowable as
deductions against trading income.(50)

2.   Loans

A loss arising from non-repayment of loans advanced to
a franchisee is an item for which a franchisor might
receive no deduction at all not even against Capital
Gains Tax. Only specific bad or doubtful debts
incurred in the conduct of a trade are deductible
revenue items.

3.   Initial Franchise Fees and Royalty Payments

(a) Front end fees will in nearly all instances be held to
be income receipts of a franchisor and taxable as such.
Legal and other expenses in granting, administering and
terminating the franchise contract are logically
therefore treated as revenue expenses. Initial
franchise fees will however nearly always be held to be
a capital expense of the franchisee.

(b)   Recurring royalty payments received by the franchisor
      in consideration for the franchisee's use of trademarks
      and other property rights will most usually be taxed as
      part of his trading income, only rarely will a receipt
      in respect of a trademark licence be a capital receipt,
      for instance, if an exclusive geographic licence is
      granted to a franchisee in circumstances where the
      franchisor is treated as receving a capital sum in
      respect of the sale of part of an underlying capital
      asset of his trade.

(c)   Apart from the wholly and exclusively test imposed on
      trading expenses the Taxes Acts only rarely impose any
      arms length dealing tests on franchisor/franchisee
      transactions where both parties are within the UK. Any
      income received by a franchisor from the sale of goods
      to the franchisee will again, simply, be treated as
      trading receipts.

D.   The U.K. Franchisee

1.   Any initial franchise fee paid will be a capital
      expense for which there is no deduction or allowance
      against tax. However circumstances do exist in which
      other and alternative items of up front expenditure can
      result in a proportionate deduction against tax.

2.   Royalty payments as such to the franchisor can be
      deducted as "charges on income" (51) payments made to
      the franchisor for administrative and managerial
      support can be deducted as a trading expense.

3.   Special and specific writing down allowances against
      tax exist for capital expenditure incurred on the
      purchase of patent rights and the acquisition of know-
      how (as defined) for use in a trade.(52)

The circumstances will be very rare when a franchisee will incur such an expense but it is just as well to bear in mind that the allowances do exist.

(vi) **Employment**

(a) Employment Protection Laws

1. (a) With few exceptions, every employee who has been in his job for a year has the right not to be unfairly dismissed (53). The employers must have a prescribed reason and be reasonable in sacking within the meaning of the Employment Protection (Consolidiation) Act 1978. If they are not, their employees can go to an Industrial Tribunal within three months and, if the Tribunal agrees with them, get their job back or an award of compensation.

(b) Where an employee terminates the contract himself either with or without notice, in circumstances such that he is entitled to terminate it without notice by reason of the employer's conduct he can claim to have been constructively dismissed by his employer.(54)

(c) There is a "deemed" dismissal when an eligible woman is attempting to exercise her rights to return to work after maternity leave and she is refused her job-back rights (55). In these circumstances she is treated as having been dismissed from the notified day of return.

2. (a) Part IV of the Act amended The Redundancy Payments Act 1965 and defines dismissal for redundancy and provides for employers to make lump sum redundancy payments to employees so dismissed. Redundancy in practice means dismissing employees, with or without notice, if the reason for dismissing them comes within

the definition of redundancy provided by Section 81 of the Act:

> "(2) For the purposes of this Act an employee who is dismissed shall be taken to be dismissed by reason of redundancy if the dismissal is attributable wholly or mainly to - (a) the fact that his employer has ceased, or intends to cease, to carry on the business for the purposes of which the employee was employed by him, or hs ceased, or intends to cease, to carry on that business in the place where the employee was so employed; or (b) the fact that the requirements of that business for employees to carry out work of a particular kind, or for employees to carry out work of a particular kind in the place where he was so employed, has ceased or diminished or expected to cease or diminish.

(b) Dismissal is presumed to be by reason of redundancy unless the contrary is proved (56).

3. Minimum periods of notice required to be given by an employer to terminate the Contract of Employment of a person who has been continuously employed for one month or more have been established (57), however, they do not affect the right of either party to treat the contract as terminable without notice by reason of such conduct by the other party as would have enabled him so to treat it before the Act was passed.

4. Employees may enjoy additional forms of protection during their period of employment by virtue of the

provisions of:-

(a) The Transfer of Undertakings (Protection of Employment) Regulations 1981.

(b) Health & Safety at Work etc. Act 1974.

(c) Equal Pay Act 1970.

(d) Sex Discrimination Act 1975.

(e) Race Relations Act 1977.

(f) The Wages Councils Act 1979.

(g) The Children and Young Persons Acts 1933 and 1963 and The Children Act 1972

(a) As a response to pressure from the European Economic Community The Transfer of Undertakings (Protection of Employment) Regulations 1981 were enacted and these regulations are designed to protect employees where the business they work in is sold or otherwise transferred, and cancel dismissal on transfer and instead transfer all the employee's contractual and related rights from the old employer to the new. They make it automatically unfair to sack any employee for a reason connected with the transfer unless for an "economic, technical or organisational reason entailing changes in the workforce". Even if the dismissal falls within the proviso, an Industrial Tribunal must decide whether the dismissal was fair or unfair in all the circumstances.

(b) Health and Safety At Work etc. Act 1974

This Act was passed with the principal intention of promoting the improvement of health and safety at work and of encouraging the maintenance of high standards in those respects. The Act established the Health and Safety Commission and is comprehensive legislation applying to employed persons, wherever they work, which, through regulations, codes of practices and guidance notes, provides a framework from which measures to improve standards in practices emerge.

(c) The Equal Pay Act 1970, The Sex Discrimination Act 1975 and The Race Relations Act 1976.

The Sex Discrimination Act 1975 and the Race Relations Act 1976 both render unlawful certain kinds of discrimination. The Acts have similar and often corresponding provisions. They are specifically designed to protect employees from discrimination in employment on the grounds of sex and race. But they are not the only anti-discrimination enactments with relevance to employment. Associated with The Sex Discrimination Act is The Equal Pay Act 1970. These two Acts together form one code, the infringement of the rights in one not giving rise to proceedings under the other. In the employment sense, The Sex Discrimination Act prohibits direct and indirect sex discrimination against men or women in respect of such matters as selection for appointment, promotion, transfer or training. For its part, The Race Relations Act also prohibits direct and indirect discrimination on racial grounds. Whereas the main objective of The Sex Discrimination Act is to promote equality of opportunity between men and women generally, The

Equal Pay Act is designed to prevent discrimination between men and women in respect of the terms of their Contracts of Employment, including pay.

(d)   The Race Relations Act 1977.

The Race Relations Act refers to racial grounds and to racial group. Racial grounds means grounds of colour, race, nationality or ethnic or national origin. "Racial Group" means a group of persons defined by reference to colour, race, nationality or ethnic or national origin. References to a person's racial group cover any racial group in which he comes. For the purpose of both definitions nationality includes citizenship (58)

(e)   The Wages Councils Act 1979

The Wages Council's Act 1979 provides for the establishment by The Secretary of State for Employment of Wages Councils where he is satisfied that no adequate machinery exists for the effective regulation of the remunertion of specific groups of workers. The principal function of a Wages Council is to fix the statutory minimum remuneration to be paid by employers and other terms and conditions of employment, either generally for the industry covered by the Council or for any particular work within the industry. Where an order is made by a Wages Council giving effect to these terms, they become minimum conditions enforceable at law.

(f)   The Children and Young Persons Act 1933 and 1963 and The Children Act 1972

These Acts lay down a number of restrictions on
the employment of young persons both generally and
in relation to specific occupations

5.   It should be noted that the foregoing rights which
have been granted by Parliament are in addition to the
Common Law rights which employees may exercise through
the Courts.

The nature complexity and diversity of the various laws
and regulations governing employment protection are
such that it is not possible to do more than give a
general overview of some of their more important
provisions, given the limited space available.

(b)   Work Permits for Foreign Employees of Franchisors

1.   (a) In general, people seeking to enter the United
Kingdom for employment must have work permits (59).
Work permits are issued by the Department of Employment
in respect of a specific post with a specific employer
(60) and only to individuals between the ages of 23 and
53 years.

(b) Representatives of overseas firms which have no
branch subsidiary or other representative in the United
Kingdom and persons in certain other categories (such
as ministers of religion doctors dentists etc) although
coming for employment, do not need work permits and may
be admitted for an appropriate period not exceeding 12
months if they hold a current entry clearance granted
for the purpose, or, where entry clearance is not
mandatory, other satisfactory evidence to show that
they do not require a work permit (61)

(c) There is also an exception for Commonwealth

Citizens if they can prove that one of their grandparents was born in the United Kingdom and Islands (62). and for nationals of members of the European Economic Community. In such a case they would normally be given indefinite leave to enter.

2. (a) It should be noted that the possession of a work permit does not absolve the holder from complying with visa requirements. The holder of a work permit is normally admitted for a maximum of 12 months. At the end of the first year of the holder's stay, the permit may be extended if he is still engaged in the employment specified in the permit or another employment approved by the Department of Employment and the Employer confirms that he wishes to continue to employ him. Where appropriate a corresponding extension will be granted to the Applicant's wife and children, usually for three years. (63)

(b) If the work permit was originally issued for less than 12 months the approval of the Department of Employment will be necessary before the original Permit can be extended.

(c) Not every type of job will qualify for the issue of a permit. There are eight categories, and a permit will only be issued for jobs requiring workers in these categories. (64) The eight categories are (a) those holding recognised professional qualifications; (b) administrative and executive staff; (c) highly qualified technicians having specialised experience; (d) other key workers with a high or scarce qualification in an industry or occupation requiring specific expert knowledge or skills; (e) highly skilled and experienced workers for senior posts in hotel and catering extablishments who have successfully completed appropriate full time training courses of at least two years' duration at approved schools abroad or, exceptionally, have acquired other specialised or uncommon skills and experience relevant to the industry; (f) entertainers and sportsmen/women who meet the appropriate skills criteria (professional sportsmen/women taking part in competitions of international standing do not normally require permits): (g) people coming for a limited period of training on the job or work experience approved by the Deparment of Employment (65) other persons only if, in the opinion of the Secretary of State for Employment, their employment is in the national interest.

FOOTNOTES

1. Section 137(2) Fair Trading Act 1973
2. Section 137(2) Ibid
3. As to the meaning of "supply of goods" See S 137 (1) Ibid and of "Supply of Services" See S.137 (3) Ibid
4. The Pyramid Selling Schemes Regulations 1973 S.1. 1973 No 1740
5. S. 26(2) Restrictive Trade Practices Act 1976
6. S. 43(1) Ibid

7. S. 43(2) Ibid and Schweppes Ltd's Agreement (No.2) (1971) All ER 1473 of pp 1487, 1488
8. S. 43(4) Ibid
9. S. 43(1) Ibid
10. See paragraph 3(2) of the Restrictive Trade Practices (Services) Order 1976 (1976 No. 98)
10a. Ravenseft Properties Ltd v Director General of Trading (1977) All ER 47
11. S.28 Ibid
12 S.30 Competition Act 1980
13. S.28 Competition Act 1980
14. S.21 (3) Restrictive Trade Practices 1976
15. S.2 Competition Act 1980
16. S.3(1) Ibid
17. S.3(10) Ibid
18. S.3(7) Ibid
19. S5(3) and 5(4) Ibid
20. S.5(1) Ibid
21. S.6(5) Ibid
22. S.7(6) Ibid
23. S.84 Fair Trading Act 1976
24. S.9(1) Competition Act 1980
25. S.10 Ibid
26. The Anti Competitive Practices (Exclusion) Order 1980
27. Full Line Forcing and Tied Sales - The Monopolies and Mergers Commission 19th March 1981 - HMSO

28.　Part I of the Resale Prices Act 1976
29.　Part II Ibid
30.　Cammell Laird & Co Ltd v Manganese Bronze and Co Ltd (1934) A.C. 402
31.　S.24(1) Resale Prices Act 1976
32.　Office Overload v Gunn (1977) FSR 39 per Denning MR at p.41
33.　Office Overload v Gunn (1977) FSR 39 per Lawton LJ at p.43
34.　Esso Petroleum Limited v Mardon (1976) 2 ALL ER 5
35.　S.2(1) Misrepresentation Act 1976
36.　S.13 Supply of Goods and Services Act 1982
37.　S.2(2) Unfair Contract Terms Act 1977
38.　Paragraph 1 (c) Schedule 1 Unfair Contract Terms Act 1977
39.　Capital Gains Tax Act 1979 S.2
40.　Grainger & Son v Gough (1896) AC 325.
41.　Maclaine v Eccott (1926) AC 424 c.f. Greenwood v F.L. Smith & Co (1922) 8 TC 193 and Firestone Tyre and Rubber Co v Llewellin (1957) 37 TC 111
42.　38 above and see s 246 Income and Corporation Taxes Act 1970 ("I.C.T.A.")
43.　S 233(2) ICTA
44.　S 485 ICTA
45.　Subject to Corporation Tax at 52%, S 246 ICTA
46.　SS 52,53, 89, 380 ICTA
47.　SS 380, 386 ICTA
48.　Introduced in Finance Act 1972
49.　Inter alia see Capital Allowances Act 1968 and Finance Act 1971
50.　See S 248 ICTA for other items, including royalties, which are deductible as "charges on income"
51.　S 248 ICTA
52.　See respectively SS 378 and 386 ICTA
53.　Employment Protection (Consolidation) Act 1978 S.54
54.　S.55(2)(c) ibid
55.　S.56 ibid

56. S.9(2) ibid
57. S.49 ibid
58. Race Relations Act 1977 SS.3(1) and 78(1)
59. See General Statement of Changes in Immigration Rules (House of Commons Papers) 1983 No 169 Part III ("HC 169")
60. H C 169 paragraph 27
61. H.C. 169 paragraphs 31-34
62. paragraph 29 ibid
63. paragraph 117 ibid
64. P 114 Immigration Law and Practice by Lawrence Grant and Ian Martin 1st Edition The Cobden Trust (1982)
65. See Leaflet 'OW 21' issued by the Department of Employment

CHAPTER 9

FRANCHISING IN EUROPE - EEC
Stanley A. Crossick

1. **INTRODUCTION**

(a) Martin Mendelsohn in "The Guide to Franchising" gives
for "franchise" a definition based on four main
features, namely:

> "1. The ownership by the franchisor of
> a name, an idea, a secret process, or a
> piece of equipment and the goodwill
> associated with it.

> 2. The grant of a licence (franchise)
> by the franchisor to the franchisee
> permitting the exploitation of such
> name, idea, process or equipment and the
> goodwill.

> 3. The inclusion in the licence
> (franchise) agreement of the regulations
> and controls relating to the operation
> of the business by which the franchisee
> exploits his rights.

> 4. The payment by the franchisee of a
> royalty or other consideration for the
> rights which are obtained and the
> services or goods with which the
> franchisor will continue to provide to

the franchisee."

(b) Franchising law cannot be regarded as a specific branch
     of law, but rather the application of several branches
     of law to specific commercial activities.

(c) As there are many different forms of franchising, the
     underlying commercial activities can be diverse.

(d) There are often wide variations in the laws of
     different Member States (particularly as between civil
     and common law countries). These laws frequently vary
     conceptually, use different terminology or use similar
     terminology differently.

(e) As will be seen from the papers presented by my
     colleagues, franchising as such receives varying
     degrees of attention in different European countries.

(f) The object of this paper is to consider the main EEC
     legal fields which may be relevant.

(g) To many, the contents of this paper will be well-known
     but it may, nevertheless, serve as a useful reference
     paper.   To some, and particularly non-European
     attorneys, it may help clarify a highly complex subject
     at EEC level.

(h) Lawyers unfamiliar with the EEC should note that the
     1957 Treaty of Rome is the principal constitutional
     document creating the European Economic Community. It
     established a separate legal order whose laws also
     directly form part of the national laws of Member
     States.   Community law prevails in the event of a
     conflict with national law. The European Court of
     Justice in Luxembourg interprets and develops the
     Treaty much like the US Supreme Court interprets the

Constitution. The Commission of the European Communities develops and implements European Community Laws and regulations.

(i) The current members of the European Community are France, Germany, Italy and the UK; Belgium, Luxembourg and The Netherlands (Benelux); Denmark, Ireland and Greece. Portugal and Spain have applied to join.

(j) This paper tries not to be too long but nevertheless to contain all relevant material. Like all compromises, it can be criticised for containing too much and too little.

2. RELEVANT LEGAL FIELDS

Jean Monnet, one of the European Community's founding fathers, said that the whole EEC Treaty is about competition. This is an exaggeration because competition is not an end in itself but is a key instrument for the fulfilment of the main aims of the Treaty. Nevertheless, his point is important.

Franchising as a commercial activity touches primarily at EEC level upon:

(a) Competition/anti-trust law and legislation.

As made clear in para 3 (b) below, franchising has no distinct treatment as such, and most of the heads of competition law have, therefore, to be examined.

(b) Intellectual and industrial property law and legislation.

Intellectual and industrial property rights have an important part to play in franchising arrangements. This is a very complex subject at European level, having regard to its interrelationship at Community level with both competition and free movement of goods, and the relationship between Community law and the national laws of the ten Member States.

3.   IS FRANCHISING A SPECIAL CASE UNDER EEC LAW AND LEGISLATION?

(a)   According to the European Communities Commission's reply on 23rd April 1980 to a question put to it on 11th February 1980 (Written Question No. 1694/79), that asked about potential problems with franchise agreements under European Common Market antitrust law:

> "The term 'franchising' covers various forms of co-operation between independent firms... Generally speaking, a franchise involves an agreement between the firm awarding the franchise (franchisor) and one or more firms thereby become the franchise holders. It allows them to use the franchisor's trade name, trademark, or other distinctive symbols and its know-how to enable them to offer products or services in an original way using specific commercial techniques."

> "These agreements... present certain features of both distribution agreements and licensing agreements for industrial and commercial property rights."

(b)   Your chairman's quotations (see above para 1(a)) and the Commission reply indicate that EEC competition and industrial property law and legislation may be relevant

they too are to be considered as restraints on competition prohibited by Article 85(1).

(iii) <u>Discriminatory pricing and selling conditions in distribution</u> (discrimination by the franchisor among franchisees in the charges offered or made for royalties, goods services, equipment, rentals etc.)

Both Articles 85(1) and 86 explicitly prohibit these practices.

Franchising agreements under which it is agreed that different prices will be charged to a purchaser merely on grounds of nationality or place of establishment are likely to contravene Article 85(1), as parallel imports may be obstructed.

In <u>Pittsburgh Corning</u> (OJ 1972 L272/35), the supplier's distributors in Belgium and the Netherlands agreed to charge a higher price for goods intended for delivery to customers in Germany and a lower price for goods intended for delivery to customers in Belgium and the Netherlands. The Commission held that discriminatory pricing of this kind, intended to hinder parallel imports, was a clear contravention of Article 85(1).

In <u>Kodak</u> (OJ 1970 L147/24) the conditions of sale contained a provision that purchasers of Kodak products situated in a given national territory should make payments to the Kodak subsidiary in that territory, at the subsidary's prices, even if the products had been obtained from a Kodak subsidiary in another territory. The Commission decided that such conditions of sale "had the effect of isolating the markets of each Member State and of excluding from competition in one or more Member States the prices charged in each of these markets."

Discrimination, by applying dissimilar conditions to equivalent transactions with other trading parties, thereby placing them at a competitive disadvantage, is also expressly prohibited in Article 86(1). Within the scope of Article 86, a dominant firm that discriminates between customers or suppliers on the ground of nationality is acting abusively.

(iv) <u>Exclusive dealing</u> (requiring the franchisee to deal only, or primarily, in products supplied or services designated by the franchisor).

Exclusive dealing agreements may fall within the scope of Article 85(1), since they limit the buyer's freedom to obtain those goods elsewhere, while at the same time the number of sales outlets open to other suppliers is reduced.

In deciding whether such agreements fall effectively within Article 85(1) the agreement must be considered in its whole legal and economic context, taking into account the existence of other agreements of the same type.

In <u>Brasserie de Haecht</u> (case 23/67 (1967)ECR 407), the European Court considered the effect of a typical "tied-house" contract whereby a Belgium cafe proprietor bound himself to obtain his supplies of beer, drinks and lemonade exclusively from one supplier in return for a loan from the supplier of BF 50,000. Considered alone, the agreement concerned only a minute proportion of the whole Belgian market. However, (as in most franchising cases) it was only one of the large number of similar contracts in which Belgian breweries had agreed like terms in respect of licensed premises in Belgium. The European Court held that the existence of these other agreements was one of the factors to be taken into consideration when examining the applicability of Article 85(1) to exclusive dealing agreement.

The agreements may however be granted an exemption under Article 85(3), since they normally contribute to improving the production and distribution of goods.

The new Commission Regulation 1984/83 on exclusive purchasing agreements establishes the conditions under which such agreements can benefit from the block exemption (see above 4(h)).

Exclusive dealing agreements may also constitute a violation of Article 86, when they are imposed by a firm in a dominant position.

(v) Other restrictive clauses

Non-Competition clauses

The obligation on the franchisee not to manufacture or sell competing products may infringe Article 85(1). However, such a restriction may be indispensable in improving distribution, by compelling the franchisee to concentrate its efforts on the sale of the franchised products and may, therefore be exempted

under Article 85(3). In any event, such covenants
are covered by Article 2(2)(a) of Regulation
1983/83.

The same conclusion may be reached as to a
covenant not to compete after the expiration of
the franchise agreement, provided that the scope
of the restriction is reasonable with regard to
time and territory.

Advertising

A restriction on advertising the franchise
products outside the territory contravenes
Article 85(1), but an obligation to advertise the
franchise products and promote them does not
infringe Article 85(1), nor does an obligation to
follow the franchisor's instructions with regard
to advertising, provided that the franchisor's
authority to give instructions does not extend to
the advertising of prices or conditions of sale.

Trademarks

Obligations to sell under the franchisor's
trademarks, and to use the franchisor's trademarks
without alteration or addition and only in a
proper manner in connection with the business, do
not in themselves fall under Article 85(1). In
any event, such covenants are permitted under
Article 2(3)(b) of Regulation 1983/83. However,
an obligation on the distributor not to challenge
the franchisor's trademark might infringe Article
85(1).

Packaging and presentation

An obligation to sell in the franchisor's original

packaging does not contravene Article 85(1). Such provisions are covered by Article 2(3)(b) of Regulation 1983/83.

Maintenance of stocks and sales network

Generally, it is not incompatible with Article 85(1) to require a franchisee to maintain a sales network and adequate stocks, and to purchase a complete range of minimum quantities. This is also permitted under Article 2(3)(a) of Regulation 1983/83.

Provision of supoporting services

Obligations on a sole distributor to provide after-sales service and to sell products with a warranty, or to employ properly qualified staff, do not fall within Article 85(1). Such provisions are also covered by Article 2(3)(c) of Regulation 1983/83.

Resale Price Maintenance controlling or suggesting the price at which goods or services must be resold by the franchisee to the public.

Price-fixing is explicitly forbidden by Article 85(1) and has never been granted an exemption.

Provision of information

An obligation on the franchisee to provide the franchisor with information as to its trading position, sales trends, market situation, stocks, expected demand and other information does not normally contravene Article 85(1).

(vi) Selective distribution systems

Many suppliers, especially those supplying
sophisticated and expensive consumer products,
wish to limit the resale of such goods to
"approved dealers" who fulfil certain qualitative
or quantitative criteria.

The Commission takes the view that selective
distribution systems do not infringe Article 85(1)
when the selection is made on the basis of
"qualitative criteria". Thus, a manufacturer may
prohibit its dealers from reselling to other
distributors who do not meet certain qualitative
requirements necessary to ensure that the goods
are sold in a satisfactory manner, at least where
the requirements are operated uniformly and
without discrimination between purchasers.
Consequently, restrictions on resale to other
distributors or dealers who do not employ
qualified staff, do not provide adequate after-
sales and guarantee services and do not maintain
suitable premises, have been found to fall outside
Article 85(1) in distribution agreements
concerning cameras, electronic equipment, watches,
perfumes and clocks.

On the other hand, elective distribution systems
under which the manufacturer limits the approved
dealers by reference to criteria which go further
than certain minimum standards objectively
required for the proper distribution of the
products, fall within Article 85(1), although an
exemption may be possible under Article 85(3).

Franchising networks are usually established in a
way similar to selective distribution systems.

In the so-called "Perfume Cases" (joined cases
253/78 and 1-3/79 (1980 ECR 2327, 37/79 (1980) ECR
2481, 99/79 (1980 ECR 2511), referred to the Court
of Justice on the basis of Article 177 EEC Treaty
concerning the possible legal effect of letters
addressed by the Commission to a few perfume
manufacturers on the selective distribution
systems they had put into force, the Court had the
possibility to consider whether such selective
distribution systems may be justified with regard
to Article 85(1).

These selective distribution systems (an exclusive
distribution agreement between the manufacturer
and his distributors - and uniform distribution
agreements between both the manufacturer and his
distributors and their authorised retailers)
although they were based mainly on qualitative
criteria, had also a few elements based on
quantitative criteria.

The Commission considered that if the illegal
clauses were banned from the selective
distribution agreements, there would be no reason
for the application of Article 85(1), despite the
fact that the quantitative criteria would still
remain. This was transmitted to the three
manufacturers through letters addressed to them by
the competent services of the Commission. Similar
letters have been addressed to other perfume
manufacturers as well.

The Court of Justice recalled its judgment in
"Metro v Commission" (case 26/76 (1976) ECR 1875)
by saying that "selective distribution systems
constitute an aspect of competition which accords
with Article 85(1) provided that re-sellers are

chosen on the basis of objective criteria of a
qualitative nature relating to the technical
qualification of the re-seller and his staff and
the suitability of his trading premises and that
such conditions are laid down uniformly for all
potential re-sellers and are not applied in a
discriminatory fashion".

The Court stated finally that "...in principle, a
selective distribution network admission to which
is made subject to conditions, going beyond
simple, objective qualitative selection falls
within the prohibition laid down in Article 85(1)
especially when it is based on quantitative
selection criteria".

The 11th Report on Competition Policy (1981)
(paragraph 2, point 10) states in regard to
selective distribution systems:

> "The Commission is now endeavouring to
> define the principles behind
> applications of Article 85 to selective
> distribution systems; proceedings under
> way in a number of individual cases are
> providing the ground work (....). The
> key factors in this connection, in
> accordance with the case law of the
> Court of Justice, are to ensure that no
> dealer satisfying objective and
> qualitative selection criteria is
> prevented from obtaining supplies and
> also that trade between appointed
> dealers in the Community is not impeded
> by restrictions on resale prices. When
> these proceedings have come to an end,
> the Commission intends to draw up

general guidelines spelling out the
restrictions which may or may not be
incorporated in a selective distribution
system."

The recent <u>SABA</u> decision of the Commission in
granting exemption under Article 85(3) is of
interest to franchising in view of the parallel
which exists between the system being considered
and franchising.

SABA sells consumer electronics equipment and
distributes its products, in Germany by specialist
wholesalers and retailers, and in other Member
States, by sole distributors supplying specialist
retailers.

SABA's selective distribution system comprises
four standard agreements:

-      the 'SABA EEC dealership agreement with
       specialist wholesalers'

-      the 'SABA co-operation agreement'

-      the 'SABA dealership agreement with
       specialist retailers'

-      the 'SABA fair service agreement'

In the distribution system set up, SABA undertakes
not to supply dealers outside the distribution
system.   SABA dealers are for their part
prohibited from supplying dealers who have not
been appointed by SABA.

Admission to the SABA distribution system is given

only to those dealers who not only fulfil general qualitative requirements, such as technical qualifications and specialist knowledge of their staff, but are also prepared to undertake specific measures of sales promotion and to achieve a particular sales performance.

Specialist wholesalers and sole distributors must maintain a trained sales force capable of marketing SABA products, allow their staff to undergo regular training with SABA, provide advices to SABA retailers, stock for whole SABA range as fully as possible, keep records on all SABA products sold.

Specialist wholesalers in the Federal Republic of Germany, who are supplied directly by SABA, must accept the obligations set out in the co-operation agreement (conclusion of annual supply contracts, acceptance of supply targets).

Specialist retailers must take supplies of and sell SABA products on a regular basis, stock the full current SABA range as fully as possible, maintain sufficient stocks of SABA products, provide technically competent aftersales service and assume warranty obligations.

Wholesalers must recognise and retailers must sign the SABA fair service agreement, under which SABA undertakes to provide technical assistance to its retailers as well as details of the spare parts service and contributes to the cost of repairing products under warranty. SABA retailers are for their part obliged to maintain a competent repair workshop or to contract with such a workshop and observe the relevant technical regulations.

SABA's selective distribution system, as described above, contains some features which are familiar areas for franchising. It establishes a continuing relationship between SABA and its dealers. SABA undertakes the obligation to provide its dealers continuing assistance in fields such as technical advice and or instruction, staff training. SABA dealers must fulfil obligations such as trained staff availability and trading requirements, marketing, sales promotion, stocktaking SABA's products as fully as possible, and after-sale service in accordance with SABA's technical regulations. SABA and its dealers are prevented from supplying dealers who are not part of the distribution system, whose integrity is guaranteed by SABA.

An exemption to SABA's distribution system is clearly a precedent which franchising agreements can follow in applying for an individual exemption under Article 85(3), even if they fall within the scope of EEC Competition rules.

5. RELEVANCE OF EEC INTELLECTUAL AND INDUSTRIAL PROPERTY LAW AND LEGISLATION

Industrial and intellectual property rights which are protected under the national laws of individual Member States raise difficult problems in Community law, in particular with regard to the fundamental rules governing unrestricted competition in a single market.

Many provisions of the EEC Treaty affect intellectual property rights: viz Articles 1, 2, 3, 5, 7, 10, 30-36, 51-62, 85-87, 100-102, 113, 116, 228, 234 and 235 but essentially those governing:

-   free movement of goods (Articles 30 - 36)

-   competition (Articles 85 and 86)

-   harmonisation or unification (Articles 100-102).

(a) General   principles   governing   intellectual   and
     industrial property rights

    (i) Intellectual and industrial property rights have
     always been considered at national level as
     privileged instruments of economic policy. The
     creation and existence of these rights are, of
     course, subject to certain conditions. However,
     from their very nature, the holders of these
     rights enjoy important prerogatives. For example,
     the holder of a national patent has, for a period
     of years, the right to exclude others from making
     use of his invention or marketing the products
     thereby manufactured.

     He has also the power to dispose of his rights to
     others, either by assigning outright to third
     parties or by licensing them to make, use or sell
     his product, usually upon payment of royalties.
     On the other hand, the law in the majority of the
     Member States allows the holder of a national
     patent to oppose the import of any product covered
     by his own patent. This is not only when the
     product is manufactured or put into circulation
     without its agreement, but also when the product
     is manufactured or put into circulation abroad by
     the holder himself, or a licensee or a holder of a
     parallel patent obtained by transfer from the
     original holder.

    (ii) The Community approach is that whereas the

existence of intellectual property rights is unaffected by the EEC Treaty (since Article 222 guarantees national systems of property ownership) the exercise of these rights is subject to all of the relevant rules of the Treaty - in particular the prohibition of measures of equivalent effect to quantitative restrictions (Article 30) restrictive practices (Article 85) and the abuse of a dominant position (Article 86).

However, Article 36, which applies directly to Article 30 and by analogy to Articles 85 and 86, permits a derogation from these rules for the benefit of the property rights conferred by national law, to the extent that those rights do not go beyond the "specific subject matter" of the property.

The criteria which determine whether or not national intellectual property rights are compatible with the Common Market are, therefore, based both on the subtle and artificial distinction between the existence and exercise of intellectual property rights - see, for example, Parke-Davis (case 24/67 (1968) ECR 55), Sirena (case 40/70 (1971) ECR 69), and Deutsche Gramophon (case 78/70 (1971) ECR 187), and on the definition of the "specific subject matter" - see, for instance, Deutsche Gramophon and Centrafarm v Sterling Drug (case 15/74 (1974) ECR 1147).

(iii) In order to define the limits of the exercise of intellectual property rights permitted under Article 36, the Court of Justice developed in a number of cases the "exhaustion of rights principle". The intellectual property owner's

exclusive right comes to an end when the product
has been placed on the market somewhere inside the
Community either by itself or with its consent.

See, for instance, in terms of patents,
Centrafarm v Sterling Drug, Merck v Stephar (case
187/80 (1981) ECR 2063), and, in terms of trade
marks, Centrafarm v Winthrop (case 16/74 (1974)
ECR 1183), Hoffmann-la Roche (case 102/77 (1978)
ECR 1139), Centrafarm v American Home Products
Corporation (case 3/78 (1978) ECR 1823), Dansk
Supermarked (case 58/80 (1981) ECR 181), and
Pfizer v Eurim-Pharm (case 1/81 (1981) ECR 2913).

Does such a principle apply to copyright? Some
argue that copyright comprises "moral rights",
i.e. the right of an author to claim authorship of
the work and to object to any action which would
be prejudicial to his honour or reputation.

However, the Court in Gema (joint cases 55 and
57/80 (1981) ECR 147), held that copyright also
comprises "economic rights" i.e. the right to
exploit commercially the marketing of the
protected work. The Gema judgment thus applied
the principle of "exhaustion of rights" to
copyright.

(b)   Licensing agreements under EEC competition law

Generally speaking, franchising agreements involve the
grant of a licence by the franchisor to the franchisee
permitting it to use the franchisor's trade name,
trademark, or other distincive symbols and its know-
how. In considering such agreements, which present
certain features of licensing agreements for industrial
and commercial property rights, account must be taken

of the general principles already discussed, namely the effect of Articles 30-36 upon the exercise of industrial and intellectual property rights. Additionally, however, the effect of Article 85(1) must be examined to see whether individual provisions of those agreements contravene Article 85(1).

(i) The application of Article 85(1) to patent licensing agreements

    (a) Exclusive manufacturing rights

        A patent licence granting exclusive manufacturing rights may fall within Article 85(1), since the exclusivity conferred on the licensee may prevent third parties from manufacturing the licensed products in the territory and subsequently exporting such products to other Member States. However, there is no *per se* rule that the grant of exclusive manufacturing rights will infringe Article 85(1), and the application of Article 85(1) will depend on the particular facts. An exemption may be given for exclusive manufacturing licences under Article 85(3), where it is found that the licensed territory is not too extensive, that there are similar products which compete in that territory and that parallel imports are still possible.

        Thus, in Davidson Rubber (OJ 1972 L143/31), which mainly concerned the grant by an American licensor of exclusive manufacturing rights under patent and know-how licences to three licenses in Germany and Benelux, Italy and France, respectively, the Commission held that the exclusive manufacturing provisions did fall within Article 85(1). Furthermore although the agreements between Davidson and its licensees provided that items covered by the contract could be sold freely as between Member States, the Commission considered that they, nevertheless, infringed Article 85(1), since they curtailed the number of suppliers and thereby produced a perceptible effect on competition and the development of trade between Member States. However, the Commission exempted the agreements under Article 85(3), recognising that, without the restriction on competition deriving from the use of exclusive licensees, the favourable objectives of the patent-licence and know-how concessions could not possibly be achieved.

Again in Kabelmetal/Luchaize (OJ 1975 L222/34), the Commission exempted, under Article 85(3) an exclusive patent and know-how licensing agreement covering the use of Kabelmetal's cold extrusion process. Kabelmetal, a German company, gave the French firm Luchaize an exclusive licence for the manufacture in France of extruded steel components and a non-exclusive licence for the sale of these goods in all Community countries. This accounted for about 20 per cent of the production in France of those components, particularly for the motor car industry.

The exemption was given because the exclusivity would help to promote technical and economic progress, by giving the licensee an incentive to work on the development of the licensed technique.

In AOIP/Beyrard (OJ 1976 L6/8) the Licensee enjoyed exclusive manufacturing rights in France under a patent licence concerning automatic starter rheostats for electric motors. The exclusivity provisions were also held to fall under Article 85(1), the licensee accounting for about 7 per cent of the French domestic market and nearly 18 per cent of French exports of the products in question.

However, an exemption under Article 85(3) was refused, as the agreement contained four clauses which were found not to be capable of exemption:

- no challenge
- non-competition
- automatic extension of the duration of the agreement
- payment of royalties even if the patent was not exploited

(b)   Exclusive sales rights and export bans

Licensing agreements, granting exclusive sales rights or imposing territorial restrictions upon the licensee, normally fall within Article 85(1), since they are direct barriers to the free movement of goods in the common market. Exemption under Article 85(3) will only be considered in special circumstances, e.g. where new products are to be manufactured and sold or a new market is to be penetrated, entailing heavy investment and considerable risk.

These principles were reaffirmed by the Commission in the AGA/Steel Radiation (in 1977 Statement of Objections. No final decision).

Steel Radiators, a British firm, was formerly a subsidiary within the AGA Group but subsequently became part of the group owned by Metal Bow Ltd. Following the sale, a patent and know-how licensing agreement was entered into whereby AGA gave Steel Radiators an exclusive licence for the manufacture and sale of its radiators in the UK.

After the Commission had issued a Statement of Objections, the parties deleted numerous clauses from the agreement which the Commission considered infringed competition rules namely:

- undertaking by AGA to refrain from manufacturing or selling the relevant products in the UK or from supplying customers who were likely to sell there

- prohibition on Steel Radiators exporting to other Member States or elsewhere in Europe

- no-challenge clause

- obligation to continue paying royalties even if one or more of the licensed patents were annulled on the application of a third party

- prohibition on Steel Radiators taking

legal proceedings against any third party holding a patent competing with one of the AGA patents were AGA had a reciprocal no-challenge agreement.

The Commission rejected the argument that the restraints imposed on the licensor as vendor of shares in the company were justified by the need to protect the goodwill assigned to the acquirer, as a considerable period of time had elapsed since the sale.

(c)   Maize Seed Case

An important judgment of the Court of Justice in respect of a licensing agreement was given in Nungesser and Eisele v Commission (The Maize Seed Case) (258/78 (1982) ECR 2015.

The applicants, Mr. Eisele and his firm L G Nungesser KG, brought an action against the Commission seeking partial annulment of a Commission decision condemning agreements made between the applicants and a French Government agency (INRA) for the development and improvement of seed varieties.

The agreements and four memoranda dated 1961 assigned the plant breeders' rights for four varieties of hybrid maize seed developed by INRA in France and the exclusive right to produce and sell the seed varieties in Germany to Mr. Eisele.

The Commission condemned the exclusive nature of the licence because it required the licensor to refrain from appointing another

licensee of the breeding rights in the
territory. The licensor also undertook not
to produce or sell itself in the territory.
In addition, third parties, including
licensees in other territories, were
prevented from importing to, or exporting
from Germany without the authorisation of
INRA and Nr. Eisele. The Commission decision
also condemned the out-of-court settlement
made in 1973 between the applicants and a
company, Louis David KG, and which attempted
to make parallel imports of the INRA seed
varieties into Germany.

The question of legality of an exclusive
licence, and its qualification of exemption,
were central issues in this case.

The Court held that:

"Having regard to the specific nature of the
products in question, the Court concludes
that, in a case such as the present, the
grant of an open exclusive licence, that is
to say a licence which does not affect the
position of third parties such as parallel
importers and licensees for other
territories, is not in itself incompatible
with Article 85(1) of the Treaty."

The point here is that the open exclusive
licence did not affect such parties as
parallel importers and licensees in other
territories. The Court held that there were
no grounds for regarding plant breeders'
rights as having characteristics so specific
as to require different treatment from other

industrial and commercial property rights. This would appear to mean that there is nothing in the nature of these rights to exempt them from the established law that absolute territorial protection is prohibited.

Complete territorial protection clearly goes beyond what is indispensible for improving production or distribution, or for promoting technical progress.

The Court also said, the following its judgment in EMI v CBS (Case 51/75 (1979) ECR 811), that:

"... an intellectual or commercial property right as a legal entity does not possess those elements of contracts or concerted practices referred to in Article 85(1) of the Treaty but, the exercise of that right might fall within the ambit of the prohibitions contained in the Treaty if it were to manifest itself as the subject, the means or the consequence of an agreement."

Thus again we see the Court saying that it is not the holding of the right which may infringe Article 85 but the exercise and enjoyment of that right.

The extent to which the Court's judgment can or will be applied by the Commission to its proposed Patent Licence Regulation (see below para 5(b)(ii) is far from clear. Plant breeders' rights are certainly far from identical to patent rights.

It would appear that licence agreements in general, which confer absolute territorial protection with the effect of preventing parallel imports, are prohibited and may not be exempted.

It is not clear whether the Court's ruling regarding the competibility with Article 85(1) of an open exclusive licence is of general application. The wording of the judgment suggests not.

(ii) The application of Article 85(1) to trade mark and know-how licences.

Generally speaking, in considering trade mark and know-how licences, the principles set out by the Commission in respect of patent licences are also relevant. In certain decisions discussed above concerning patent licences, know-how was licensed. In these cases no separate treatment was accorded to the know-how aspects.

A non-exclusive licence to use the licensor's trade mark will not ordinarily infringe Article 85(1). However, the exercise of a trade mark right deriving from an agreement to prevent parallel imports from another Member State may contravene Article 85(1).

Thus, in Advocaat Zwarte Kip (OJ 1974 L237/12), the Commission made clear that it would use its powers under Article 85 to oppose any attempts to partition markets through the assignment or use of trade marks.

Following a complaint from a parallel importer,

the Commission condemned an agreement to assign a trade mark insofar as it was used to prevent imports of products bearing the same trade name.

A Dutch firm, Van Olffen, assigned in Belgium and Luxembourg to SA Cinoco its rights over a trade mark relating to egg liqueurs (Advocaat Zwarte Kip). In an exchange of letters between the parties, the assignee was assured that it would have absolute territorial protection. SA Cinoco brought an action for infringement of the trade mark right against a Belgian who imported from the Netherlands advocaat manufactured and marked by Van Olffen under the trade mark. The agreement was found to have the effect of segregating the Benelux markets.

(iii) Exemption under Article 85(3)

A licensing agreement which falls under Article 85(1) and is duly notified may benefit, like any other type of agreement, from an exemption under Article 85(3) if the requirements of that provision are satisfied (see above para 5(b)(i).

The Commission also has powers under Regulation 19/65 to make Regulations granting exemption to certain categories of agreement.

A proposed Regulation on the application of Article 85(3) to certain categories of patent licensing agreements was published in March 1979 (OJ C58/79).

It aims at introducing provisions for block exemptions in the application of competition rules to patent licences, and at establishing a clear

distinction between those clauses which are
permissible in agreements and those which are not.

Article 1 lists the obligations in restraint of
competition imposed on licensors and licensees
which are exempted from the prohibition in Article
85(1). It generally exempts exclusive rights to
manufacture and to use specified products. The
proposal also fixes a turnover limit above which
undertakings cannot benefit from group exemption.
This provision aims to exclude a number of firms
which have large financial resources and which
hold the bulk of the patents in force in the
Community.

Article 2 lists cluases which will not stand in
the way of exemption, such as the obligation not
to divulge business secrets, an obligation to
respect quality standards, grant-back clauses, or
restrictions on the field of use.

Article 3 lists the restrictions and clauses which
may not be inserted in agreements, such as no-
challenge clauses, clauses stating that the
licence is for an indefinite duration, competing
products clauses...

The Commission reasserts strongly that exclusive
sales rights and related export bans can only be
allowed if they are necessary for ensuring the
expansion of technical progress. The benefit of
the proposed Regulation is extended to patent
licensing agreements containing provisions
concerning the assignment of the right of the use
of know-how or secret manufacturing processes
which are related to the use or application of
industrial technology.

The proposed Regulation has been subjected to much critisism and the Commission is now envisaging major changes to the first draft as to:

-   the type of know-how included in the licence, e.g. removal of all references to ancillary know-how

-   the field-of-use restriction. The provision might be extended to cover know-how. It would mean that the licensee cannot use know-how gained under the licensing agreement, after it expires, for a related use

-   the removal of Article 3(11) which permitted the use of secret know-how by the licensee after the expiration of the agreement.

In revising its original proposal, the Commission is currently considering the effects of the decision of the Court of Justice of 8th June 1982 in the Maize Seed Case (see above para 5(b)(i)(c))

6. RELEVANCE OF OTHER EEC LAW AND LEGISLATION

(a) Problems could also arise in connection with fields of Community law other than competition/anti-trust and intellectual/industrial property. For example: tax and insurance.

However, an analysis of other Community law fields is, practically speaking, beyond the scope of this paper. Free movement of goods aspects might briefly be considered, given their importance in the functioning of the common market and their interrelationship with both competition and industrial property. A few words on consumer protection are also necessary.

(b)   The EEC Treaty provides for the elimination, as between
      Member States, of customs duties and of quantitative
      restrictions on the import and export of goods, and of
      all other measures having equivalent effect. The free
      movement of goods is a cornerstone of the EEC Treaty
      whose primary aim is to establish a common market
      uniting the different national markets into a single
      market.

      On customs duties, Article 12 provides that:

           "Member States shall refrain from introducing
           between themselves any new customs duties on
           imports and exports or any charges having
           equivalent effect, and from increasing those which
           they already apply in their trade with each
           other."

      On quantitative restrictions, Article 30 provides that:

           "Quantitive restrictions on imports and all
           measures having equivalent effect shall, without
           prejudice to the following provisions, be
           prohibited between Member States."

      However, Article 36 provides for important exceptions
      to the basic prohibitions on grounds of (inter alia)
      public morality, public policy or public security,
      protection of health and life of humans, animals or
      plants, protection of industrial and commercial
      property. Furthermore, the European Court admitted in
      Cassis de Dijon (Case 120/78 (1979) ECR 649) that
      national provisions which apply equally to imports and
      domestic goods may fall outside the prohibition in
      Article 30 if they are necessary to satisfy mandatory
      national requirements.

Goods which are subject to a franchising arrangement must, therefore, be admitted into the territory of the Member State where the franchisees are operating, subject to the exceptions provided for in the EEC Treaty and the case law of the European Court.

(c) The Consumer Protection Directorate General (XI) of the European Commission has not so far specifically considered franchising.

Franchising schemes do sometimes involve fraud or unreasonable exploitation of the consumer. Were the incidence of these schemes to increase substantially, the Commission might decide, or be persuaded, to act.

7. CONCLUSIONS

Perhaps it is useful to conclude with the check-list of basic questions which a lawyer should ask himself when considering a franchising agreement, remembering that such an agreement will form part of a network of agreements, containing one or two tiers.

(a) Is competition within the Common Market prevented, restricted or distorted? (see para 4(a))

(b) If yes, is trade between Member States affected? (see para 4(a))

(c) If yes, are competition and intra-Community trade affected to an appreciable extent? (see para 4(a))

(d) Is there an abuse of a dominant position in the market of relevant products? (see para 4(c))

(e) Do the exclusive distribution provisions fall within the block exemption under Regulation 1983/83? (see para 4(g))

(f) Do the exclusive purchasing provisions fall within the
     block exemption under Regulation 1984/83? (see para
     4(h))

(g) If no to 7(e) or 7(f), does the agreement nevertheless
     quality for individual exemption under Article 85(3)?
     (see para 4(b))

(h) Should the agreement be notified in order to benefit
     from individual exemption under Article 85(3)? (see
     para 4(d))

(i) Does the exercise of the exclusive rights conferred
     upon the franchisee infringe Article 85(1)? (see para
     5(a))

(j) Do the provisions granting exclusive rights qualify for
     individual exemption under Article 85(3)? (see para
     5(b))

     Finally, just as in national law, other fields of law
     which are of general application, may also apply to
     franchising (see paras 6(b) and 6(c))

INTERNATIONAL FRANCHISING – AN OVERVIEW
M. Mendelsohn (editor)
© Elsevier Science Publishers B.V. (North-Holland), 1984

CHAPTER 10

FRANCHISING IN EUROPE - FRANCE
Olivier Gast

France is the European country in which franchising has developed the most, with approximately 500 franchisors. A considerable amount of literature exists on the subject with books and articles, and jurisprudence is starting to take it seriously.

I intend to limit myself to the legal aspects and business considerations which govern the practice of franchising in France at the present time, from the particular view point of a foreign franchisor who wishes to set up in France.

This franchisor and his lawyer will therefore be pleased to learn that France is extremely propitious to franchising, in all forms. But it is more particularly favourable to the "business format franchise". Franchising in the strict term, that is, the business format franchise which is becoming well known, even by the public, should be distinguished in France from the other methods of distributing products or services. The use of the name "franchising" in America and Canada covers methods of distribution which have already existed in France for many years but which are known under clearly differentiated names.

-    concession,
-    licensing,
-    voluntary associations of business firms,

and in which the commercial partners are also independent,
by contrast with branch managers who are salaried staff.

But these methods do not all benefit from the reputation and
the favourable opinion of franchising. On the contrary,
with regard to concessions, a series of resounding law suits
have taken place which have tarnished the brand image of
this technique leading to a mistrust of potential
concessionaries. These were caused by conflicts between oil
companies and concessionary service stations which threw
light on the state of subjection to which the
concessionaries were reduced.

The business format franchises or, more simply, franchising,
is very favourably known, perhaps too much so, because
certain businessmen, a little too clever, unscrupulous or
ill-advised, have played on its reputation giving the name
of "franchise contracts" to contracts which have none of the
elements of a franchise. They have to take advantage of the
misdescription of the transaction by the use of the word
"franchise".

This explains why franchisee candidates who are sometimes
aware of this fact, are occasionally more suspicious than
might be expected and pose irrational questions which might
surprise a serious franchisor conscious of the value of his
products.

The fact that there is no law in France at present governing
the right of franchising causes a legal void which, combined
with jurisprudence which is still in a state of formation,
unfortunately and inevitably leads to abuse.

The French Government is therefore considering, and have
been doing so for three years, passing a law on franchising.
A new commission, succeeding the first two, is being
assembled again to examine this problem. Several proposals

for laws have previously been drawn up but have never been voted.

It is too soon to say what form the proposed law will take. There are two possibilities which are being discussed:

- the one that I support is an American type imposing disclosure of information before contracting,

- the other one proposes that the franchisees merge into associations, with which the franchisor would be obliged to negotiate agreements and disputes.

But we are not sure what will happen. In my view, at least three or four years will be necessary before a decision can be made, which could be no law being passed at all as the Home Trade Department's view is that such a law may not be needed.

This prospect is still far off and will not worry American lawyers who are accustomed, with their FTC and their UFOC, to having clients who are reliable in business, a reliability that the French should do well to prectice more often.

I should now like to refer to an aspect of franchising in France which is generally neglected because it is not a material, legal or economic fact - mental habits.

French people are, from many viewpoints, Latins and somewhat indisciplined for this reason. This is why, in order to succeed with franchising in France, not only is a well written contract certainly needed - the more so that there is more chance of having to produce it in Court - but also an enthusiastic and dynamic sales team to make the franchisee candidates and the recruited franchisees understand the advantages and the how and the why of

everything and, particularly, to give them the impression
that they are taking part in decisions, even if this is not
quite true, so that their naturally critical spirit is not
awakened.

In my opinion, this mental attitude governs a good part of
the decisions which have to be taken on the methods of
setting up and operating a franchise in France.

To be more concrete, what is the best way of setting up in
France for the foreign franchisor?

There are three possibilities:

- direct licencing,
- founding of a company,
- the Master franchise.

Direct licencing is, legally, perfectly reasonable with no
major disadvantages. French law allows the parties to
subject the contract to French law or to foreign law, at
their choice, with French or foreign courts holding
jurisdiction.

I nevertheless believe that this method should be
discouraged. First, because it requires a multiplicity of
individual contracts and of contracting parties and, second,
because of the complexity of management resulting for the
franchisor irrespective of the problem of recruiting each
franchisee.

Mamagement of such a portfolio of contracts would in
practice be difficult if not impossible. The formalities
would be multiplied by the number of contracting parties,
registration of contracts with "L'Institut National de la
Propriete Industrielle" (I.N.P.I.) for licencing of trade
names, bank formalities for repatriation of royalties,

difficulties of supplying commercial and technical
assistance to each of the franchisees.

Bank formalities concern:

- repatriation of royalties made under Bank control and
  after registration of the agreement at I.N.P.I. without
  which exchange control authorities will not authorise
  the transfer of royalties abroad,

- repatriation of royalities is also subject to VAT and
  withholding tax. The rate is usually thirty three and
  one third per cent (33,1/3%). But France has signed
  various tax treaties providing either an exemption or a
  reduced rate. For instance, the Franco-American
  convention provides a 5% rate instead of 33,1/3%
  (Convention of 28th July 1967 signed in Paris, Art.
  11); the convention signed on the 22nd May 1968 between
  France and Great Britain provides there shall be no
  withholding tax in France except if the beneficiary of
  royalties owns a permanent office in France (Art.12).

- customs and import-export controls:

All imports of foreign goods of a value equal to or greater
than 125,000 FF must be transacted through an "intermediaire
agree" (authorised intermediary). They usually are Bank
agencies authorised by the Ministry of Economy.

If the franchisor wants to keep active of the chain, it is
more convenient to set up a company in France with French
partners. There is no insurmountable obstacle to this but,
nevertheless, I believe that the method should be reserved
for the biggest companies which possess the required
financial facilities and who have decided to make the
necessary investments in personnel and in capital.

I believe that the third method, the Master franchise, is best for the majority of cases because it gives the greatest technical flexibility and therefore relatively close control of the Master franchisee.

It is moreover the Master franchisee method which is most commonly used by foreign franchisors in France. Master franchise contracts can, of course and as in the case of direct franchising, be subject to French law or to foreign law and to the jurisprudence of French or foreign courts.

If foreign law is chosen, it is advisable to ascertain whether:

(a)   it contains any provisions contrary to French law and order (which is relatively rare) which could cause the contract to be void or unenforceable under French law;

(b)   the foreign law stipulated in the contract can be applied by the French courts or a decision taken by a foreign court can be enforced in France.

If French law is chosen, care must be taken to avoid the traditional traps of French contractual law of which the most important are the following:

-     abusive clauses of which the meaning is difficult to define and which can only be decided by courts in the last resort; An example of such a clause would be one which sought to restrict the liability of the franchisor.

-     in the event that the contract provides that the Master franchisee shall draw supplies exclusively from the franchisor or from a supplier designated by it, the contract must contain a price clause which determines

the price of the future merchandise or at least makes
it determinable. Such a provision must not be capable
of existing for more than ten years otherwise the whole
agreement will be null and void;

- a possibility that the contract may be treated as a
  contract of employment or as one with an *ipso facto*
  corporation. This risk is very frequent in matters
  governed by domestic law but is practically nil in the
  case of a Master franchisor residing abroad, at least
  with regard to a work contract. The risk is further
  reduced by providing that a Master franchise contract
  is entered into with a company and not an individual.

In the event that the franchisor should interfere too
greatly in the business of the Master franchisee, it is
still possible that the Court could hold that the essence of
the arrangement created an ipso facto corporation and treat
the contract on that basis. The problem is aggravated by the
foreign element and it is difficult to judge how the court
will respond in such a case.

An important formality relating to the law of trade names
must not be neglected:

- firstly, it is plain that a trade name which is owned
  by the Master franchisor must be registered in France
  to obtain maximum benefit of legal protection.

- secondly, and this aspect is sometimes neglected, the
  contract by which the trade mark is licenced to the
  Master franchisee must be registered at the I.N.P.I.
  The Master franchisee must also register each of the
  contracts by which it sub-licences the name to its own
  franchisees. This is a simple formality which is not
  costly. If this is not done, regretably problems of
  procedure may arise if legal action is needed in France

for infringement. Neither the franchisee nor the Master franchisee will be able to take action against infringers and only the Master franchisor will be able to act which will evidently have considerbale effect on the amount of damages because only the injury suffered by the Master franchisor will be taken into consideration when the assessment of damages is made.

As a French lawyer and considering the matter from the point of view of the Master franchisee, I have frequently found that Master franchisors make the same mistakes. I have not yet met an American franchisor who has decided to sell his Master franchise in France after first carrying out a serious market study of the French market compared with the American market, or after setting up a store directly with the object of testing the reaction of French consumers when faced with the imported products and services.

The result is almost invariably that the market potential is miscalculated usually resulting in an overestimate of the potential. This leads to clauses relating to quotas or to rates of market penetration in the Master franchise contract which are much too onerous and unrealistic. The Master franchisee will probably not, in practice, effectively impose the clauses but it remains a fact that they usually cause tension in the relationships between Master franchisor and Master franchisee. The Master franchisee almost invariably is disappointed because he has not anticipated the relatively long time required for consumer acceptance needed for success in France to be compatible with that of the product or services in the United States or in England.

When the Master franchisee has paid a relatively high price for his Master franchise and when he has devoted all his forces to it, the feeling of disappointment inevitably causes embarrassment and friction between the franchisor and the franchisee, even if the franchise is successful but on a more moderate scale than contemplated by the parties.

With regard to the other problems resulting from French domestic law, it is the Master franchisee who will be responsible for drawing up his own franchise contract in conformity with applicable law. He must notably take pains to respect the official policy on prices and also the law on competition.

I advise that the Master franchise contract should stipulate that the Master franchisor has the right to approve the contract written by the Master franchisee so that he can make sure that the basic interests of the franchise chain and of its public image are respected.

The problem of Master franchises is that of the choice of a partner. This is the crucial problem of the technique because the success or failure of the transaction depends on it. The public image which the franchise system will acquire in France depends heavily on this choice of partner.

INTERNATIONAL FRANCHISING – AN OVERVIEW
M. Mendelsohn (editor)
© Elsevier Science Publishers B.V. (North-Holland), 1984   389

CHAPTER 11

FRANCHISING IN EUROPE - GERMANY
Dr. Walther Skaupy

I. INTRODUCTION: GERMAN LAW AND FRANCHISING

German law is a statute law. Most of it is contained in
general codes or special statutes. The majority of the basic
laws like the Civil Code (BGB), the Commercial Code (HGB)
and the Criminal Code (StGB) have been in in existence for
more than 80 years, some of them for more than a hundred
years. Gradually, in accordance with the development of
modern society and technical progress new statutes were
enacted , e.g. the Unfair Trade Practices Law (UWG) and the
Antitrust Ordinance (KartellVO). All such statutes have been
amended or remodelled from time to time and will also in the
future be adapted to the necessities of the changing times.

The German legislature - this is in most relevant aspects
the Federal Parlament (Bundestag, formerly Reichstag) - has,
however, taken care not to over-regulate the matters it had
to deal with. Jurisdiction, customs and legal practice play
an important part in the interpretation of the statutes
which is broad, not formal. A typical example of a matter
not regulated by law is licensing which is even not
mentioned in the Trademark Law. Numerous judgments and
decisions of the courts have dealt with trademark licensing
problems and will probably continue to do so. Thus, much of
the law is indeed judge-made. Such case law has been
developed mainly to complete and to refine statutory
provisions, particularly in areas where social and economic

conditions have changed, and statutory regulation has been
either missing or inadequate.

Since licensing and franchising have quite a number of
common aspects - a franchise agreement necessarily includes
the licensing of certain rights - it is understandable that
we have no German franchising legislation which is not
contemplated in the near future. Certainly, franchising
raises more problems than the pure licensing of a patent or
a trademark. But these problems, whether civil or criminal,
can be dealt with by existing laws.

There are certainly abuses just as they have always existed
in the field of distribution. Sometimes the same kind of
imposters who make people sign up contracts obliging them to
pay entrance fees or make down-payments for joining a
seemingly profitable sales organisation which have indeed
had the audacity to call their fraudulent organisation a
"franchise system". But legally such cases are just frauds
which can be speedily taken care of by the criminal courts.
So far, we have no information about any cases in court
labelled as franchising or involving a real, but deceitful
franchise system.

Thus we do not think we need, for the time being, any
particular franchising laws. We are even rather happy that
our authorities have taken but little interest in
"regulating" this matter. I am aware that many States in the
U.S.A. have adopted franchise laws and they were certainly
convinced of the necessity of such legislation. Every
country must judge the necessity of such laws for itself.

As far as I see, the business communities and most lawyers
in European countries do not like the idea of franchising
laws. The EEC Commission seems, however, be inclined to

regulate the matter on the European level.*

II. DEFINITION AND SCOPE

In the absence of a statute, it is obvious that there exists no legal definition of franchising in Germany. A comprehensive definition which appears to be generally accepted has been proposed by the author. Translated into English it reads as follows:

> "In exchange for a direct or indirect fee, the franchisee, a legally independent trader or entrepreneur is granted, within the framework of a continuing relationship, the following rights in connection with the distribution of certain goods and/or services:
>
> (a) The use of the franchisor's image, name, registered or unregistered trademark rights, trade dress, marks, symbols or other protectible rights;
>
> (b) the use of the franchisor's commercial and/or technical know-how.
>
> Additionally, the franchisee is obliged to comply with the franchisor's developed organisation and marketing system. The franchisor is obliged to supply training,support (Beistand) and advice to the franchisee and to supervise the maintenance of his business concept by contractual specifications (Weisungen) and control."

---

* There does not seem to be any confirmation by the European Commission of this assertion by Dr. Skaupy - Editor

It should be added that the granting of a franchise does not necessarily include an exclusive right, territorial or otherwise. Furthermore, it is understood that the franchisor is obliged continuously to develop the organisation and marketing system on which the success of the franchise is necessarily based.

It will be noted that the German definition resembles the American business format concept to a considerable extent while a contractual structure which could be compared to the American concept of "product distribution franchising" would rather be called a dealership (see below).

Another definition of franchising which is also accepted in Germany is the one contained in the European Code of Ethics which had been drafted in 1981 by the European Franchising Federation and presented to the EEC Commission. In the English version the definition, reads as follows:

> "Franchising is defined within the framework of this Code as a method of contractual collaboration between parties which are legally independent and equal: on the one hand a franchising firm, the Franchisor, and on the other hand one or several firms, the Franchisee(s).
>
> As far as the franchising firm (the Franchisor) is concerned, it implies:
>
> 1. Ownership of a Company Name, a Trade Name, Initials or Symbols (possibly a Trade Mark) of a business or a service, and Know-how, which is made available to the franchised firm(s) - the Franchisee(s).
>
> 2. Control of a range of Products and /or

Services presented in a distinctive and original format, and which must be adopted and used by the franchisee(s), the format being based on a set of specific business techniques which have been previously tested, and which are continually developed and checked as regards their value and efficiency.

The main object in establishing a franchising agreement between the two parties is to give benefit to both the Franchisor and the Franchisee(s) through the combination of their human and financial resources, without in any way affecting the independence of either party.

Implicit in any franchising agreement is that there shall be a payment made in one form or another by the franchisee to the franchisor in recognition of the service supplied by the franchisor in providing his name, format, technology and know-how. Franchising is therefore something more than a sales agreement or a concession agreement or a Licence Contract in that both parties accept important obligations to one another, over and above those established in a conventional trading relationship."

III. **DEALERSHIPS AND AGENCIES**

Mainly in the field of technical products, the distribution in Germany has been taken care of for a long time by dealers (Vertragshandler, Eigenhandler). These traditional dealerships resemble in many ways the American Product Distribution Franchising and the French "Concessions

Commerciales".The main difference as compared to franchise systems is the lack of a strict marketing and organisation concept imposed on the dealer, and the absence of a uniform group image although also a dealer is obliged to use name, trademarks and other symbols of the enterprise he represents. Furthermore, the supervision of the dealer and the enforcement of a marketing concept through contractual specifications is unknown within the framework of dealerships. As a rule, most dealers are, contrary to a great number of franchisees, technical and commercial experts in the field of the products they sell, and they have been selected as dealers just for that reason by the manufacturers of those products.

The dealerships will probably continue to exist for a long time. Many dealers are well-to-do businessmen who would probably refuse to abide by the rules and restraints which are customary in franchise systems. In quite a number of cases, a lawyer would therefore advise the creation of a dealership system rather than a franchise system. Dealerships are not regulated by law; they have developed within the framework of civil law and controversial problems have so far been dealt with satisfactorily by the courts.

The distribution of goods and services is, moreover, to a large extent being effected through company-owned organisations, very often in connection with franchised units, and mainly through agencies. The Commercial agents are, under German law (Sec. 84 of the Commercial Code-HGB), independent businessmen,but they never operate for their own account like a franchisee, but in the name and for the account of the enterprises which they represent.

The relationship of commercial agents to the firms which they represent is basically that of a service agreement and the agent's powers are subject to this agreement. Mandatory provisions of the Commercial Code give the agent the right to obtain a commission for his transactions (Sec.87). Other provisions which have been included in the Commercial Code in recent years give the agent the right to extra payments after expiration of a contract if it contains a non-competition clause (Sec.90a) and finally - this is the most important amendment to the Commercial Code in recent times - a claim for "reasonable compensation" (Ausgleichsanspruch) after the termination of the agreement (Sec. 89b).

This "Ausgleichsanspruch" is a form of indemnification intended to compensate the agent for the business and the goodwill created through his activity. The amount of such claims depends upon the length of the services and the turnover and profit made. There is a ceiling amount, however, based upon average income and length of service which will never exceed one year's total income based on his average income in the last five years of his activity. The claim cannot be waived effectively in advance and will be denied only if the agency relationship was terminated through the agent's fault or if the agent terminated the agreement on his own without being motivated by the principal's fault.

It may be emphasized that the afore-mentioned mandatory provisions have, in recent years, not only applied to situations where a representative acted as a commercial agent, but also where the representative was a dealer or distributor and his agreement with the manufacturer (or wholesale dealer) was such that in case of termination his clients would more or less automatically fall to the latter. Such jurisdiction "adapted" the dealers "by analogy" more and more to commercial agents. It must be assumed that also franchisees could be entitled, under this jurisdiction to compensation in quite a number of cases (see below, VII).

IV. **OTHER DISTRIBUTION ORGANISATIONS**

Among further organisations of the associated trade co-
operatives and voluntary trade groups (Handelsketten) may be
mentioned. Mainly the cooperatives have had a long tradition
in the food trade, but in recent times they are more and
more inclined to incorporate franchising structures within
their widespread organisations because they lack the strict
set up and marketing scheme which makes franchising so
efficient.

The fact that the distribution of products and services has
for a long time successfully been carried through by the
various aforementioned organisations explains why
franchising originally developed rather slowly. The
situation has, however, changed in the last few years and
franchising is now steadily progressing and its development
has indeed recently picked up to a considerable extent. New
franchise systems are increasingly being set up or planned
in many sectors of the German economy. Quite a number of
distributorships and branch systems are being restructured
and converted into new distribution systems in which the
concept of franchising is introduced in one way or another.

V. **THE STATUS OF FOREIGNERS IN THE FEDERAL REPUBLIC OF
GERMANY**

Before discussing the various methods a foreign franchisor
may consider, if he decides to export his franchise to
Germany, some general remarks on the legal status of
foreigners and foreign partnerships and corporations will
certainly be useful. Generally speaking, German law does not
distinguish between Germans and foreigners including foreign
enterprises. Under the constitution (Grundgesetz), everyone
in Germany is indeed entitled to most "basic rights", such
as, personal freedom, freedom of trade, free competition,
freedom of speech and faith, etc. The contractual liberty

has been a cornerstone of civil law for a long time being restricted however, by certain laws designed to protect the freedom of enterprises, like the Cartel Law.

There are, of course, quite a number of legal problems which require special provisions for the legal treatment of foreigners, and the classic definition of the foreigner by nationality is still applicable with respect to certain constitutional rights or other public law as well as to certain aspects of private international law. But almost all forms of economical and commercial activity are open to the foreigner without discrimination.

The German economy is almost entirely liberalised. Currency restrictions of any type have been abolished by the Foreign Trade Law of 1961 (Aubenwirtschaftsgesetz). A free flow of capital allows the export and import of all currencies, all transactions, however, being subject to notification to the competent authorities which is usually carried through by the banks.

As far as imports and exports of goods are concerned, it should be noted that no extraordinary import quotas,import licensing requirements nor other restrictions are known, all imports being, however, subject to import turnover taxes at rates identical to those of the added value tax. With respect to a number of products, certain technical, health or other requirements must be observed. Otherwise, no extraodinary regulations will restrict the free flow of goods.

On the other hand, it must be noted that, in spite of his equal treatment in commercial aspects, a foreigner cannot stay indefinitely in the Federal Republic of Germany. A foreigner may only stay three months without a particular visa as a tourist or businessman. He may repeat the three month stay after each departure from the country. If a foreigner intends to stay for a longer period and/or wishes to become employed with a foreign or domestic enterprise in the Federal Republic he must first obtain a residence permit from the police (aliens' registration office) which will normally be granted for a year.

At the present time such permits are very difficult to obtain, except for EEC nationals and to a certain extent nationals of the U.S.A, Switzerland and Austria. A justified interest to take up a residence in Germany must be shown, otherwise the application is not likely to be successful. Once a residence permit has been obtained it is easier to obtain a working permit from the appropriate Arbeitsamt ("labor office"). As a rule, permits will be obtained both by the employer and the employee. Joint application forms are usually filed by the employer. The permission to employ a foreign national is limited to 12 months and must be renewed after that period.

VI.   **METHODS OF INTERNATIONAL FRANCHISING**

There are different methods a foreign franchisor may choose if he decides to export his franchise to Germany. In the first place, there is the direct method which is, as a rule, certainly the simpler and less costly one as compared to the indirect method. No affiliate is being created in Germany, but the franchise is being granted to an independent businessman or a company/corporation on the basis of a customary franchise agreement. This method should only be adopted if the franchisor resides in a neighbouring country and will be in a position to supervise and to attend to the franchised outlets in a sufficient manner.

The indirect method consists in setting up an affiliate (company, corporation) or permanent establishment in Germany from where franchising may be commenced. The shares of an affiliate may be totally held by the foreign franchisor who may even nominate foreign (non-German and non-resident) directors or managers, one or several German executive employees being, of course, necessary to take care of the day-to-day work. There is, indeed, no requirement of local participation in ownership or management.

There has been a lot of talk about "master franchises" or "master licenses". This may be considered as a third method of franchising in another country although it appears to resemble more or less the direct method. In such cases the franchisor selects an independent businessman or enterprise residing in the other country to whom the franchise is granted. However, a much higher degree of independence must be given to such a "franchisee" than to a "normal" franchisee since he is supposed to develop a distribution network on his own and independently from the foreign franchisor. A "master franchisee" is a kind of "sub-franchisor" in his country. A master franchise agreement should therefore spell out the general obligations and rights of the franchisee without going into the details of a customary franchise agreement. In most cases, it would, in my opinion, be better to speak of "master licensees" or "general licensees" because the franchisor will, as a rule, indicate to such master franchisees only the general lines of the organistion and marketing scheme which they have to observe and develop on their own in accordance with the legal and economical requirements of the country.

There are, moreover, quite a number of additional methods of penetrating the German market to distribute goods and/or services there. The franchised associate may e.g. be company affiliated or partnership related. If the franchisor owns a majority share of the franchise company, the organisational supervisory and control rights normally reserved by contract are instead exercised by the franchisor's majority shareholder position in the franchisee company. Similarly, if the franchisor is a general partner and the franchisee a limited partner (Kommanditist), the franchisor exercises control partially through specifications in the partnership agreement (Gesellschaftsvertrag). Use of the share participation or partnership is considered to assure the franchisor of greater control over the franchisee and continuity of the franchised business. In the case of such structures the underlying concept is often referred to as "quasi franchising".

If, on the other hand, the franchisor owns merely a blocking minority share of 26% in the franchise company, we are inclined to consider such structure as genuine franchising. In most cases, the franchsior intends here to prevent, through such participation, undesirable changes within the franchise company in the interests of the whole system keeping the franchisee as majority share holder and sole responsible manager at the top of his franchise business.

A foreign investor may also take a participation in a joint venture or commonly owned company (sometimes referred to as "joint venture company"). We do not consider such structures as franchise systems because the partners do not form part of a centralized, strict open end marketing organistion in which all participants offer the same goods and services. A joint venture or a commonly owned operation is, as a rule, formed by a limited number of partners getting together on the same level and contributing various types of products or services. It is, of course, possible that a foreign investor gets together with a German businessman within the framework of a joint venture which starts franchising along the lines suggested by the foreign investor.

A franchisor who intends to greate a subsidiary in Germany has the choice of a variety of enterprise forms, namely several kinds of partnerships, companies and corporations. The ideal form for the subsidiary is a limited liability company (GmbH) the minimum capital of which is DM 50,000,-.

Since January 1, 1981 only one shareholder will be required for the formation of the GmbH. Thus a foreign franchisor may own the corporation all by himself. As already mentioned, he may also be the only legal representative without having a residence in Germany.

VII. **CIVIL AND COMMERCIAL LAW PROBLEMS**

Franchise agreements must, like many other types of contracts not dealt with by a particular statute, be in accordance with the general rules of law and public order as well as with certain special laws, ordinances or regulations which may be applicable in certain fields and aiming e.g. at the sanitary and technical protection of individuals. There is, in the first place, the obligation to act in good faith and not to cheat or to get the better of the other party. Contracts must be, as the Civil Code puts it (Sec.242), in line with "good morals" ("gute Sitten") and they can be declared as null and void by the courts if they violate this basic principle of the Civil Code (Sec. 139). This refers particularly to contracts called "Knebelungsvertrage", meaning oppressive contracts restraining the economic freedom of the other party and dishonestly taking advantage of it. If only a single clause of a franchise agreement is considered to violate "good morals", e.g. an over-restrictive non-competition clause, such clause can be declared null and void while the remainder of the agreement may be upheld.

The termination of franchise agreements, dealership contracts or commercial agent's agreements has, to my knowledge, never given rise to any particular legal problems except the claims resulting from such termination. If a freely stipulated contract comes to an end in accordance with its dispositions, e.g. if one party has given notice in due time, there is no chance for the party to demand its extension or renewal. It would be considered as a

contradiction to the principle of contractual liberty
(Vertragsfreiheit), if one party could force the other
party to extend the duration of a terminated contract. If
the parties themselves have not provided for regulation
of the matter - and it should be strongly recommended that
they do so - a franchisee in many cases would have a chance
to get a "reasonable compensation" within the framework of a
commercial agent's legal rights, as mentioned above (see
IV). Such claim will be granted if and so far as:-

1.   the entrepreneur also had substantial advantages from
      the business relations with new customers whom the
      commercial agent had recruited, after expiration of the
      contractual period,

2.   the commercial agents by reason of termination of the
      contractual relationship lost rights to commissions
      which he would have had, had the contractual
      relationship continued, out of already concluded
      business or business to be concluded in the future with
      those customers whom he had recruited, and

3.   the payment of compensation is equitably appropriate
      taking into consideration all circumstances.

These prerequisites may appear to be rather onerous for a
commercial agent, but as a rule he will have a very good
chance to have his claims acknowledged in court.

The legal situation of a franchisee and a dealer is a little
more difficult. He must additionally prove that his
situation may be compared to that of a commercial agent in
order to justify the application by "analogy" of a legal
provision originally designed to protect commercial agents
only. However, the Federal Supreme Court has in recent years
handed down quite a number of judgments in favour of dealers
extending the area of application of Sec. 89b of the

Commercial Code more and more. Up to now we have had no case in court where a franchise claimed "reasonable compensation", but it may be fairly assumed that his lawsuit would have the same result. The few lawsuits involving franchise agreements have had different problems to deal with, e.g. the lack of promised support from a franchisor, the lack of adequate publicity, the validity of a non-competition clause, etc.

VIII. **ANTITRUST CONSIDERATION**

A discussion of the problems a foreign franchisor may encounter if he starts exporting his franchise to Germany must necessarily include a look at the German antitrust legislation. The Cartel Law (Gesetzgegen Wettbewerbsbeschrankung - GWB) prohibits, like most other antitrust laws, any horizintal restrictive agreements including price fixing, although it provides for the authosization of certain "Kartelle" which are deemed to be useful and innocuous, such as agreements with respect to rationalization, specialisation, interbrand co-operation, export cartels, etc. (Sections 1 to 8 of the Cartel Law).

On the other hand vertical restraints including e.g.exclusive dealing requiring the franchise to deal only, or primarily, in products supplied or services designated by the franchisor are not prohibited. But the Cartel authorities have the power to intervene in cases deemed to constitute an "abuse". In this respect Sec. 18 (1) of the Cartel Law authorises the Cartel Authority to declare a vertical restraint of trade to be ineffective and to prohibit:-

"the implementation of new obligations of the similar kind, insofar as such agreements

1. restrain a party to the agreement in the

use of the supplied goods, other goods or commercial services: or

2. restrain a party to the agreement in the purchase from or the sale to third parties of other goods or commercial services; or

3. restrain a party to the agreement in the resale of the supplied goods to third parties; or

4. oblige a party to the agreement to purchase goods or commercial services which are, by their nature or in commercial practice, non-related

and further insofar as

(a) enterprises in a number significant in relation to competition in the market are thereby bound in the same manner and inequitably restrained in their freedom to compete; or

(b) other enterprises are thereby inequitably restrained in entering the market; or

(c) the competition in the market for these or other goods or commercial services is substantially impaired through the scope of such restraints.

(2) A restraint is deemed not to be inequitable within the meaning of subsection (1) lit b) if it is insignificant in relation to supply and demand opportunities which continue to exist for other enterprises."

The rather complicated clauses of Section 18 constitute indeed the cornerstone of antitrust law regarding vertical restraints. With the exception of the restrictions to be mentioned below, nothing is "per se" prohibited, and in cases where the Cartel Authority intervenes, there are often many chances to arrive at some kind of consent settlement.

The principles of Section 18 are applicable in all cases of exclusive dealing, territorial and customer restrictions, tie-in sales as well as limitations on restricting sources of supply and restrictions imposed on the franchisees as to their purchases with the franchisor or suppliers who will make the product to the franchisor's specifications or standards.

As in many countries, resale price maintenance is strictly forbidden in Germany. Excepted are only the products of publishers. However, a manufacturer or importer is permitted to suggest prices with respect to brand products (not services) under certain conditions. The products must openly carry the inscription "unverbindliche Preisempfehlung" (non-obligatory price recommendation).

Another aspect of German antitrust law being of considerable interest to certain franchisors are the special dispositions regarding technical licenses (including secret technological know-how) which are much stricter than in the case of customary franchise agreements. In accordance with Section 20 of the Cartel Law, agreements concerning the use of patents and utility models are ineffective insofar as they impose upon the licensee any restrictions on his business conduct which go beyond the scope of the protected right. Restrictions pertaining to the type, extent, quantity, territory or period of exercise of such rights are not deemed to go beyond the scope of the protected right. Likewise, certain further restrictions are also permitted, e.g. insofar and so long as they are justified by the

licensor's interest in a technically satisfactory
exploitation of the protected right;furthermore, the
obligation of the licensee for improvement in, or the
applied use of, an invention insofar as such obligation is
in accordance with identical obligations of the licensor;
moreover, the obligation of the licensee not to challenge
the protected right, etc.

The Cartel Authority may, however, authorise agreements
containing additional restrictions if the freedom of
economic action of the licensee or other enterprises is not
unfairly restricted, and, if competition in the market is
not substantially impaired by the extent of the restrictions
involved. The same rules apply to agreements concerning the
use of unprotected inventions and technical know-how insofar
as they constitute trade secrets (Sec.21 of the Cartel
Law).

Further antitrust provisions being of interest to a foreign
franchisor deal with boycotts, refusals to sell and
discrimination. In accordance with Section 26 of the Cartel
Law,

> "enterprises and associations of enterprises
> may not, with the intent to affect specific
> enterprises inequitably and adversely,
> request another enterprise or associations of
> enterprises to refuse to sell or refuse to
> buy.
>
> Market-dominating enterprises or associations
> of enterprises.... shall not unfairly
> hinder,directly or indirectly, another
> enterprise in business activities which are
> usually open to similar enterprises, nor in
> the absence of facts justifying such
> differentiation,treat such enterprises,

directly or indirectly, in a manner different from the treatment accorded to similar enterprises. The same rules shall apply to enterprises and associations of enterprises insofar as suppliers or purchasers of a certain type of goods or commercial services depend on them to such an extent that sufficient and reasonable possibilities of dealing with other enterprises do not exist."

As far as market-dominating enterprises are concerned, the Cartel Authorities may prohibit abusive practices and declare agreements to be of no effect. Prior to such action the Cartel Authority shall request the parties involved to discontinue the abuse to which objection was raised (Section 22 (4,5) of the Cartel Law).

IX. **CONCLUSIONS**

Concluding my modest presentation, it may be once more useful to point out that foreign individuals and enterprises have a variety of methods at their disposal if they intend to set up a franchise system in Germany. There are no particular legal or administrative obstacles which would deter a foreign investor or franchisor from doing business in Germany since he will in all respects be treated as a German entrepreneur. The prospects for international franchising are steadily increasing in Germany provided that really new or better products or services are being offered to the consumer.